LEAVING CERTIFI

LESS STRESS
MORE
SUCCESS

Geography Revision

Patrick O'Dwyer

g GILL EDUCATION

Gill Education
Hume Avenue
Park West
Dublin 12
www.gilleducation.ie

Gill Education is an imprint of M.H. Gill & Co.

Design by Liz White Designs

Illustrations: Andriy Yankovskyy

At the time of going to press, all web addresses were active and contained information relevant to the topics in this book. Gill Education does not, however, accept responsibility for the content or views contained on these websites. Content, views and addresses may change beyond the publisher or author's control. Students should always be supervised when reviewing websites.

For permission to reproduce photographs, the authors and publisher gratefully acknowledge the following:

© Alamy: 10, 24, 36, 41T, 61, 120, 150, 154, 199, 210, 217T, 218, 227, 230, 232, 253, 271, 283, 296, 96, 101T; © Barrow Coakley Photography: 70, 80, 81, 83; © Collins Agency: 166, 205; © Daniel Beltrá: 239; © Getty Images: 27, 62, 125, 143, 176, 188, 211B, 242, 302, 312; © iStock: 15, 32, 94, 95, 101B, 106, 112, 113, 114, 126, 139, 144, 184, 211T, 212, 217B, 250, 293T, 293B, 294T, 294C, 294B, 307; © Kevin Dwyer: 72; © Ordnance Survey Ireland: 71, 74, 76, 78, 187; © Real Ireland: 41B. Ordnance Survey Ireland Permit No. 9107 © Ordnance Survey Ireland/Government of Ireland.

The author and publisher have made every effort to trace all copyright holders, but if any have been inadvertently overlooked we would be pleased to make the necessary arrangement at the first opportunity.

The paper used in this book is made from the wood pulp of managed forests.
For every tree felled, at least one tree is planted, thereby renewing natural resources.

CONTENTS

Introduction

The purpose of this book is to help you recall the key points from your class textbook on the main areas of the course and to offer you some sample answers that are focused on the exam marking scheme. Practical skills, such as exam tips, key points and map work are also covered to maximise your choices and improve your performance in the examination. There are some choices of topics: these are marked 'OR' to suit the main textbooks used in different schools.

 Note: Material that is to be studied only by those taking higher level is indicated in the text.

Exam breakdown

CORE
ALL STUDENTS MUST COVER
Core Units 1 and 2 (pages 1–156)

ELECTIVES
ALL STUDENTS MUST COVER *ONE ELECTIVE*
Either
Elective 1: Chapters 15–19 inclusive (pages 158–191)
Or
Elective 2: Chapters 20–25 (pages 192–232)

OPTIONS
HIGHER LEVEL STUDENTS ONLY
must cover *one* option
Either
Option 1: Chapters 26–29 (pages 235–260)
Or
Option 2: Chapters 30–33 (pages 262–290)
Or
Option 3: Chapters 34–36 (pages 292–320)

The Geography exam booklet

All students must do the short-answer questions.

 Higher level students must do **four** other questions:

- one multi-part question from Physical Geography
- one multi-part question from Regional Geography
- one multi-part Elective question
- one Option question.

Each question is worth 80 marks.

Ordinary level students must do **three** other questions:

- one multi-part question from Physical Geography
- one multi-part question from Regional Geography
- one multi-part Elective question.

Each question is worth 100 marks.

Allow 10 minutes to read the paper carefully and another 10 minutes at the end to check over your script. This will give higher level students **30 minutes** for each full question and ordinary level students **40 minutes** for each full question. Careful timing of your answers during the exam will help you gain maximum marks.

Structure of core and elective questions

These are all multi-part questions and they all have **three parts**.

- Part A is a skills-based question, e.g. sketch maps, map-reading, charts, skills.
- Parts B and C test syllabus-based material and skills.

Ordinary level marks are generally:

Part A – 30 marks

Part B – 40 marks

Part C – 30 marks.

Give *at least* 8 significant relevant points (SRPs) for parts B and C and name examples.

Higher level questions are generally marked:

- Part A – 20 marks
- Part B – 30 marks
- Part C – 30 marks.

Think in terms of 12 to 15 SRPs for parts B and C.

For both ordinary and higher level, write your SRPs in paragraph format. Bullet points may lose you marks for lack of cohesion. Give a labelled diagram to explain a point if time permits.

The **Option answer** must be in **essay format**. You should divide this answer into sections using **three or four headings**. For each heading write a well-developed paragraph (*not* bullet points) that has at least eight SRPs. Cohesion is vital. **Focus on your headings** and **stay with the topic**.

What are SRPs?

SRPs are **significant relevant points**. They are statements of factual information. **Each SRP is worth 2 marks**.

An SRP may be:

- A fully explained statement or short paragraph.
- A statistic with some associated explanation.
- A relevant diagram or chart.
- Extra labels on the diagram that are not already mentioned in your answer.
- A full explanation of a geographical term.

Structure of the exam paper and questions

All students must do the following:

Question Structure	Marks	Timing for Higher Level
12 short-answer questions on Core Units 1, 2 and Elective (only 10 required). Do all 12 questions.	Higher level: 80 marks Ordinary level: 100 marks	30 minutes – 12 × 2.5 minutes 40 minutes – 12 × 3.25 minutes
One question from **each** of the following multi-part questions: • Core 1 **Physical** Section • Core 2 **Regional** Section • **Elective** Section	Higher level: 3 × 80 = 240 marks Ordinary level: 3 × 100 = 300 marks	3 × 30 minutes, each 30 minutes divided into 6 + 12 + 12 minutes (for a 30-mark question) or 16 minutes (for a 40-mark question)
Option section (higher level only) Do **ONE** question from **ONE** of the following: • Global Interdependence • Geoecology • Culture and Identity	80 marks	30 minutes

Higher level students do one **additional** Option question.

Preparing for the exam

- Make sure you have all your equipment with you: pens, pencils, rubber, ruler, etc.
- Get to bed early and get up early.
- Have a good healthy breakfast.

What to do in the exam

1. **Carefully** read each question.
2. **Make sure** you can attempt **all** parts of the questions you have chosen to do. Don't rush in only to find you can do only two parts.

3. Watch the **timing** for each answer.

4. Don't waste time using lots of colour in sketch maps. Colour is helpful but not essential.

5. **Make notes** on the paper near the question to structure your answer and recall key words.

6. Write notes on the topics you have chosen as soon as you think of them. It's so easy to forget things under pressure in the exam.

7. Spend only a limited time on sketch maps. Write/mark **only** what is asked of you. Get the shape of the sketch map correct.

8. Do the question/Option question you know best first.

SECTION 1
Core Units

CORE UNIT 1
Patterns and Processes
in the Physical Environment

CORE UNIT 2
Regional Geography

All students must study
both of these units (pages 1–156).

 **The Tectonic Cycle**

 aims You need to know about:
- the structure of the earth
- plate tectonics (in detail).

 key point

The earth is made up of layers: the **crust**, the **mantle** and the **core**.

The crust is broken into **plates**. These plates move. They **separate**, **collide** and **slide past** each other.

The plates are carried about by **convection currents** in the mantle.

The crust

The crust is composed of the continents, the ocean floors and the rigid upper mantle. This is called the **lithosphere** and all its rocks are solid.

The continents are formed mostly of light, granite-like rocks. They are 45 km thick on average, and up to 70 km thick under the mountain ranges.

The ocean floors are formed mostly of **basalt**, which is heavy. They have an average thickness of 8 km, but may be as thin as 3 km in places.

The mantle

- The **upper mantle** is solid rock.
- The **middle and lower mantle** consist of plastic-like rock that moves to form convection currents. The plates of the lithosphere move about on these slow-moving currents. The rock in the lower mantle is in a semi-liquid state because its temperature is very high.

 key point

The lithosphere is formed of the crust and upper mantle.

The core

The core is made up of **nickel and iron**. It is the hottest part of the earth: temperatures are greater than 4,000°C.

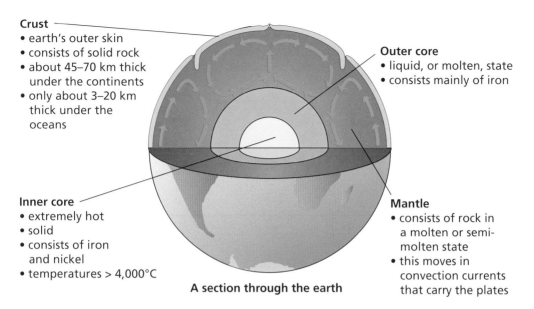

Crust
- earth's outer skin
- consists of solid rock
- about 45–70 km thick under the continents
- only about 3–20 km thick under the oceans

Outer core
- liquid, or molten, state
- consists mainly of iron

Inner core
- extremely hot
- solid
- consists of iron and nickel
- temperatures > 4,000°C

Mantle
- consists of rock in a molten or semi-molten state
- this moves in convection currents that carry the plates

A section through the earth

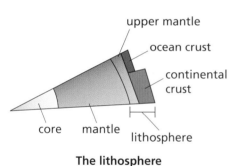

upper mantle

ocean crust

continental crust

core   mantle   lithosphere

The lithosphere

key point

- Forces within the earth are called **endogenic forces.** *Examples:* convection currents, subducting plates.
- They create, change and destroy landforms on and within the earth's surface.

WHAT WAS PANGAEA?
- All continents were joined together to form a single continent called Pangaea.
- It was surrounded by a single ocean called **Panthalassa**.

Proofs of seafloor spreading

- Mid-ocean ridges form at the boundaries of construction.
- New rock forms at mid-ocean ridges.
- The oldest ocean rock is closest to the continents.

exam focus

Make sure you know these basic facts about plate tectonics theory.

Proofs of continental drift

- Matching rocks found on continents that are thousands of miles apart.
- Matching fossils found in precise locations where the continents were once joined together.
- Edges of continents along the continental shelves fit together like a jigsaw.

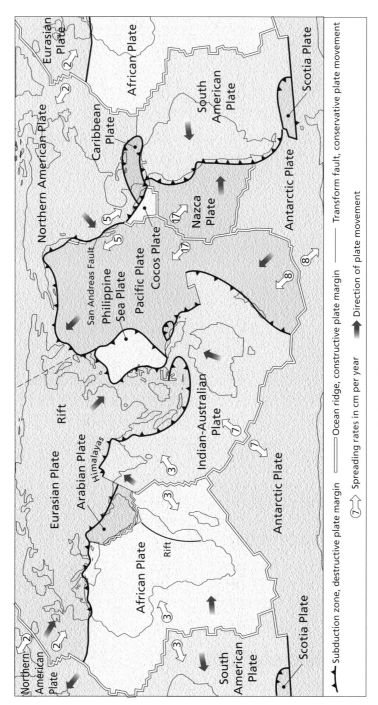

Plates of the earth's crust

Northern American Plate

Eurasian Plate

African Plate

Caribbean Plate

South American Plate

Scotia Plate

San Andreas Fault

Philippine Sea Plate

Pacific Plate

Cocos Plate

Nazca Plate

Antarctic Plate

Eurasian Plate

Rift

Arabian Plate

Himalayas

Indian-Australian Plate

African Plate

Rift

Antarctic Plate

Scotia Plate

South American Plate

Northern American Plate

Subduction zone, destructive plate margin —— Ocean ridge, constructive plate margin —— Transform fault, conservative plate movement

7⤳ Spreading rates in cm per year ➤ Direction of plate movement

Plate boundaries

There are three types of plate boundary: **divergent or constructive, convergent or destructive** and **transform or passive**.

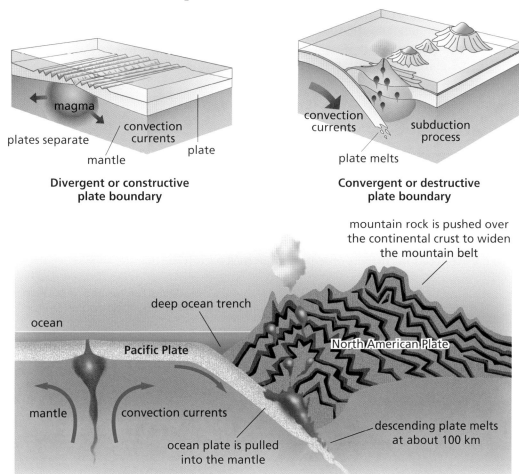

Divergent or constructive plate boundary

plates separate
magma
convection currents
mantle
plate

Convergent or destructive plate boundary

convection currents
subduction process
plate melts

mountain rock is pushed over the continental crust to widen the mountain belt

deep ocean trench

ocean

Pacific Plate

North American Plate

mantle

convection currents

ocean plate is pulled into the mantle

descending plate melts at about 100 km

Convergent or destructive plate boundary

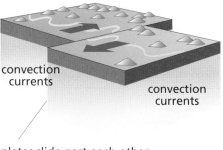

convection currents

convection currents

plates slide past each other along the transform fault

Transform or passive plate boundary

Plate tectonics states that the earth's crust is divided into plates and these plates move, driven by convection currents of semi-molten rock within the mantle.

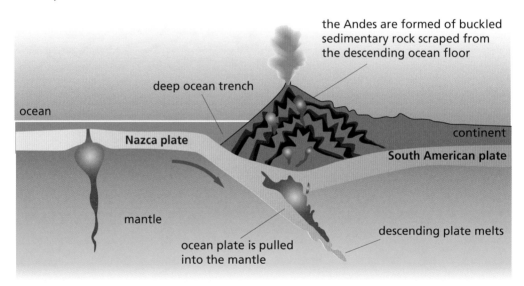

Subduction – a boundary of destruction associated with *continental drift*

These currents carry the plates of the earth's crust in a **piggy-back motion**.

At divergent or constructive boundaries the plates move apart, and at convergent or destructive boundaries the plates collide.

Seafloor spreading

- The **rifting** of a continent occurs when a continent is pulled apart and new narrow seas form. *Example:* the **Red Sea**.

- These new seafloors become boundaries of construction along their centres.
- New rock is formed from magma where the plates separate.
- It cools instantly on contact with the cold seawater and forms basalt rock. This widens the sea.
- The new rock is carried away from the ridge by **convection currents**. **Transform boundaries or faults** help this sideways movement to fit the shape of the earth.

> **key point**
>
> This answer also explains how fold mountains form.

Continental drift

- Continents are pushed across the globe by expanding ocean floors and convection currents to locations where they collide with other continents. *Example:* along the **Peru Trench**.
- These form **boundaries of destruction** where ocean floors, such as the **Nazca plate**, are sucked into the mantle and are destroyed by the process of subduction.
- As the ocean plates sink into the mantle they heat up and eventually **melt at a depth of 100 km** to form magma.
- The sinking plates are **saturated with seawater**, which helps melt the rock.
- Sediments on the ocean floor are **scraped off** the descending plate and are crushed and buckled upwards against the continent to form **fold mountains** of sedimentary rock. *Example:* the **Andes**.
- The **magma** from the melted plates **rises up through the folded rock** to create batholiths and volcanoes. *Example:* **Cotopaxi**.
- The **batholiths** form **granite rock** within mountains and the volcanoes form basalt and lava at the surface.

> **exam focus**
>
> You can refer to the causes of earthquakes at plate boundaries (see page 14) to extend an answer on continental drift.

Summary: Plate Boundaries

Type	Example	Process
Divergent or Constructive	Mid-Atlantic Ridge	• Separation • American and Eurasian plates move apart • New rock formed
Convergent or Destructive	Nazca/South American plates	• Collision • Fold mountains formed • Volcanoes, earthquakes
Transform or Passive	Pacific/North American plates	• Sliding past each other • Earthquakes along the San Andreas Fault in California

SAMPLE EXAM QUESTION AND ANSWER

Question: Discuss the geographical distribution and impacts of constructive plate boundaries. (2016, 30 marks)

Marking scheme:

- Impact identified – 2 marks
- Reference to geographical distribution – 2 marks
- Discussion – 13 × SRPs
- Relevant labelled diagram – 1 × SRP
- Credit relevant extra information on labelled diagram for 2 × SRP.

Note: Draw a simple diagram or diagrams with a few labelled sentences/SRPs

1. A new sea floor is created as the rising magma forms basalt when it meets the cold ocean water

2. Ocean water spills in and fills the newly created valley to form a narrow sea

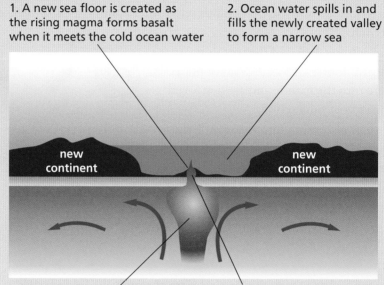

3. The rising magma current pushes each newly created continent apart

4. A mid-ocean ridge forms at the centre

A mid-ocean ridge is a boundary of construction associated with seafloor spreading

Answer: Most volcanoes form at boundaries of destruction.

Distribution

- Constructive plate boundaries are locations where **plates separate** and **rift valleys** are created. These constructive plate boundaries form on continents in some cases, but mostly on ocean floors.
- The best-known continental plate boundary occurs at the East African Rift Valley but it is in the early stages of separation. **This process is known as continental rifting.** This is causing the continent of Africa to move away from Arabia by forming the Red Sea and causing Africa to split apart, forming a separate new plate that is now called the **Nubian Plate.**
- Separating plates generally **form a Y-shape**, in this case creating the **Red Sea** and the **Gulf of Aden** which the sea has flooded, and the **East African Rift Valley** which has not fully developed. The process that drives this separation is **a plume of magma**, forming a **Hot Spot** that rises towards the surface from the mantle.

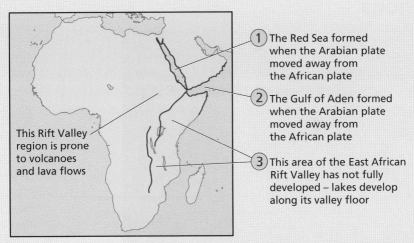

1. The Red Sea formed when the Arabian plate moved away from the African plate

2. The Gulf of Aden formed when the Arabian plate moved away from the African plate

3. This area of the East African Rift Valley has not fully developed – lakes develop along its valley floor

This Rift Valley region is prone to volcanoes and lava flows

- The more southern section of the East African Rift Valley has many large lakes that formed on its floor, e.g. Lake Tanganyika and Lake Malawi.
- **Mid-ocean ridges** are formed from new rock at constructive boundaries on ocean floors. This new rock pushes continents apart in a process called **continental drift**. The best known to Irish students is the **Mid-Atlantic Ridge** that pushes Europe and Africa away from the Americas.
- Mid-ocean ridges are located in all the major oceans; examples include: The Mid-Atlantic Ridge in the Atlantic Ocean, the Mid-Indian Ridge in the Indian Ocean, and the East Pacific Rise in the Pacific Ocean.
- As continents move apart, the new rock accumulates into high mountain ridges that sit on the ocean floor. The **Mid-Atlantic Ridge** is a mid-ocean ridge in the Atlantic Ocean. This new rock forms on both sides of the separating plates, thus increasing the width of the ocean floor. Sea floor rock is always youngest nearest to these separating plates and oldest at continental edges.
- The magma beneath the ocean ridges is hot and light and it pushes the thin seabed upwards, making the mountains higher. Most igneous rock is formed at these locations when magma cools quickly to form **basalt**.
- Iceland is an island that formed at a hot spot on the Mid-Atlantic Ridge, and the rift valley on the Atlantic Ocean floor continues on land through the island. Volcanoes regularly occur in Iceland. Magma close to the surface provides thermal energy for the island and heats homes and greenhouses.
- The island of Surtsey is a nearby island that formed from the sea bed in 1963 during a volcanically active period in Iceland.
- **Earthquakes** also occur along constructive plate boundaries. These earthquakes are rarely very powerful because new rock breaks easily under low strain so there is little build-up of tension sufficient to create a powerful earthquake.

exam focus

The best way to revise volcanoes is by using past questions and sample answers.

Volcanoes

Volcanoes at hot spots throw pyroclasts into the air

key point

Most volcanoes occur at subduction zones where plates collide. Some volcanoes also occur at hot spots.

SAMPLE EXAM QUESTION AND ANSWER

Question: Discuss how plate tectonics has increased our understanding of the global distribution of volcanoes. (30 marks)

Note: draw a **simple** diagram or diagrams with a few labelled sentences/SRPs.

Marking scheme:
- Two global examples – 2 marks each
- Plate tectonics examined – 13 SRPs @ 2 marks each.

Answer: Most volcanoes form at boundaries of destruction.

- The earth's crust is divided into plates and these plates move due to seafloor spreading and continental drift.
- Convection currents carry the plates of the earth's crust in a piggy-back motion.
- The plates collide at boundaries of collision or destruction.
- **Most volcanoes form at two types of destructive plate boundaries: (a) where an ocean plate collides with a continental plate; and (b) where two ocean plates collide.**
- As plates approach each other, the intervening ocean floor plate is subducted into the mantle. As it descends, it melts at a depth of about 100 km.
- The continental plate scrapes layers of sediment from the descending ocean floor and they are forced upwards, buckled and compressed into fold mountains.
- The melting descending plate creates magma that rises through the folded rock above.
- Small amounts of this magma rise and collect into huge masses of magma called batholiths.
- These batholiths are the source of magma, which creates volcanoes at the surface in fold mountains such as Cotopaxi in the Andes.

- Most volcanoes are located around the western edge of the Pacific Ocean where ocean plates collide. They form part of the Pacific Ring of Fire.
- The sinking plates melt, forming magma.
- Eventually, the compressed gases and liquid magma are blasted through the ocean floor and build up volcanic cones, such as those in the Philippines and Japan.

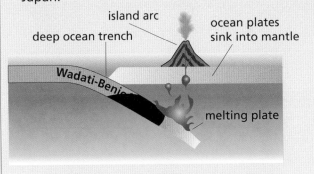

island arc
deep ocean trench
ocean plates sink into mantle
Wadati-Benioff
melting plate

Ocean–ocean boundary: Western Pacific

exam focus

You should:
- write at least 15 SRPs (2 marks each)
- name two plates that collide to cause subduction
- name a volcano.

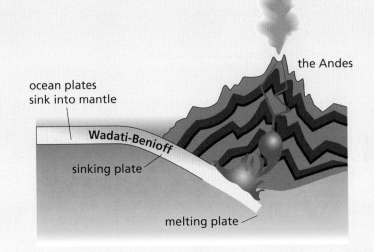

ocean plates sink into mantle
Wadati-Benioff
sinking plate
melting plate
the Andes

Ocean–continent boundary: Eastern Pacific

Some volcanoes occur at **hot spots**. These are areas where large batholiths are close to the surface at locations away from plate boundaries. *Examples:* Yellowstone National Park, USA.

exam focus

A question on hot spots may appear in short-answer questions.

- Black smokers are chimney-like openings at mid-ocean ridges.
- Very hot water containing **dissolved minerals** gushes from these openings.
- Hot spots are localised areas of volcanic activity that may be far from plate boundaries.

Effects of volcanoes

Positive

- Lava soils are rich in iron, which is good for coffee production.
- Geothermal energy can be generated from hot rock and geysers.
- Mineral ores and veins are important resources.
- New land is created on volcanic islands.
- Tourists visit volcanic regions. *Examples:* Iceland; Mount Etna, Sicily.

Negative

- People can be killed by **nuées ardentes** (clouds of poisonous gases and ash).
- Lava flows destroy houses and towns.
- Eruptions force people to evacuate their homes.

- Earthquakes usually occur at plate boundaries as a result of plate tectonic processes.
- There are three types of earthquake: shallow-focus, intermediate-focus and deep-focus.
- Some earthquakes, like those in Ireland, occur on old faultlines.

Earthquakes

Causes of earthquakes

Tectonic plates

Strain builds up in tectonic plates as they get stuck when they try to move past, apart or under each other. This strain suddenly releases and readjusts itself. This readjustment is felt on the surface as an earthquake.

The Ice Age

Thousands of metres of ice pressed down the land surface. When the ice sheets melted at the end of the Ice Age, the land gradually bounced back to its original level. This change still causes earthquakes from time to time.

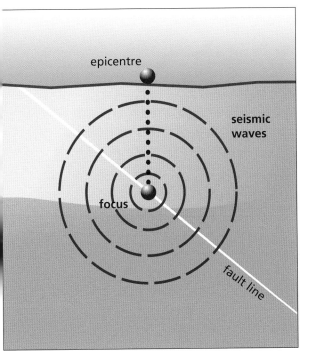

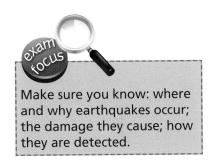

Make sure you know: where and why earthquakes occur; the damage they cause; how they are detected.

Important terms at an earthquake location

Ancient faults

Plates move along ancient faults that lie buried deep beneath the earth's surface.

Rising magma

Magma rushes towards the surface through the vent pipe just before a volcanic eruption. This movement creates numerous small earthquakes.

The measurement and effects of earthquakes

- A **seismologist** is a person who studies earthquakes.
- A **seismograph** is an instrument that records and measures earthquakes.
- The **focus** is the spot at the origin of an earthquake.
- The **epicentre** is a spot on the earth's surface directly above the focus.
- **Seismic waves** radiate from the epicentre.
- There are two types of seismic (earthquake) waves: **body waves** and **surface waves**.
- Surface waves make the ground move in two ways at the same time: (a) in a rolling motion like waves on the sea; and (b) in a snake-like sideways movement.
- Buildings roll and twist at the same time.
- The **Richter scale** indicates the size or magnitude of an earthquake.
- An earthquake measuring 7 on the Richter scale is 10 times more powerful than one measuring 6, and 100 times more powerful than one measuring 5.
- The **Mercalli scale** measures earthquake damage on a 12-point scale: 1 = no damage; 12 = total destruction.

SAMPLE QUESTION AND ANSWER

Question: Discuss how plate tectonics has increased our understanding of the global distribution of earthquakes.

Answer:
Most earthquakes occur along major plate boundaries (faultlines).

- For every 30-mark question, write at least 15 SRPs @ 2 marks each.
- Draw a simple diagram with a couple of labels as SRPs.
- Give examples.

- Earthquakes occur along all major plate boundaries: these boundaries are called faultlines. Most earthquakes occur along the Pacific Ring of Fire around the Pacific Ocean.
- As the plates collide, the heavier ocean plate **subducts** beneath the lighter continental plate.
- All earthquakes at these boundaries of destruction occur along the line of the descending plate. This is called the **Wadati-Benioff Zone**.

Draw this diagram

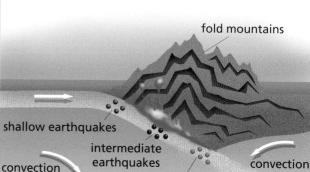

Earthquakes occur along the Wadati-Benioff Zone

- Three categories of earthquake occur along this zone: **shallow-focus earthquakes**; **intermediate earthquakes**; and **deep earthquakes**.
  - **Shallow-focus earthquakes** occur near the surface.
  - **Intermediate earthquakes** occur where the descending plate melts to form magma.
  - **Deep earthquakes** occur when chemical and mineral changes occur within the rocks of the descending plate.
- Plate edges at all boundaries tend to grind against each other as they slide past. Sometimes the plates get jammed, for example along the **San Andreas Fault** in California.
- This causes the rock within the plates to stretch but it will eventually break and the plates snap back to a spot where there is no stress. This process is called 'elastic rebound'.
- This movement releases seismic waves, or shock waves, to radiate through the earth from the focus, so creating an earthquake.

Learn some facts about two recent earthquakes in contrasting regions.

Case study: The Japan earthquake and tsunami of 2011

Sendai in Japan after the earthquake and tsunami. Tsunami are caused by earthquakes that occur offshore beneath the ocean seabed.

Cause

- The 2011 earthquake off the Pacific coast of Tohoku occurred at 2.46 p.m. on Friday, 11 March 2011. Its epicentre was approximately 70 km east of the Oshika peninsula of Tohoku, at a depth of 30 km beneath the seabed. It measured 9.0 on the Richter scale.
- It was the **most powerful earthquake ever recorded** to have hit Japan, and the fourth most powerful earthquake in the world since modern record-keeping began in 1900. It happened where the Pacific Ocean plate that moves about 9 cm per year subducts under the lighter Eurasian plate.
- An estimated **500 km of fault line ruptured** and the earthquake lasted for 6 minutes. The city of Sendai was the nearest major city to the earthquake.

Consequences

- The earthquake was preceded by numerous foreshocks, the largest of which was 7.2 magnitude. Many aftershocks were also felt, one of which measured 7.7 magnitude.

- Powerful tsunami waves reached heights up to 40.5 metres (over 133 feet) and travelled as much as 10 km inland.
- The waves overtopped and destroyed specially designed protective tsunami seawalls at several locations and a number of three-storey buildings where many people had sought safety from tsunami waves.
- The World Bank estimated economic cost of the damage was US$235 billion, making it the **costliest natural disaster in world history.**
- The tsunami caused a cooling system failure at Fukushima Daiichi Nuclear Power Plant that led to a nuclear meltdown and release of 300 tonnes of radioactive materials. Approximately **16,000 people were killed,** most by drowning. More than **2,500 are still missing.**
- The earth's axis was shifted slightly, and the island of Honshu was shifted eastward by 2.4 metres. The Pacific plate slipped westward by 24 metres.

How to reduce the effects of earthquakes

- Enforce strict building regulations in earthquake-prone regions.
- Install earthquake-proof technology in new tall buildings.
- Practise emergency earthquake drills and regional emergency plan procedures.
- Develop tsunami warning stations for all countries throughout the Pacific and Indian Ocean regions.

Predicting volcanic eruptions and earthquakes

- **Scientific instruments** (e.g. strain meters, lasers) are placed in susceptible regions.
- **Seismic gaps** are places that have not had an earthquake for a long time but are bordered by areas of recent earthquake activity. Seismic gaps are the most likely spots for future earthquakes.
- A **dating pattern** of past earthquakes and volcanoes can help to predict the likelihood of new ones.
- Observations of **animal behaviour** – animals are sensitive to tremors.

Plate boundaries:
Questions 3B, 2014; 3C, 2016.
Volcanoes:
Questions 1B, 2011; 3C, 2013.

2 The Rock Cycle

aims What you need to know:

- Rocks are classified into groups, according to how they were formed. These groups are: **igneous**, **sedimentary** and **metamorphic**.
- Some are formed, changed and destroyed by forces within the earth (**endogenic** forces).
- Weathering and erosion (**exogenic** forces) destroy rocks, and their sediments form new rock on the surface.
- All these forces create the rock cycle.

- Learn how rocks are formed, modified, destroyed and reformed as part of the rock cycle.
- You should also know about the impact of human interaction with the rock cycle.

The rock cycle

1. The first rocks were igneous rocks, which formed from magma.
2. All rocks are broken down by weathering and erosion.
3. Their sediments are deposited, compressed and hardened to form sedimentary rocks.
4. Some sedimentary, igneous and metamorphic rocks are heated by other hot igneous rocks and changed to new rocks. These new changed rocks are metamorphic rocks.
5. So some metamorphic rocks can be changed to new metamorphic rocks.
6. Igneous rocks can be changed to metamorphic rocks and sedimentary rocks can be changed to metamorphic rocks.
7. Rocks are destroyed and melt to form magma at subduction zones.

Write out a detailed account of this rock cycle, starting with igneous rocks. Make sure you have at least 15 SRPs (each worth two marks in the exam).

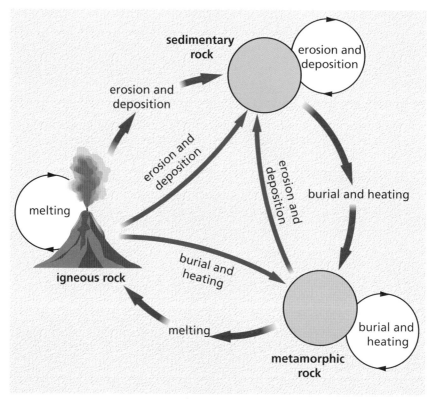

The rock cycle

Types of rock

Igneous rocks

- Igneous rocks form from **magma** when it cools and hardens.
- **Plutonic** rock cools slowly within the earth. *Example:* granite.
- **Volcanic** rock cools on the earth's surface. *Examples:* basalt and lava.

Rock type	Origin	Location
Granite	*Plutonic:* • Magma in batholiths • Large crystals	Wicklow Donegal Connemara
Basalt	*Volcanic:* • Lava cooled quickly • Tiny crystals	Giant's Causeway, Antrim

SAMPLE EXAM QUESTION AND ANSWER

Question:

Explain how igneous rocks form.

Answer:

- Most igneous rocks form from hot molten magma that comes from the mantle.
- Most magma forms at **subduction zones** when ocean plates sink into the mantle.
- Some magma forms when other igneous, sedimentary or metamorphic rocks melt.
- This magma rises and gathers in great masses to form **batholiths** within fold mountains. *Example:* Wicklow.
- The magma in batholiths **cools very slowly** and forms granite.
- Granite is a **plutonic** rock because it formed within the earth's crust.
- Granite has **large crystals** – mica, feldspar and quartz.
- Some magma finds its way to the surface through a vent. At the surface this magma is called **lava**.
- Lava cools quickly and forms **small crystals**, so lava is a volcanic rock.
- Some magma is blasted into the air and forms **volcanic ash**.
- The ash and lava form **volcanic cones**.
- Some lumps of magma harden quickly in the air to form **volcanic bombs**.
- Some lava pours out through **fissures** (cracks/tears) onto the surface to form **basalt**. *Example:* Antrim.

> **exam focus**
> - Give at least 15 SRPs for a 30-mark question.
> - Use Irish examples.

Sedimentary rocks

Sedimentary rocks form from cemented deposits of rock particles.

Rock type	Origin	Location
Limestone	Coral and shells in warm tropical seas	• Burren, Co. Clare • Central Plain
Sandstone	Deposited rock particles, mostly quartz	• Galtees • All mountains in Munster
Shale	Clay particles	• Wicklow • South Co. Clare

> **exam focus**
> 'Describe how one rock type is formed and how it produces a distinctive landscape' is a question that appears regularly. (See page 37 for how to answer this question using limestone as an example.)

How sedimentary rocks form

SAMPLE EXAM QUESTION AND ANSWER

Question: Describe the formation of one sedimentary rock that you have studied and briefly explain how this rock may be transformed into a metamorphic rock. (30 marks)

Marking scheme:

- Name one sedimentary rock – 2 marks
- Name one metamorphic rock – 2 marks
- Formation of sedimentary rock – 11 × SRPs
- Formation of metamorphic rock – 2 × SRPs
- Credit relevant diagram for 1 SRP
- Credit extra relevant information on labelled diagram for 2 × SRPs.

See also how limestone forms on page 37.

Answer:

How sandstone formed:

- Any tiny grains of rock between 1/16 and 2 mm in diameter that are cemented together form what is called sandstone. So, sandstone grains are all about size. Sandstone is composed of medium-sized rock particles.
- However, because quartz is so resistant to weathering, most sandstone grains are quartz.
- Sandstone forms from beds of sand deposited under the sea or in low-lying areas on the continents. As these beds subside into the earth's crust, usually pressed down by overlying sediments, they are heated and compressed.
- Hot groundwater then flows slowly through the spaces between the sand grains, where it deposits dissolved minerals, such as quartz, calcium carbonate and iron oxide. These minerals crystallise around the sand grains and cement them together into sandstone. This is called the process of **lithification**.
- Most sandstone formed during the **Devonian period** (about 400–350 million years ago), when this tropical region had a hot desert climate. At that time Ireland was located at 20°S, about where the Kalahari Desert is today.
- The region had occasional heavy downpours that eroded the Caledonian mountains and washed their sediments in flash floods to lowland areas.
- Sandstone formed from sandy delta deposits, river channel and flood-plain deposits, beach sand and sand dunes. Large deposits of **gravel** (stream-bed deposits) formed **conglomerate rock**. Each flood deposit is separated from the next by a hairline crack called a **bedding plane**.
- **Iron oxide** dissolved in ground water gave sandstone a red colour, so all these sandy deposits that were formed at this time are called **Old Red Sandstone**.

- Then the land level fell and the sea covered all of these sandstone deposits. Limestone formed in this warm sea and covered the sandstones. Eventually, earth movements pushed up all of these deposits into mountains such as the mountains of Munster, the Galtees and the Comeraghs.

How sandstone changed into metamorphic rock:

- Sandstone changes to quartzite when magma rises from the earth's interior during a period of mountain building. The magma then bakes or cooks the sandstone. In some instances, when the **magma touches off the sandstone**, it bakes it.
- This is called **contact metamorphism**. In other instances, it cooks it by **heat and pressure** in a process called **regional metamorphism**.
- This process occurred in our **oldest mountains in Co. Wicklow**, in the **Twelve Bens**, in Connemara, Co. Galway, and at **Croagh Patrick** in Co. Mayo.

How limestone formed:

- See page 37.

Metamorphic rock

- Metamorphic rock is rock that has been changed in its structure while it is still solid rock. It **has not melted** to make this change.
- Metamorphic rocks form when rock is subjected to extreme heat and/or pressure.
- See how sandstone changes to quartzite above, or how slate forms on page 22.

SAMPLE EXAM QUESTION AND ANSWER

Question: Explain the formation of metamorphic rocks, with reference to examples from Ireland. (30 marks)

Marking scheme:

- Name two metamorphic rocks – 2 + 2 marks
- Explanation – 13 × SRPs
- Credit relevant labelled diagram for 1 × SRP
- Credit extra relevant information on labelled diagram for 2 × SRPs
- Credit 3rd named metamorphic rock for 1 × SRP
- Diagram without labelling – 0 marks.

A labelled diagram is worth at least 1 SRP.

Examples:

Slate at Kilcavan in the Wicklow mountains; Portroe in Co. Tipperary, near Killaloe; Valentia Island Co. Kerry

Quartzite in the Connemara Mountains or the Twelve Bens. Croagh Patrick Co. Mayo; Mount Errigal Co. Donegal; the Sugar Loaf in Co. Wicklow

Answer:

How metamorphic rock is formed:

- Metamorphic rock is rock that has been changed in its structure while it is still a solid rock. It **has not melted** to make this change.
- Metamorphic rocks form where rock is subjected to extreme heat and/or pressure or stress. Generally this occurs at boundaries of destruction. This heat is often generated by the presence of magma in a batholith nearby.
- Some metamorphic rocks also form where low heat levels and pressure alone are generated by earth movements such as folding.
- Some metamorphic rock such as slate may form new metamorphic rock such as schist when conditions change.
- Surface rock is buckled and pushed upwards where plates collide. More buckled rock is pushed downwards by as much as 40 km deep into the earth's crust, and its temperature rises at about 25°C for every km of depth.
- Some metamorphic rocks form at temperatures as low as 250°C because the atoms that make up their minerals vibrate and break their chemical bonds. This allows these atoms to move a short distance, only to reattach themselves to another atom or atoms. These moving atoms eventually rearrange themselves to form new rock crystals that are more stable at this new temperature and/or pressure.
- Over time, the entire original rock may change to a new rock type composed of the newer rock crystals.
- Sedimentary rock or some metamorphic rocks change when they touch off or are pushed near to magma. For example, limestone changes to marble, sandstone changes to quartzite and shale changes to slate.
- The mineral composition of a sedimentary rock determines which new rock it changes to. Limestone, for example, is composed of only one mineral, calcium carbonate. So it has a limited choice of rocks to change into and can only form marble which is also formed of calcium carbonate. Sandstone also has a similar limited range of metamorphic rocks to change into so it forms quartzite which is made of quartz just like sandstone.
- Slate, however, is composed of many minerals and it may form any new rock type or colour determined by its mineral composition, the amount of heat and/or pressure or both. It can change to phyllite, schist or gneiss. The clay minerals that form slate may contain mica, quartz calcite, pyrite, hematite and other minerals.
- Heat radiating from the earth's core raises ground water temperature. This warm groundwater has the ability to dissolve some minerals and carry them in solution to new locations where it may deposit them or attach them to new minerals to make new rock crystals. This is how metamorphic rock at low temperatures may form.

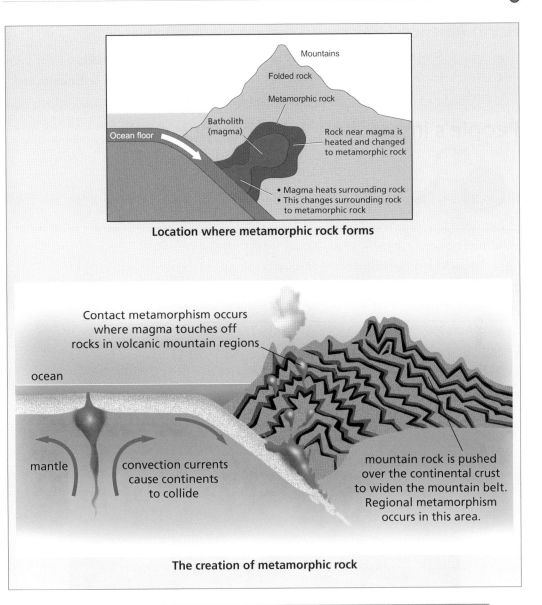

Location where metamorphic rock forms

The creation of metamorphic rock

Rock type	Origin	Location
Marble	Heated limestone	Connemara
Slate	Heated shale	• Wicklow • Valentia Island • Portroe, near Killaloe
Quartzite	Heated sandstone	• Donegal • Connemara • Croagh Patrick, Co. Mayo • Sugar Loaf, Co. Wicklow

North American active and trailing plate margins

- America's west coast is **tectonically active** and has **new igneous rocks**.
- America's east coast is **not tectonically active** and has **new coastal sediments and rock**. This is America's trailing plate margin.

People's interaction with the rock cycle

You need to study **only one** of the following:
- mining
- extraction of building materials (quarrying)
- oil and gas exploration
- geothermal energy.

Extraction of building materials (quarrying)

Irish example: Roadstone quarry, Ballyneety, Co. Limerick.

Quarrying is the process of blasting rock from quarry faces (man-made cliff faces) or excavating it from the ground and preparing it for the construction industry.

**Quarrying is carried out in many locations throughout Ireland.
Roadstone, for example, has many quarries making rock aggregates.**

Sands and gravels

- Excavated from ridges (**eskers**), and other deposits of sands and gravels that were laid down by rivers that flowed at the end of the Ice Age.

- Sand is generally **mixed with cement** to make mortar and concrete.
- Gravel is also used in concrete. It is used as filling in housing, for surfacing paths, and as subsurface material in road construction.

Limestone and sandstone

Parallel lines of holes are drilled along the top of a quarry face. Explosive charges are placed in these drill-holes. Controlled explosions release thousands of tonnes of limestone or sandstone rock that fall to the base of the quarry face. Loads of these shattered rocks are removed by dumper truck to crushers. They are then broken down into smaller particles of stone of various sizes called aggregates. The angular nature and hardness of these particles allows them to be used:

- to make concrete and concrete products, such as concrete blocks and roofing tiles
- for road surfacing
- as filling for passages and driveways.

Powdered limestone – lime – is used as a fertiliser.

Gypsum

- Quarried at Kingscourt, Co. Cavan.
- Used to make plaster slabs for house construction.
- Has both insulating and fireproofing characteristics.

Marble

- Quarried in Connemara.
- In industry, the term *marble* refers to any polished rock.
- Pure marble forms from metamorphosed limestone.
- Also quarried at Carrara, Tuscany. In its purest form it is white. It is used for flooring, wall tiles and fireplaces. Marble from these quarries was used by Renaissance sculptors such as Michelangelo.

The rock cycle:

Questions 2C, 2011; 3B, 2011; 1B, 2012; 1B, 2013; 2C, 2013; 1B, 2014; 2B, 3C, 2015; 1B, 2016.

3 Weathering Processes

aims You need to:

- know the difference between physical and chemical weathering
- know two examples of each type and a location where each occurs
- be able to recognise each on a diagram or photograph.

Weathering is the breaking down of rocks that lie on or near the earth's surface. There are two types of weathering: **mechanical** and **chemical**.

Mechanical weathering

Joint formation (jointing)

The removal, by erosion, of surface rock reduces the weight on deeply buried rocks. Joints develop and this breaks rock into large and small rectangular blocks.

Sheeting/exfoliation

Sheeting and exfoliation occur due to stresses and strains that act within rock. Granite was formed deep within fold mountains, under extreme pressure from great forces that squeezed it from all sides. Later, after overlying rock layers and pressures were removed by erosion, the rock expands and the granite batholiths split into onion-like sheets when exposed at the surface. This is called **sheeting** or **exfoliation**.

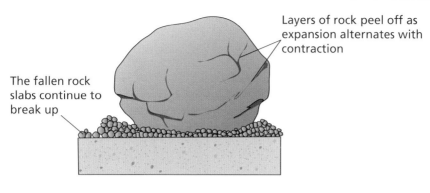

Layers of rock peel off as expansion alternates with contraction

The fallen rock slabs continue to break up

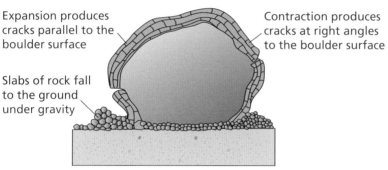

Expansion produces cracks parallel to the boulder surface

Contraction produces cracks at right angles to the boulder surface

Slabs of rock fall to the ground under gravity

When exfoliation affects rocks, their outer shells break off

Exfoliation of granite is also called sheeting

Freeze-thaw

When water freezes in cracks or joints in bedrock it widens the cracks and so helps to break up rock.

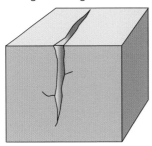

Trapped water freezes during winter at night on high mountains

Surface water fills cracks in rocks

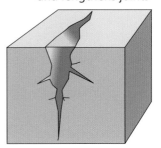

Ice expands by about 9 per cent and lengthens joints

Freeze-thaw action shatters rocks

Plant roots

Plant roots penetrate joints, cracks and crevices, widening them as the roots thicken with age.

Surface flaking

Water soaks into rock in buildings, walls and bedrock. As the rock dries, mineral crystals grow. These mineral crystals push out surface rock grains to cause flaking.

Chemical weathering

Chemical weathering is most active in hot, wet regions. Types of chemical weathering include **carbonation**, **oxidation**, **hydration** and **hydrolysis**.

Carbonation

Rainwater is weak carbonic acid. As it trickles through rock joints it changes the limestone to calcium and bicarbonate minerals. These are soluble in water and are washed away in solution. (For more detail on carbonation, see pages 38–39.)

Oxidation

This is the rusting of minerals. It is particularly effective in rocks that contain iron. Most iron in rocks is in the form of a bonding/cementing agent. Iron reacts with water to become iron oxide. Because oxides are soluble in water the iron oxide is washed away in solution and the rock crumbles.

Hydration

Some minerals absorb water. This creates stresses in rock and over time the rock shatters.

Hydrolysis

This affects granite. Water bonds with micas and feldspar to form clay minerals. These become oxidised and lose their bonding effect; the remaining minerals are separated and the rock crumbles.

4 Landforms Influenced by the Tectonic Cycle

 You need to know about volcanic and plutonic landforms.

Volcanic and plutonic landforms

Rifting and subduction form **volcanic** and **plutonic** landforms.

- **Volcanic landforms** form on the earth's surface. They include volcanic cones, basalt plateaus and fumaroles.
- **Plutonic landforms** form beneath the earth's surface, within the crust. They include batholiths, dykes, sills, laccoliths and lopoliths.

Volcanic landforms

SAMPLE EXAM QUESTION AND ANSWER

Question: Describe the processes that have led to the formation of any two volcanic landforms. (30 marks)

Answer:

1. Basalt plateau

Irish example: Antrim Plateau.

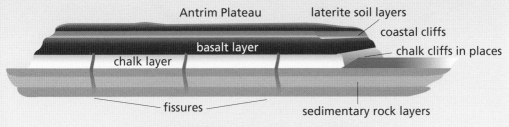

The basalt plateau in Antrim is a volcanic landform

- About 65 million years ago a new hot spot caused **rifting** and the American and Eurasian continents began to split apart.
- The Mid-Atlantic Ridge extended northwards over what is now the Norwegian Sea.
- The crust was stretched and cracks or **fissures** appeared on the surface.
- Hot lava poured out through the these fissures from the batholith underneath. There were many successive lava flows and each flow cooled quickly to form basalt.

- Because the lava flows were 5–40 metres thick, they formed five-sided basalt columns such as those at the **Giant's Causeway**.
- Basalt is a fine-grained volcanic rock with tiny crystals that are not visible to the eye.
- Eventually the basalt layers built up to form a flat-topped plateau.

2. Volcanic cone
Example: Cotopaxi (the Andes) or Mount Etna (Sicily).

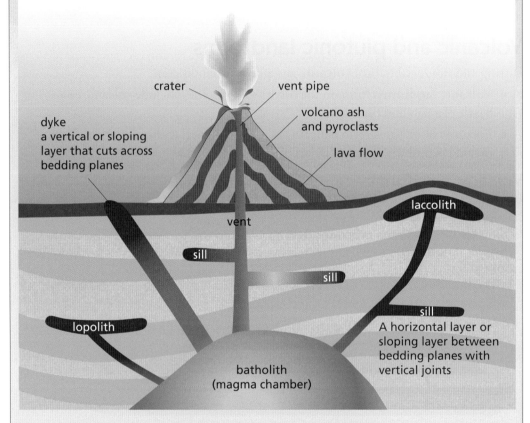

A volcanic cone is a volcanic landform. Some plutonic landforms form part of a volcano. Can you name them?

- Magma gathers in a **batholith** within fold mountains when an ocean plate sinks beneath another plate.
- The magma contains **compressed gases** that are under extreme pressure. This magma finds its way to the surface through weaknesses in the folded rock.
- As magma rises, the gases expand and create huge pressure that forces the magma upwards. Eventually it reaches the surface through an opening called the vent.
- An explosion blasts ash and molten rock high into the air; this then falls back to the surface and gathers around the **vent**.
- Lava flows pour out through an opening at the top called the **crater**.
- Alternate layers of ash and lava build up a cone-shaped mountain around the vent.

Plutonic landforms

SAMPLE EXAM QUESTION AND ANSWER

Question: Describe the process that has led to the development of any one plutonic landform.

Answer:

A batholith

Irish example: the Wicklow batholith.

- A batholith forms in fold mountains where two plates collide at a destructive plate boundary.
- An ocean plate is subducted under a continental plate into the mantle.

> Most of these bullet points can be used to answer several different questions on the tectonic cycle.

- Layers of sediment are scraped off the descending ocean plate and are pushed up and buckled against the continent, forming high fold mountains.
- As the plate sinks into the mantle it gets hotter and melts at a depth of about 100 km, forming magma.
- Magma rises up through the folded rock layers above because it is less dense (lighter) than surrounding rock.

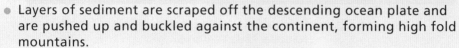

batholith cools slowly to form granite

fold mountains

ocean

magma masses join to form a batholith

ocean plate subducts beneath continental plate

magma masses rise because they are lighter than cool surrounding rock

sinking plate melts at 100 km depth

Batholiths form at destructive boundaries

Half Dome is an exposed batholith in Yosemite National Park, California

- The presence of gas bubbles makes the magma more buoyant, so it rises easily.
- As the magma melts its way upwards, much of the surrounding rock melts into the magma, making it rich in silica (up to 70 per cent).
- The magma gathers within the fold mountain into one large mass to form a batholith that may be many kilometres wide.
- The magma cools slowly and forms large crystals of **mica, feldspars and quartz**.
- The cooling magma heats the surrounding rocks and metamorphoses them. Sandstone changes to quartzite, limestone changes to marble and shale changes to schist and slate.
- Over millions of years the overlying rock is eroded away and the granite batholith is exposed at the surface.
- The granite weathers by shedding thin layers or shells of rock in a process called sheeting or exfoliation.
- Distinctive exfoliation granite domes develop. *Example:* Half Dome in Yosemite National Park, California
- Tors form on granite hilltops and create a distinctive landscape. *Example:* Dartmoor, England.

Landforms of sedimentary rock

key point

Plate collision creates landforms by **tilting, faulting** and **folding** sedimentary rock.

exam focus

Make sure you also know the landforms created by tectonic forces.

Tilting

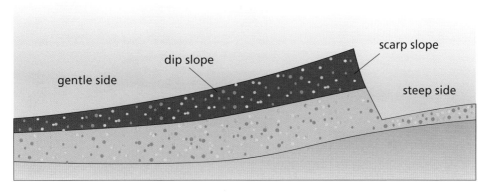

An escarpment has one gentle side and one steep side

Escarpment

One side is steep and the other has a gentle slope. *Examples:* the Dartry-Cuileagh uplands and the Brecon Beacons in Wales.

Faulting

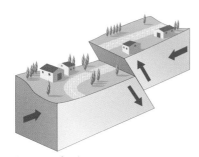

Reverse fault

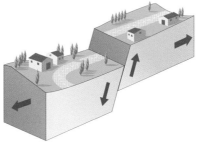

Normal fault

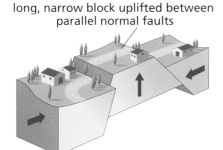

Block mountain (horst) – compression

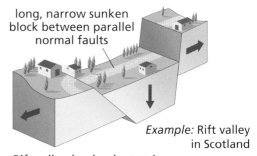

Rift valley (graben) – tension

**Block mountain (horst – compression/squeezing laterally); rift valley
(graben – tension/stretching laterally)**

Folding

Compression buckles and shortens rock layers.

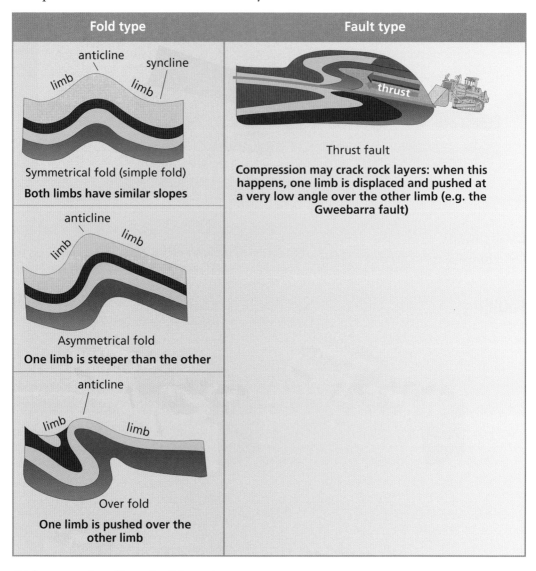

Fold type	Fault type
Symmetrical fold (simple fold) Both limbs have similar slopes	**Thrust fault** Compression may crack rock layers: when this happens, one limb is displaced and pushed at a very low angle over the other limb (e.g. the Gweebarra fault)
Asymmetrical fold One limb is steeper than the other	
Over fold One limb is pushed over the other limb	

Ridges and valleys in Munster

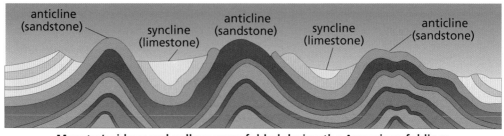

Munster's ridges and valleys were folded during the Armorican foldings

- Forces of compression folded the land in Munster into a series of anticlines and synclines.
- This occurred during the **Armorican (Variscan) foldings**.
- Today the ridges are of sandstone and the valleys of limestone.
- These ridges and valleys run **west to east** across Munster.
- Each rock layer is separated from the next by a **bedding plane**.
- Where folding was severe, an **overthrust fold** was formed.

The Paris Basin

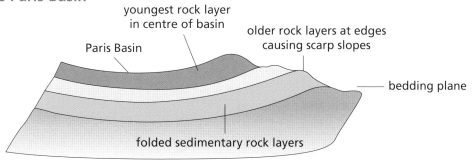

The Paris Basin is a saucer-shaped structure

- Forces of compression folded the rock layers.
- This occurred during the **Alpine foldings**.
- The centre sagged after folding, so the basin is dish-shaped, level at its centre, and with steep slopes called **scarps** at its eastern edges.
- The oldest rock layers are exposed on the eastern scarp slopes.

Doming

The Weald, southern England

A dome was created here by folding. Weathering and erosion of the youngest rocks have exposed the older rocks in the centre.

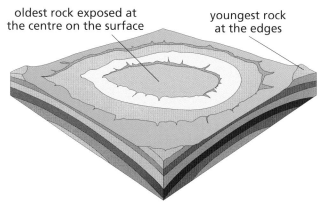

A dome landform in the Weald, southern England

exam Q

Questions 1C, 2014; 1C, 3B, 2015.

5 Landforms Influenced by Rock Type

aims You need to know about:

- the formation of rock types, e.g. limestone
- how limestone weathers to form a distinctive **karst** landscape
- how limestone bedrock produces specific surface and underground landforms
- how granite weathers to produce a distinctive **rounded** landscape with **tors** on top.

exam focus

You should know how at least one major rock type is formed; how this rock type weathers to form a distinctive landscape, with an Irish example.

Landforms of limestone rock

Limestone pavement displays grikes and clints that allow water to drain through freely from the surface

SAMPLE EXAM QUESTION AND ANSWER

Question:

With reference to any **one** rock type, explain how it was formed **and** how it can produce a distinctive landscape. (30 marks)

Answer:

How limestone and karst landscape formed. Example: the Burren in Co. Clare.

How limestone forms

- Limestone is formed from the mineral calcium carbonate or calcite. Its chemical formula is $CaCO_3$.

- It is found throughout the Central Plain and the Burren in Co. Clare in Ireland.

- Limestones formed when low-lying regions of the continents were submerged beneath shallow seas in the tropics about 350–300 million years ago.

- Some limestones formed from calcium carbonate from seawater that collected around tiny sand grains floating or rolling back and forth in shallow lagoons near the tropics.

- More limestones also formed from **billions of shells and skeletons** of organisms such as coral and seashells that lived in warm seas near the Equator.

- These organisms made calcium carbonate by extracting it from seawater to grow protective shells and skeletons.

The Burren, Co. Clare

The Burren in north-west Co. Clare

exam focus

- Name a rock type – 2 marks.
- Name a distinctive landscape, e.g. karst landscape – 2 marks.
- Describe its formation – 14–16 marks.
- Describe how it produces a distinctive landscape – 10 marks.

- Later, other sediments such as sand were washed into the sea and they covered the limestone with layers of sandstone that squeezed it into hard rock.

- The seabed eventually stopped sinking and began to rise into shallow waters. With erosion, the limestone that was once deeply buried was eventually exposed at the surface, where we find it today.

- There is less pressure at the surface so the limestone developed obvious **horizontal bedding planes** and vertical cracks called **joints**.

- Some limestones have a dark colour from dead plant matter that mixed with the rock while it formed.

- Pure limestone is white.

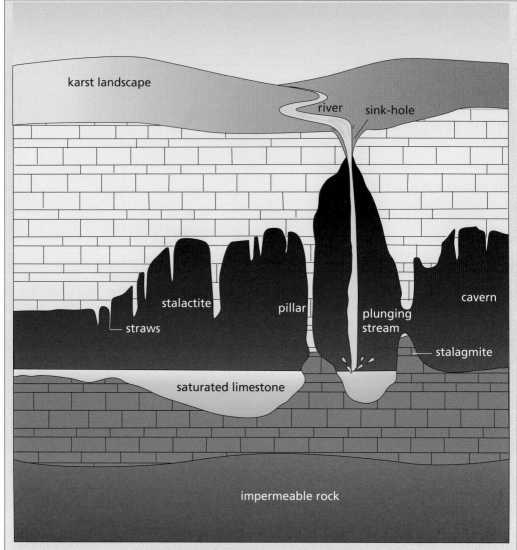

Limestone features in a karst landscape

How does limestone develop a distinctive landscape?
Carbonation

- **Karst** only develops where limestone rock is exposed at the surface. The **Burren** in Co. Clare is a karst landscape.
- Because limestone is formed of only one mineral (calcite), it weathers evenly, forming a **level landscape**.
- Rainwater is a weak acid, carbonic acid, which forms when carbon dioxide joins with moisture in the air. Once it falls on limestone it forms a chemical reaction, called carbonation, that dissolves the rock.
- This type of reaction is visible when hydrochloric acid is dropped on limestone. The acid releases carbon dioxide from the rock and the gas bubbles or fizzes as it is released.

- Rainwater trickles through the vertical **joints** and horizontal **bedding planes** in the limestone and widens them through solution.
- The joints at the surface widen to form **grikes**: the remaining rock between the grikes forms **clints**. Together they form **limestone pavement**.
- Underground, the rainwater continues to dissolve the limestone, forming narrow **passages that form the routes of underground streams**.
- The beds of surface streams regularly collapse into these passages, creating **sinkholes** or **swallow holes**. Poulnagolm in the Burren is an example.
- These sinkholes create **dry valleys** downstream from the sinkhole as surface water no longer flows through them.
- Large **caverns** are formed when limestone bedrock lies below the water table and large masses of it are washed away in solution.
- **Stalactites**, **stalagmites** and **columns** form from dripping water when calcite is deposited on cavern surfaces.

exam focus

In **ordinary level** papers, some questions ask for two surface or two underground landforms in a limestone region. **Always give Irish examples.**
Higher level papers may ask for just one landform, so describe it with 15 SRPs.

Some other limestone landforms

Sinkholes

Examples: Poulnabunny, Co. Mayo; the Cradle Hole in the Cuilcagh Uplands, Co. Fermanagh.

- Rainwater is a weak acid, **carbonic acid**, which forms when rain absorbs carbon dioxide in the atmosphere.
- The parallel vertical joints allow the rainwater to trickle through the rock.
- When underground, the flowing **ground water dissolves** the limestone and **sediment erodes** the rock through abrasion along these lines of weakness. These processes create underground **passages** that begin under the river bed.
- The joints and bedding planes divide limestone into blocks. Some blocks fall from the ceiling of these passages, eventually leading to a collapse of the rock on the river bed above.
- This creates an **opening from the passage to the surface**, through which the river plunges vertically downwards.
- This opening, which swallows up the river, is called a **sinkhole**.
- The remaining river valley downstream of the sinkhole becomes dry and so is called a **dry valley**.

Caverns

Examples: Marble Arch Cave, Co. Fermanagh; Mammoth Cave, Kentucky, USA.

- Limestone is composed of calcium carbonate, which is soluble in water.
- Most caverns form in the **zone of saturation**.
- The flowing ground water dissolves away the limestone.
- This process creates huge cavities that become enlarged by other processes over time: **sediment** in flowing ground water erodes the rock by **abrasion**; **collapsing limestone blocks** from the ceilings of small caverns increase the height of the cavern.
- **Melt-water** from melting ice sheets and glaciers at the end of the last Ice Age released vast amounts of melt-water that carried sand, rocks and boulders into these underground channels through sinkholes and enlarged them into enormous caverns.
- Many of these caverns are dry because of a fall in the water table or tectonic uplift.

Stalactites and stalagmites

Examples: Marble Arch Caves, Co. Fermanagh; Mitchelstown Caves, Co. Tipperary.

- Ground water in limestone regions is saturated in dissolved **calcium atoms** and **bicarbonate atoms**. Ground water is also **supersaturated in carbon dioxide**.
- Calcite is deposited where the water drops from cracks in cave roofs. Initially, calcite gathers around the outside of the drip, forming a delicate hollow stalactite, called a **soda straw**; but eventually the hollow fills up or gets blocked with grit, and water seeps around the hanging stem to form a more massive, solid **stalactite**.
- Where the drip hits the floor, it splashes, and the resulting calcite builds up to form an upward-pointing cone called a **stalagmite**.
- If this process continues over a very long time the stalagmites and stalactites join to form limestone **columns**.

Granite landscapes

The weathering of granite – Unloading, hydration and gravity

- Granite forms under extreme pressure deep within fold mountains. It contains three minerals: mica, feldspar and quartz. It forms from a magma batholith that gathered from melted ocean plates.
- Weathering and erosion removes the surrounding mountain rock. Eventually the granite reaches the surface. This reduces the weight of overlying rock and so expands in a process called **unloading**. Unloading creates joints/cracks in the granite. Ground water and rainwater seep into the joints. Two new processes then weather the rock:
  - ○ **Hydration** allows micas and feldspars to absorb water. This creates stresses within the rock and helps to break it up.
  - ○ **Hydrolysis** occurs when ground water, which is acidic, reacts with the feldspars in granite. Some atoms in the feldspar dissolve in the ground water, while others join with new atoms to form entirely new minerals to create clay. So the rock crumbles apart.
- **Gravity** moves the weathered particles downslope.

Granite tors

Example: Dartmoor, south-west England.

Tors are like blocks of granite stacked on each other. The cracks that divide them are called joints.

Tors are found on the **summits of granite hills and mountains**. They are blocks of granite that have their joints widened. The joints open for two reasons:

1. Pressure is released because the granite is no longer deep within a mountain where pressure is severe. This released pressure allows the rock to expand, creating the joints.
2. Weathering of the feldspar and mica minerals along the joints widens them even more so the granite splits into stacked blocks. *Example:* Wicklow Mountains.

Quartzite peaks

Example: Sugarloaf peaks, Co. Wicklow.

Croagh Patrick in Co. Mayo is formed from quartzite. It is pointed because of freeze-thaw action.

Pointed mountain peaks of quartzite rock are found close to granite landscapes. The granite batholith **metamorphosed** nearby **sandstone** layers and changed them to quartzite. When quartzite weathers on mountain tops, the freeze-thaw process sharpens the peak and scree gathers at its base.

exam Q

Questions 3B, 2012; 3B, 2013; 2C, 3C, 2014; 3B, 2016.

6 Landforms Influenced by Surface Processes

aims You need to know about all the surface processes of mass movement – ice, rivers and seas; and you should be able to **identify** the landforms that form from them on a photo/diagram/map.

exam focus

Study all surface processes, pages 42–44.

Make sure you study **at least two landforms in detail**.

exam focus

This question has appeared in every exam since 2006:

Examine, with the aid of a labelled diagram/diagrams, the processes that have shaped one/two Irish landforms of your choice.

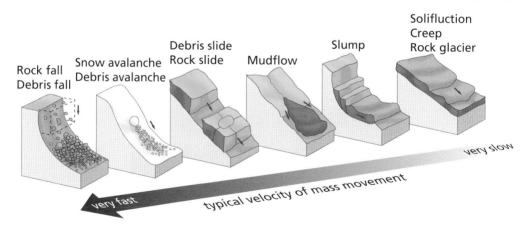

Rock fall / Debris fall — Snow avalanche / Debris avalanche — Debris slide / Rock slide — Mudflow — Slump — Solifluction / Creep / Rock glacier

very fast ← typical velocity of mass movement → very slow

Processes of mass movement

Slow movements

Soil creep

This is the movement of soil particles downslope. It occurs due to the influences of:

- **gravity** – pulls soil particles downslope
- **solifluction** – some soil particles swell as a result of absorbing ground water. This swelling pushes neighbouring particles away from each other.
- **frost heave** – ice crystals form under stones and move them to the surface.

Fast movements

Gravity

This pulls large rocks, boulders and soil downslope to create rock falls and landslides.

Earth flows

These occur when soil is saturated with water on gentle slopes.

Lahars or mud flows

Lahars occur when enormous amounts of soil, rock, trees and other debris move rapidly downslope. They are triggered when volcanic eruptions on ice-capped volcanic mountains cause large masses of ice to melt.

Slumping

This happens when cliff edges collapse; as they slip downwards there is a rotational movement of the falling material.

Glacial processes

Plucking

Water from melting ice trickles into cracks at the base of a glacier and then freezes. The glacier becomes attached to the rock under it. When the ice moves, rock particles are plucked from the ground.

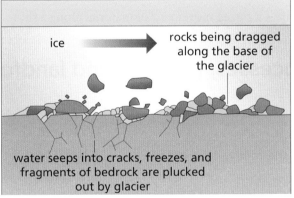

Rock fragments and bedrock are plucked out and somewhat rounded by movement of a glacier

Abrasion

The glacier moves these plucked rocks, which erode the base and sides of valleys, making them deeper.

It also involves the scouring of lowland areas, leading to the removal of soil in some regions.

Basal slip

The sliding movement of a glacier over its rock floor.

Freeze–thaw

During the day melt-water seeps into cracks in rock; at night the water freezes and expands, breaking up the rock.

River processes

- **Hydraulic action** – rocks are broken up by the force of moving water.
- **Corrasion or abrasion** – a river's load erodes the banks and bed of the river.
- **Cavitation** – bubbles of air collapse and form tiny shock waves against the outer bank of a river.
- **Deposition** – eroded material is dropped on the bed or flood plain of a river when the slope, the speed or the volume of a river is reduced.
- **Attrition** – fragments of stone are rounded and made smaller by hitting off each other.
- **Slumping** – rotational movement of a collapsing river bank as it is undermined by a river.

Coastal processes

- **Abrasion** – boulders, pebbles and sand are pounded by the waves against the coastline.
- **Hydraulic action** – the direct impact of strong waves on a coast.
- **Compression** – air is squeezed in cracks and caves, breaking up the rock.
- **Attrition** – fragments of stone are rounded and made smaller by hitting off each other.
- **Longshore drift** – a zigzag movement of material along a shore. It builds up bars, spits and lagoons and leads to the development of salt marshes.

Surface processes, patterns and landforms

Study only **one** of the following in detail:
- Mass movement processes, patterns and landforms: pages 45–47.
- Glacial processes, patterns and landforms: pages 47–50.
- River processes, patterns and landforms: pages 50–55.
- Coastal processes, patterns and landforms: pages 55–57.

You should be able to **identify** all surface landforms by name or from a diagram/photo/map and know the processes that formed them.
- By explaining the processes you can increase your number of SRPs.
- Make sure your SRPs are cohesive.
- Relate your SRPs to the landform formation.

Mass movement processes, patterns and landforms

Factors that influence mass movement

- Steepness of slope: the steeper the slope, the faster the movement.
- Type of material: loose material slips faster than compacted material.
- Water content: the higher the water content, the faster the movement.
- Vegetation cover: plant roots help to bind surface material to reduce movement.
- Earth movements: earthquakes shake and loosen material to aid movement.

Processes of mass movement

Soil creep

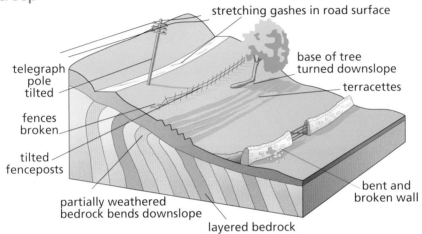

The effects of soil creep

This is the movement of soil particles downslope. It occurs because of the influences of:

- **gravity** – pulls soil particles downslope
- **solifluction** – some soil particles swell when they absorb ground water. This swelling causes neighbouring particles to move away from each other
- **frost heave** – the movement of soil particles by ice crystals that form under stones and move the soil particles to the surface.

Gravity

This pulls large rocks, boulders and soil downslope to create rock falls and landslides.

Earth flows

These occur when soil is saturated with water on gentle slopes.

Lahars or mud flows

Lahars occur when enormous amounts of soil, rock, trees and other debris move rapidly downslope. They are triggered when large masses of ice melt as a result of volcanic eruptions on ice-capped volcanic mountains.

Landforms of mass movement

Terracettes

These are parallel ridges of soil on a steep slope, much like long steps of a flight of stairs. They form because of:

1. Wet–dry periods: moisture increases the weight and volume of soil, causing expansion and the movement of the soil downhill under the pull of gravity. When the soil dries it contracts.
2. Freeze–thaw: when a soil freezes, its water particles expand and push up the soil at right angles to the slope. When the soil thaws, the material slips downslope under the pull of gravity. This is the slowest form of mass movement.

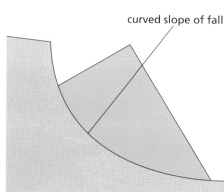

Terracettes are like steps on a steep slope

Sloping cliffs due to slumping

Slumping is caused by undermining of a slope. When this happens, areas such as coastal cliffs and river cliffs collapse and slip, and as they do there is a rotational movement of the falling material. *Example:* chalk cliffs at Garron Point, Co. Antrim.

Slumping occurs when steep slopes are undercut

Flows

Flows are moving masses of soil, stones, mud and water.

Bog bursts

Blanket bogs that cover hill and mountain tops may flow after spells of continuous heavy rain. *Example:* Derrybrien, Co. Galway.

Lahars

A lahar is a particular type of mud flow that occurs when hot lava or hot ash from a vent falls on great deposits of snow or ice on a high, snow-capped volcanic peak. The water from the melted snow or ice saturates the ground, which then rushes downhill rooting up soil, trees and other material on its journey.

Landslides and rock falls

Landslides

These occur when soil, stones and clay become loose and fall downhill owing to the pull of gravity. Water may or may not be an influencing factor. Landslides leave a **concave scar** on the slope where the material originated, and a **convex mound** of material where it ended.

Rock falls

Rock falls occur when loose boulders are set free on a slope and roll downhill. They may become loose for a number of reasons, including earthquakes or the erosion of surrounding soil or stones. Weathering and erosion of base rocks undermines cliffs, creating rock falls.

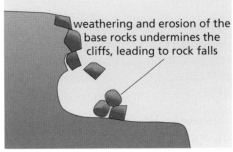

weathering and erosion of the base rocks undermines the cliffs, leading to rock falls

Weathering and erosion of base rocks undermines cliffs, creating rock falls

Glacial processes, patterns and landforms

Causes of Ice Ages

Ice Ages occur because of three factors that happen to occur at the same time. These are:

- changes in the tilt of the earth's axis – every 41,000 years
- the orbit of the earth changing from a circular path to a more elliptical one – every 100,000 years
- the tendency of the earth to 'wobble' – every 23,000 years.

DEFINITIONS

Arête: a knife-edged ridge created where two cirques form side by side.

Crevasse: a long, narrow, deep crack in the surface of a glacier.

Erratic: a large boulder that was carried a long distance from its place of origin.

Fjord: a glaciated valley that has been drowned by sea water.

Glaciated valley: a steep-sided and flat-floored valley (U-shaped) formed by the action of a glacier.

Glacier: a very slow moving river of ice.

Outwash plain: a large, gently sloping area of sand and gravel that was deposited by streams flowing from the front of an ice-sheet.

Overflow channel: a V-shaped valley cut by water that flowed from an ice-dammed lake.

Pyramidal peak: a peak pointed by frost action formed when there were three or more cirques back to back (e.g. Carrauntoohil, Co. Kerry).

Landforms of glacial action

Landform: U-shaped glaciated valley

Highland erosional landform

Example: Gap of Dunloe, Co. Kerry.

Formation

- Ice moved downslope under **gravity** through river valleys from snowfields and cirques high in the mountains.
- Melt-water seeped between the base of the ice and the bedrock.
- This allowed glaciers to slide downslope in a process called **basal sliding**.
- This melt-water regularly froze when the ice stopped moving. **Freeze-thaw** then occurred.
- When the glacier moved again it **plucked** large boulders and rocks from the bedrock surface.
- Rocks fell to the glacier surface gathered along the valley sides to form lateral moraines.
- These originated from freeze-thaw action above the glacier and gravity dragged them downslope. The ice used them to erode and deepen the valley by **abrasion**.
- The process of abrasion created **truncated spurs** on the valley sides by eroding the fronts of interlocking spurs.
- **Erosion** and **plucking** created long, deep hollows that later filled with water to form **ribbon lakes** on the valley floor.
- **Hanging valleys** formed where smaller glaciers entered the main valley.
- These end abruptly on the sides of the main valley, often causing waterfalls to form. *Example:* Torc Waterfall in Killarney.
- Some deep glaciated valleys in coastal areas were drowned by the sea. These inlets are called **fjords**.

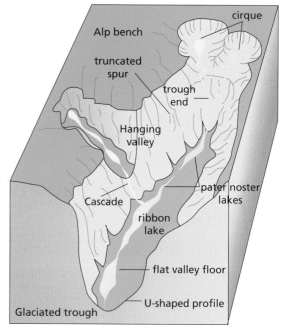

A glaciated valley or trough. These are the characteristic features of a glaciated valley.

Processes involved: plucking, abrasion, gravity, basal sliding.

Landform: Moraine

Upland and lowland depositional landforms

Example: Cumeenduff Glen, Co. Kerry.

All rock material transported by a glacier, including boulder clay, is called **moraine**. Rock fragments range in size from large boulders to particles of dust.

Formation

Moraine consists of **unsorted debris** of rounded and angular boulders, stones, soil and sand deposited by glaciers.

Processes involved: transportation, deposition, ablation (melting of ice).

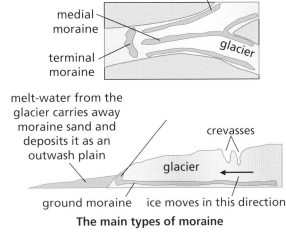

The main types of moraine

This material was **plucked** or **abraded** from the landscape over which the glaciers passed. It may be divided into three main types:

- **Lateral moraine** formed **long sloping ridges** of material deposited **along valley sides**.
- **Medial moraine** is an uneven, long ridge of similarly unsorted material that runs along the centre of valleys.
- **Terminal moraine** formed **crescent-shaped ridges** of unsorted debris across valleys and plains where glaciers or ice sheets stopped and melted for a long time. They represent the **furthest advance** of the ice.

Landform: Esker

Lowland depositional landform

Examples: Eiscir Riada, near Clonmacnoise, Co. Westmeath.

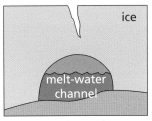

1. As ice melts, melt-water channels form under the ice.

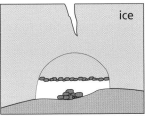

2. Sand, gravel and boulders are deposited, depending on the speed of melt-water flow.

Processes involved: transportation, deposition, ice action.

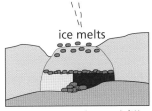

3. Melt-water channel fills with deposits as the ice melts.

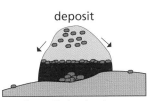

4. After all the ice has disappeared, esker slopes slump and stabilise, leaving a ridge of sand, gravel and boulders.

Formation of an esker

Formation

- Melting ice sheets produced vast amounts of melt-water, some of which flowed through tunnels under the ice.
- The **fast flow** of the water allowed it to pick up **large quantities of sediment** from the ground moraine beneath the glacier.
- It washed and cleaned the sediment and carried it along, some in **suspension**, some by **saltation** and more by **traction**.
- The silt and clay particles were carried far from their source to lakes or the sea.
- But the **sand and gravel particles** were laid down in **alternate sorted layers** on the beds of these enclosed rivers and streams.
- Layers of fine sediment, such as **fine sand**, were deposited during times of **low water**. **Gravels** were laid down during periods of **rapid ice melt**, such as in summer.
- These sub-glacial rivers formed a **winding course** across level plains beneath the ice, just as rivers do when they **meander** in their late stage of development.
- So their deposits today form winding ridges of sand and gravel across lowland regions.

OR

River processes, patterns and landforms

River patterns

A **basin** is the area drained by a river. The pattern of drainage in a basin may be:

- **dendritic** – the tributaries form a pattern like the branches of a tree
- **trellised** – tributaries run parallel to each other towards the main course and meet the main river at right angles

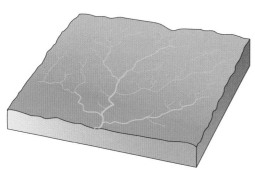

Dendritic drainage is tree-shaped

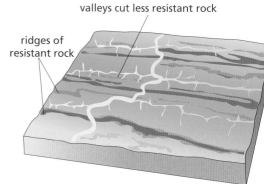

valleys cut less resistant rock

ridges of resistant rock

Trellised drainage shows tributaries that meet the main river at right angles

- **radial** – streams flow downhill, radiating from a central hilltop or mountain top.

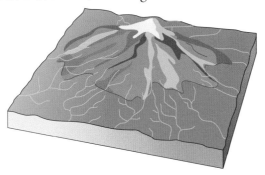

In radial drainage, rivers radiate outwards from a central area

DEFINITIONS

Basin: the entire area drained by a river and its tributaries.

Confluence: the place where rivers join.

Estuary: that part of a river's course that is tidal.

Mouth: the place where a river enters a sea or lake.

Source: the place where a river begins.

Tributary: a river that joins a larger river.

Watershed: the high ground that separates one river basin from another.

Landforms of river action

SAMPLE EXAM QUESTION

Question:

With the aid of a labelled diagram, examine the processes that have led to the formation of any one Irish landform of your choice.

Note: you may be asked for **two** landforms.

You should:

- Know at least two landforms from rivers – one from erosion and one from deposition – and explain the processes.
- Write 15 SRPs (2 marks each) if you are asked for **one** landform, and eight SRPs for each landform if you are asked for **two**.
- Include a simple sketch with three labels/SRPs.
- Give an Irish example of each landform.

Landform: V-shaped valley

Landform of erosion, upper course

Examples: upper Liffey Valley, upper Blackwater Valley.

Formation

- Water flows quickly on steep slopes so it rushes down slope and winds and twists its way around obstacles.

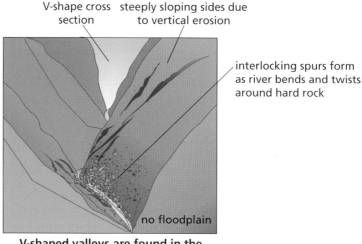

V-shape cross section

steeply sloping sides due to vertical erosion

interlocking spurs form as river bends and twists around hard rock

no floodplain

V-shaped valleys are found in the upper stage of a river's course

- The force of the rushing water, called **hydraulic action**, causes vertical erosion of the channel.
- Through **abrasion**, the load of the river also **erodes vertically** so that eventually a V-shaped valley is formed.
- The water **erodes laterally** (sideways) where the channel bends and twists around obstacles.
- The current erodes most strongly on the outside of the bends, causing **undercutting** and **slumping** of the bank.
- The sediment is constantly removed by hydraulic action.
- The bends and twists become more pronounced, creating **interlocking spurs**.
- **Gravity** and rainfall on the valley sides supplies the channel with sediment, which is removed, making the valley deeper.
- Bands of hard rock may lie across the path of the stream. Waterfalls form at these locations by eroding the soft rock downstream of the hard rock.
- **Plunge pools** form at the base of the waterfalls due to abrasion and hydraulic action.
- As a waterfall retreats upstream it leaves a steep-sided channel called a **gorge** below the falls.
- **Potholes** form by abrasion where **eddies** (swirling pools) occur.
- The pebbles and sediment are rounded by attrition as they are moved downstream.

Landform: Waterfall

Landform of erosion; upper course
Examples: Asleagh Falls on the Erriff River; Torc Waterfall in Killarney.

Formation

- A waterfall usually occurs in the upper course of a river.
- It forms where a layer of **hard rock** that lies across the riverbed is **horizontal** or **tilted upward**.

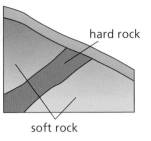 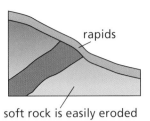 

The formation of a waterfall

Processes involved:
hydraulic action, abrasion,
traction, eddying, solution,
rejuvenation.

- Due to the **uneven hardness** of the bedrock there is **differential erosion**. The softer rock is eroded at a faster rate than the hard rock layer.
- The softer rock undergoes severe erosion due to **hydraulic action** and **abrasion**.
- This causes a vertical drop on the river's bed where the hard rock ends and the softer rock begins.
- As the falling water strikes the soft rock on the riverbed, its erosive power gouges out a deep pool called a **plunge pool**.
- This pool deepens gradually, caused by the **eddying** or swirling of the water and its **load**, which creates **abrasion** within the pool.
- **Large chunks** of the hard rock **break away** from the capstone and fall to the base of the waterfall. This occurs due to undermining or the opening up of the rock's joints by hydraulic action.
- In some regions where extremely cold conditions are experienced and the river freezes over, some **frost wedging** may loosen these rock chunks.
- In this way the waterfall **retreats upstream** leaving a deep, steep-sided narrow channel downstream from the waterfall. This landform is called a **gorge**.
- Some waterfalls are formed when sea level falls or land level rises and new profiles and waterfalls form at knickpoints.

Landform: Flood plain

Landform of erosion and deposition, middle and lower course

Example: River Shannon in the Midlands, Blackwater Valley near Fermoy.

Processes involved:
undercutting, divagation,
deposition.

Formation

- When a river reaches lowland it **slows down** and starts to swing from side to side. This lateral wandering of the river to and fro is called **divagation**.
- This creates **lateral erosion** and begins the process of removing its interlocking spurs. The processes of **hydraulic action**, **cavitation** and **abrasion** are very active at this stage.

- As the river flows around a bend it **erodes** most strongly on its **outside**, forming a **river cliff**.
- **Undercutting** of the bank occurs and parts of it **slump** into the river.
- Little erosion occurs on the inside of the bend, but there is often deposition, forming a gravel beach or **point bar**.
- Over time a wide and flat valley floor is created.
- During times of flood, such rivers **overflow** their channels and spread across this flat valley floor.
- Each successive flood over thousands of years builds up a thick blanket of the sediment called alluvium to form a level plain.
- High banks develop close to the channel. These are called **levees**.
- In delta regions these levees may retain a channel that is at a higher level than the surrounding floodplain.

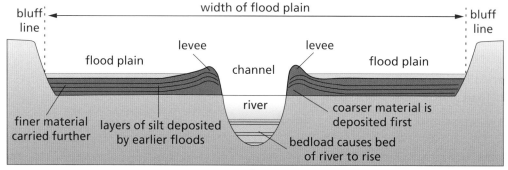

Levee formation

Landform: Ox-bow lake

Examples: River Moy near Foxford, Co. Mayo; Shannon at Leitrim town.

| A neck of land separates two concave banks where erosion is active | Neck is ultimately cut through: this may be accelerated by river flooding | Deposition seals the cut-off, which becomes an ox-bow lake |

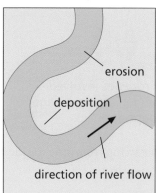

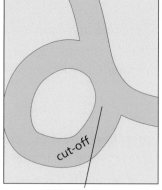

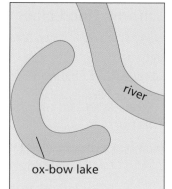

deposition begins to seal up the ends of the cut-off

Ox-bow lakes form in the lower stage of a river's course

Formation

- **Meanders** develop on mature and old river valleys where slopes are gentle or flat.
- As meanders move downstream they erode most strongly on the outside of bends by abrasion.
- This creates a loop in the river's course, enclosing a **peninsula** of land.
- Over time this peninsula develops a narrow neck as the meanders approach each other.
- Finally, during a period of flood the river cuts through this neck and continues on a straight and easier route, leaving the river loop to one side.
- Deposition occurs at both ends of this loop to form an ox-bow lake.
- After a long time these ox-bow lakes become filled with silt from floodwater, and finally they dry up.

key point

Processes involved: hydraulic action, corrasion/abrasion, cavitation, deposition.

OR

Coastal processes, patterns and landforms

Coastal Processes: see page 44.

DEFINITIONS

Backwash: the return of the water down the beach.

Load: mud, sand and shingle carried along the shore by the sea.

Longshore drift: the movement of material along the shore.

Swash: water that rushes up a beach following the breaking of a wave.

Wave: wind causes water particles on the surface of the sea to move in a circular motion and form a wave shape. This disturbance is transmitted to neighbouring particles, and so the wave shape (not the actual water) moves forward.

exam focus

- Always write at least 15 SRPs @ 2 marks each.
- Draw a simple diagram with a few SRPs as labels.
- Give an Irish example.

Landforms of coastal action

Landform: Cliff

Landform of erosion

Example: Cliffs of Moher, Co. Clare.

Formation

- Wave action cuts a **notch** on any new land surface that is exposed to the force of the sea.
- Air is forced into joints and bedding planes in rock surfaces that are exposed to wave action.
- The air is **trapped and compressed** by the force of incoming waves. This is called **hydraulic action**. As each wave retreats, the air instantly expands.
- Its 'explosive' expansion enlarges the cracks, and eventually shatters the rock into small and large blocks and boulders.
- The rock particles are removed by the crashing waves and fall to the seabed.
- **Strong waves** pick up these shattered rock particles and strike them off the coast. Most of this action takes place at or below high tide level. This process is called **abrasion**.
- The combined processes of hydraulic action and abrasion eventually cut a notch in the coast that creates an **overhanging rock ledge**.
- Once this notch lengthens, the overhanging rock mass becomes too heavy to be supported and collapses into the sea.
- This leaves a vertical 'wall' of rock along the water's edge, which is called a cliff.
- As the cliff 'retreats', a level rock surface is formed at the base of the cliff. This surface is called a **wave-cut platform**. It may be exposed at low tide in some places.

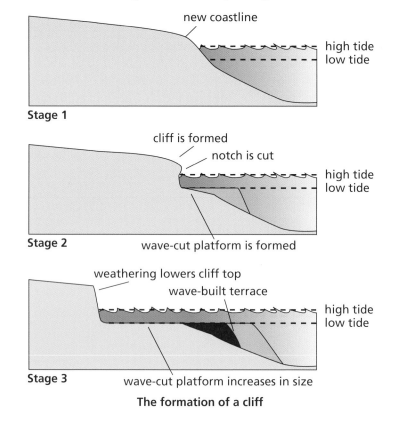

The formation of a cliff

Landform: Beach
Landform of deposition
Example: Tramore Beach, Co. Waterford.

> **key point**
>
> Processes involved:
> deposition, longshore drift.

Formation

- A beach is formed by the process of **longshore drift**. This refers to the **zigzag movement** of beach material, such as sand and shingle, along a shore.
- As a constructive wave approaches a shore, part of the wave 'touches ground' and slows down. The remainder of the wave in deeper water continues at its original faster speed. So a wave tends to **bend** as it approaches a beach and breaks at an **oblique angle**.

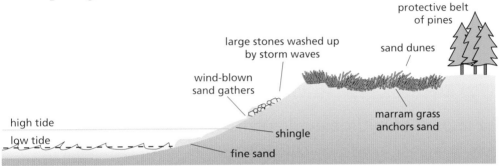

Composition of a beach

- The water that rushes up a beach is called the **swash**, and it deposits sand along the shore.
- Constructive waves commonly occur on beaches with a **low angle**. They have a wide area to cross, so their swash loses its energy quickly. This leaves a weak backwash, so sand and shingle is slowly, but constantly, moved up the beach. Less material is pulled down the beach by the **backwash**.
- The force of the backwash is called the **undertow**.
- During storms, sea level is higher than normal, due to low atmospheric pressure. Waves are also stronger and they regularly throw large rocks, broken shells and driftwood on to the shore above normal high tide levels. This forms the **backshore** or **storm beach**.
- The **foreshore** is composed of **fine sand** and small shell particles. It has a gentle gradient and is regularly covered by the tide each day.
- Some beaches may form in crescent-shaped pocket bays or coves.
- Others are long and narrow and may run parallel to the shore along spits or bars.

exam Q

Question 2B, 2012; 2B, 2013; 2B, 2014; 2B, 2015; 2B, 2016.

7 People's Interaction with Surface Processes

 aims You need to know how people interact with **one** of the following:

- river processes: page 44
- coastal processes: page 44
- mass movement processes: pages 42–44.

 **exam focus**

- The easiest topic to learn and to write about is how people interact with river processes.
- You should make sure you are able to write about two examples, with 14 SRPs each.
- Give two examples.

River processes (fluvial processes)

The impact of hydroelectric dams

Hydroelectric dams are built across river valleys to dam water in order to generate electricity. This interferes with the natural processes of river action.

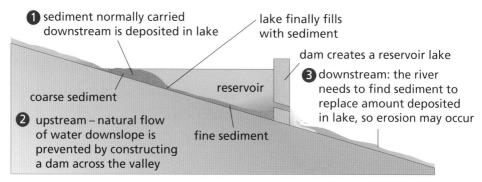

① sediment normally carried downstream is deposited in lake

lake finally fills with sediment

dam creates a reservoir lake

③ downstream: the river needs to find sediment to replace amount deposited in lake, so erosion may occur

coarse sediment

reservoir

② upstream – natural flow of water downslope is prevented by constructing a dam across the valley

fine sediment

Dams interrupt a river's natural processes

SAMPLE EXAM QUESTION AND ANSWER

Question:

Examine human interaction with surface processes in reference to one of the following:

- The impact of dams on river processes
- The impact of coastal defence work on coastal processes
- The impact of human activity on mass movement. (30 marks)

Marking scheme:
- First impact on processes identified – 2 marks
- Examination – 14 SRPs
- Discussion/SRPs may be positive or negative
- Second impact – 2 marks
- Two examples (specific locations) @ 2 marks each
- Three relevant extra SRPs on labelled diagram @ 2 marks each
- Make sure all SRPs relate to impacts by people on river processes.

Example 1: Building dams on the River Rhône

The aims of this project were:
- To control flooding
- To improve navigation on the River Rhône and connected waterways
- To generate hydroelectric power
- To use irrigation to improve agricultural output.

How people impacted with natural processes

*This is an example of an **integrated development** that has had many different positive impacts on the Rhône Valley region.*

- More than **20 dams** were built on the Rhône and its tributaries. **These dams** and artificial lakes **have interrupted or stopped the natural transportation of rocks, gravels, sand and silt downstream** from its source in the Alps to its delta region in the Mediterranean Sea.
- **The natural seasonal fluctuations of water levels no longer exist today.** The dams help **regulate water levels** throughout the year. This allows barges of up to 5,000 tonnes to carry bulky goods between the river port of Lyon and the deep-water seaports of Fos and Sete.
- **The natural movement of water downstream has been channelled through turbines to generate hydroelectric power.** This process increases the speed of the water that rotates the turbines and generates electricity.
- Up until the 1950s the Rhône flooded frequently, especially in early spring when alpine snow melted. Its floods devastated towns such as Arles and Avignon on the lower course of the river.
- **Parts of the Rhône delta were so marshy as a result of flooding that they became breeding grounds for mosquitoes that infected people with Malaria.**
- The regular floods also hindered navigation on the river.
- **Diversion canals were built along the Rhône.** These canals, such as those at Bollène and Châteauneuf, allowed barges to bypass narrow gorges that had previously hindered river traffic.
- Agricultural output has increased dramatically in the Rhône Valley. Irrigation water is supplied to the fertile alluvial soils of the Camargue that were once marshland only.
- Crops such as rice, apples, peaches and early vegetable flourish. Farm-related spin-off industries, such as food processing and fertiliser manufacture have developed in towns such as Nimes and Montpellier.

Example 2: Building artificial levees on the Mississippi River

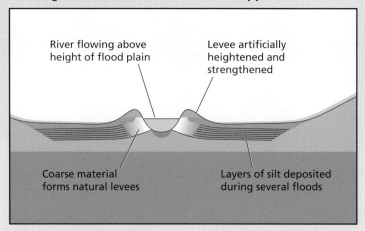

River flowing above
height of flood plain

Levee artificially
heightened and
strengthened

Coarse material
forms natural levees

Layers of silt deposited
during several floods

Levees are either natural or man-made raised banks

- **Artificial levees up to 10 metres high** are built to protect the floodplains and to move floodwaters downstream. They run a distance of 1,600 km from the confluence of the Ohio and Mississippi Rivers all the way south to the delta region in the Gulf of Mexico.
- **The river's load is diverted away from the floodplains** where it originally fertilised the soil and is now transported directly south to the Gulf of Mexico.
- Because **flooding is now controlled**, swamps have been drained and reclaimed and most of the Mississippi floodplain has been converted to agricultural production.
- The levees have in-built **flood gates** that, in severe flooding, are opened to divert water back to the floodplains to protect urban regions from flooding.
- **Sections of the Mississippi** that had looping meanders **have been canalised**. This change helps remove floodwater more quickly. It has also straightened the river and deepened its channel with a minimum depth of 20 metres that allows ocean-going vessels to have access to the port of New Orleans.

OR

Coastal processes

The impact of recreation

Groynes

- Long piles of large rocks are built at right angles to the coast in places to trap sand.
- These are called groynes. *Example:* Rosslare Strand, Co. Wexford.
- Longshore drift is interrupted by these barriers and coastal currents deposit sand, leading to the creation of new beaches.

Water quality

Naturally clean water may become polluted as recreation centres increase along a seashore. Water bodies can accept a certain level of pollutants and remain clean, since natural processes are able to break down pollutants such as human waste. However, when pollutants increase, seas become polluted, leading to poor water quality and contaminated beaches.

Coastal construction

The construction of hotels and holiday homes along sand dunes and sandspit environments leads to a change in natural ecosystems and damage to the coastal environment. Increased human traffic damages coastal grasses, leading to the erosion of sand dunes.

What evidence in this photograph suggests that tourism may be hindered by this type of coastal development?

Coastal defences

An increase in coastal storms and surges as a consequence of global warming has led to great damage in some coastal areas. *Example:* Rosslare Strand, Co. Wexford. Groynes and breakwaters are used to reduce such storm damage by breaking the force and size of waves as they approach a shore.

Sand dune management

Wave energy is released by waves as they crash and run up a beach. It is a natural process that keeps coastal regions in balance – so beaches should be preserved in their natural form in order to maintain this balance.

Removal of sand by people, traffic, or any measure that interferes with this balance must be eliminated or reduced to protect coastal environments.

Natural wildlife protection

Mudflats, sandflats, coastal marshes and other environments that support wildlife should be protected as part of nature's heritage. They add to the attraction of coastal regions for bird watchers and tourists.

OR

Mass movement

The effect of overgrazing on mass movement processes

Desertification leads to soil erosion on a large scale

- The overstocking of land can lead directly to soil erosion. Overgrazing reduces heather and grass cover and the soil is no longer protected from the direct impact of raindrops. Rain strikes the soil and loosens it, causing it to be washed downhill.
- Since the 1990s Irish mountainsides such as the Galtee and Mweelrea mountains have been subjected to increased mass movement, as overstocking of sheep has led to soil erosion.

The effect of overcropping on mass movement

- Overcropping occurs when soils in areas that are not suited to tillage are exposed to wind and rain.
- The **Sahel** in North Africa (see pages 242–244 and 288–290), south of the Sahara, became vulnerable to erosion when overgrazing by cattle herders, overcropping by tillage farmers and drought conditions left the soil exposed to dry winds from the Sahara. This led to a cycle of drought, famine, disease and loss of life that continues today.

8 The Process of Isostasy, Adjustment to Base Level and Landforms

aims You need to understand that all landforms represent a balance between forces within and on the earth's surface; and that this balance may change over time.

The earth's crust is made up of rocks of different densities (weights).

- The continents are composed of light rocks, called **sial**.
- The ocean floors are made up of dense rocks, called **sima**. A continent 'floats' on a layer of sima that runs under the continents and along the floors of the oceans.
- When erosion of continents occurs, the eroded sediment is deposited on lowlands. This increases weight in this area, so lowlands are pressed down.
- This action also reduces weight in mountain regions, so the mountain regions float higher on the sima layer.
- Together these actions cause a levelling of the landscape. This process is called **isostasy**.

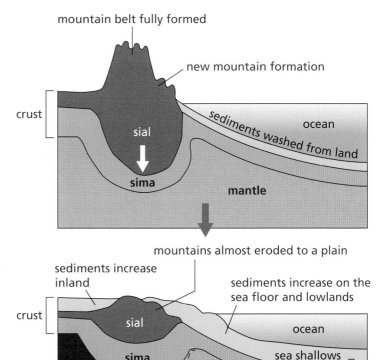

Erosion causes a levelling of the land surface over time

Landforms caused by changes in sea level

The process of **isostasy** causes raising and lowering of land relative to the level of the sea. This can lead to some landforms being drowned, or partially drowned, by the sea. Other landforms may be raised above sea level.

Emerged coastal features

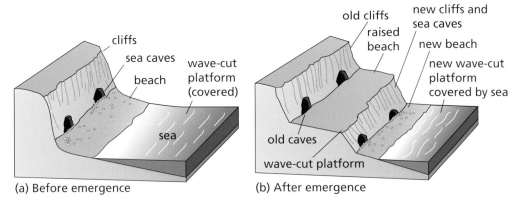

(a) Before emergence   (b) After emergence

Raised beach and wave-cut platform exposed due to isostatic uplift

Raised beaches and wave-cut platforms

- The sea level, relative to the land, changes over time.
- If the level of the sea falls or the land rises, coastal features such as beaches or wave-cut platforms may now be well above sea level.
- Step-like terraces may also form when sea levels change.

Submerged coastal features

Rias

Rias are submerged river valleys. They occur in south-west Ireland. *Examples:* Dingle Bay, Bantry Bay.

As the American plate moved away from the Eurasian plate, the west coast of Ireland lost its support, tilted seawards and was drowned by the sea. This process created the rias of the south-west.

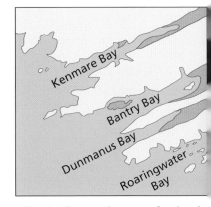

Rias in the south-west of Ireland

Fjords

During the last Ice Age, glaciers carved deep, U-shaped valleys in coastal mountain ranges. When the Ice Age ended, the water stored in the ice flowed back into the sea, causing the sea level to rise and flood some of these valleys, forming fjords. Killary Harbour is Ireland's best example of a fjord. There are many fjords in Norway.

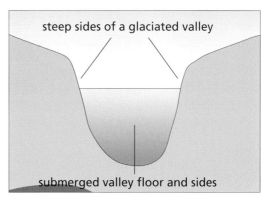

Features of a fjord

Adjusting to base level

- When earth movements raise land, the rivers in that region will erode to create a new curve or profile. Rivers begin cutting their new curve or profile from their estuaries upstream.
- This process is called **rejuvenation**.
- Waterfalls or rapids on a river near to its estuary indicate that **uplift** has taken place recently. In Co. Donegal in Ireland, the rejuvenation was caused by loss of weight on the landscape when the Ice Age ended.

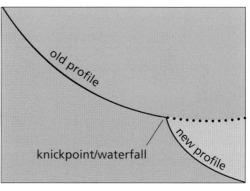

Waterfalls develop where old and new river profiles meet

- Waterfalls occur where the old profiles and new profiles meet. This is called the **knickpoint**.
- When rivers in their old stage are rejuvenated, they start to erode or cut into their old flood plain. This creates **incised meanders**.

Cycle of landscape evolution

- As new, level landscapes are exposed to weathering and erosion, they come under attack from rivers, wind, rain, frost and mass movement.
- The rivers open up channels, and the other processes combine to divide the original level land into separate ridges and valleys.
- These ridges gradually become worn down until they are just barely visible as raised land separating valleys that are in their lower stages of development.
- These almost perfectly flat landscapes are called **peneplains**. *Example:* South Cork.

9 Ordnance Survey Maps, Photographs, Graphs and Charts

 You need to be able to:

- draw sketch maps
- use grid references
- identify land uses and town functions
- understand scale
- find direction
- measure distance and area
- describe the location of a town on maps.

Scale

Scale is the relationship between a distance on the map and its corresponding measurement on the ground.

- Maps with a scale of 1:20,000,000 or 1:1,000,000 are **small-scale maps** showing large regions in little detail, e.g. major roads and cities (a road map).
- Maps with a scale of 1:2,500 or 1:1,000 are **large-scale maps** showing small areas in great detail, e.g. named streets and individual buildings.

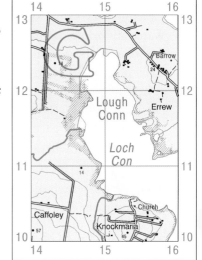

Area

To find the area of an OS map:

1. Count the number of grid squares across the top of the region.
2. Count the number of grid squares along the side of the region.
3. Then multiply the number along the side by the number across the top.

The area of this map is 3 × 2 = 6 sq km.

To find the area of an irregular-shaped region on an OS map (e.g. a water region):

1. Count the number of squares that have 50 per cent or more covered by water. Omit all others.
2. This number will represent the approximate area of the water region.

On this map, there are two squares at least half-filled with water. So the area of water is approximately 2 sq km.

Scale on a map

SCÁLA 1:50 000   SCALE 1:50 000

1 KILOMETRES 0   1   2   3   4   5   6   7   8
1 STATUTE MILES 0   1   2   3   4   5
2 ceintiméadar sa chiliméadar (taobh chearnóg eangaí) 2 centimetres to 1 kilometre (grid square side)

Scale on a map

- **Statement of scale.** The scale is stated. (In this case it is 2 cm to 1 km.)
- **Representative fraction** (RF) is given as a ratio. The RF 1:50,000 tells us that any one unit of measurement on the map corresponds to 50,000 similar units on the ground.
- **Linear scale** is a line divided into kilometres and parts of a kilometre (or miles and parts of a mile).

How to locate places on an OS map

Grid references

A grid reference is made up of:

1. **Letter** (**L**). It is coloured blue on every map and should be named first.
2. **Eastings** (**AT**). These are the vertical grid lines. They are numbered at the top and bottom. They should be named second.
3. **Northings** (**AS**). These are the horizontal grid lines. They are numbered along the sides. They should be named last.

How to locate a specific place on a map

Always look across the top first. Then look along the side. Remember **LATAS**:

L = letter
AT = across the top
AS = along the side.

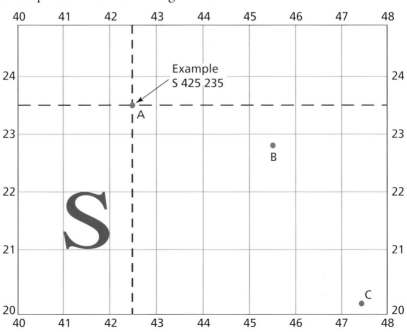

Examples of grid references: A = S 425 235; B = S 455 227; C = S 474 202

Locating regions on maps

Four-figure grid references are used to locate a single square on a map.

The grid reference used to do this is:

- the sub-zone letter
- the easting on the west side of the square
- the northing on the south side of the square.

For example, the Mass Rock is located in region L 70 39.

Locating regions within Ireland

The **national grid** is used to locate places or regions on Ordnance Survey (OS) maps. This national grid is **displayed on -the legend** attached to your OS map in an examination. By identifying the **sub-zone** letter on your map you can identify the location of that region in Ireland.

For example, the sub-zone letter on this map extract is **S**. This sub-zone on the national grid is located in the **south of Ireland**.

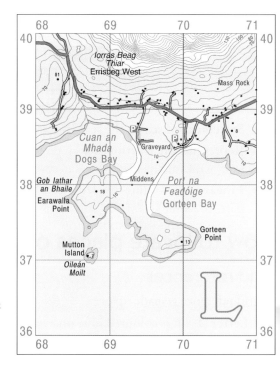

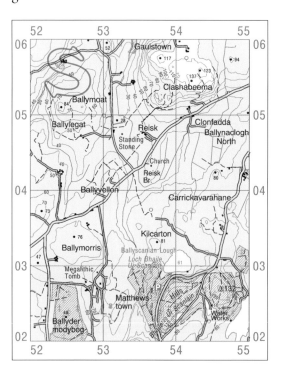

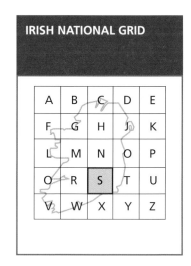

Directions on maps

Directions are usually given in the form of compass points. Place a cross representing north, south, east and west on the location you wish to get directions from, for example from Goatstown to Blackwood Cross Roads (see map). Then use the compass points to find your answer (*answer: north-west*).

Now identify each of the following directions on the map:

- from Goatstown to Robertstown
- from Goatstown to its nearest graveyard
- from Goatstown to Mondello Park
- from Blackwoods Cross Roads to Goatstown.

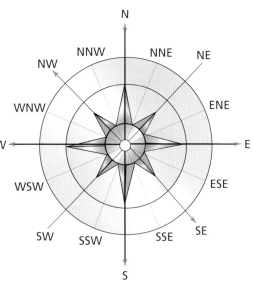

▲ Compass points

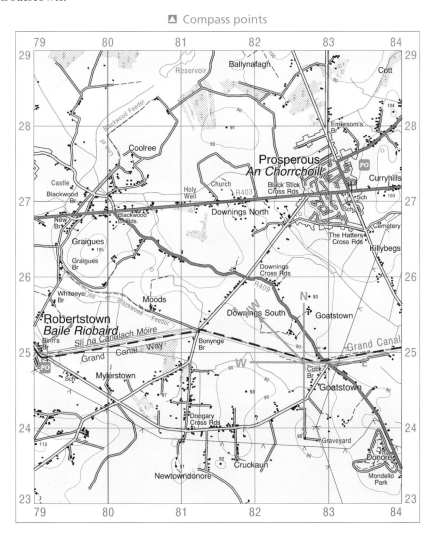

How to locate places on photographs

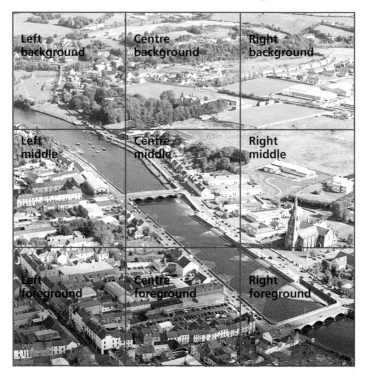

Oblique photograph with no north symbol

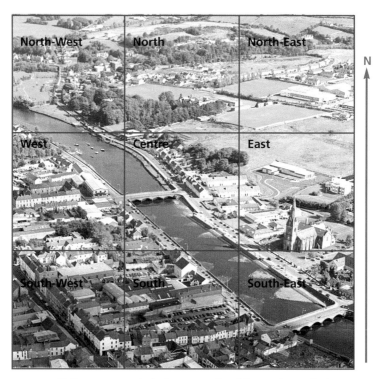

Oblique or vertical photograph with north symbol

N

Oblique or vertical photograph with north symbol

Drawing sketch maps

1. **Draw a frame** for your sketch map. This frame should be the **same shape** as the photograph or map.
2. Then draw in guidelines lightly on both the sketch map and the OS map or photo.
3. Alternatively, you can draw in the grid lines from your map. **Draw these lines lightly**.

Draw all sketch maps on the graph paper supplied in the exam if you are asked to do so.

Grid lines help to draw accurate sketch maps

Drawing sketch maps from Ordnance Survey maps

exam focus

1. Always draw – **on graph paper** – if you are asked, and then draw a frame similar in shape to that of the map.
2. **Never** trace a map. A sketch map must be drawn freehand.
3. 'Mark' and 'name' (or 'label') are different directions, and marks will be awarded for each separately.
4. Never draw a very large sketch map, as it is more difficult to draw and it takes up too much time.
5. Practise different types of sketch map, and time yourself.
6. Use a soft lead pencil.
7. Use colour **only** if you have enough time.
8. To identify individual physical regions on a map it is often helpful if you squint your eyes; the separate regions may then become clearer.

Drawing sketch maps of maps to half scale

1. Measure the width of the map. It is generally 18 cm wide.
2. Measure the length of the map. It is generally 24 cm long.
3. Draw a box 9 cm wide x 12 cm long.

A sketch drawn to half scale will be one-quarter the size of the original map.

Case study 1: Kenmare region (2015)

Sample question:

Examine the 1:50000 Ordnance Survey map of the Kenmare region on page 74. Draw a sketch map of the area shown to half scale. On it, correctly show and label each of the following:

- The entire route of the waymarked walk called the Béara Way shown on the map
- The entire area of coniferous plantation at V 85 72
- The entire area of land above 300 metres at Letter South
- The entire area of Kenmare River shown on the map. (20 marks)

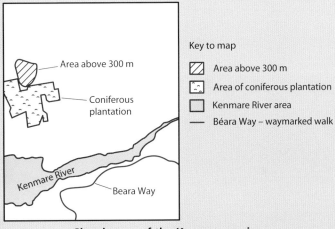

Sketch map of the Kenmare region

Marking scheme:

- Sketch outline – 4 marks
- Four features @ 4 marks each – shown 3 marks (graded 3/1/0)
- Label – 1 mark

Notes:

1. If sketch is traced or only a section of the map is drawn, lose 4 marks for sketch outline and lose 3 marks for showing per item. Allow labelling marks only.
2. Sketch outline means to half scale. Required size is 9 cm x 12 cm, but allow a difference of 0.5 cm on each side.
3. If aerial photograph is used instead of Ordnance Survey map, 0 marks are given.

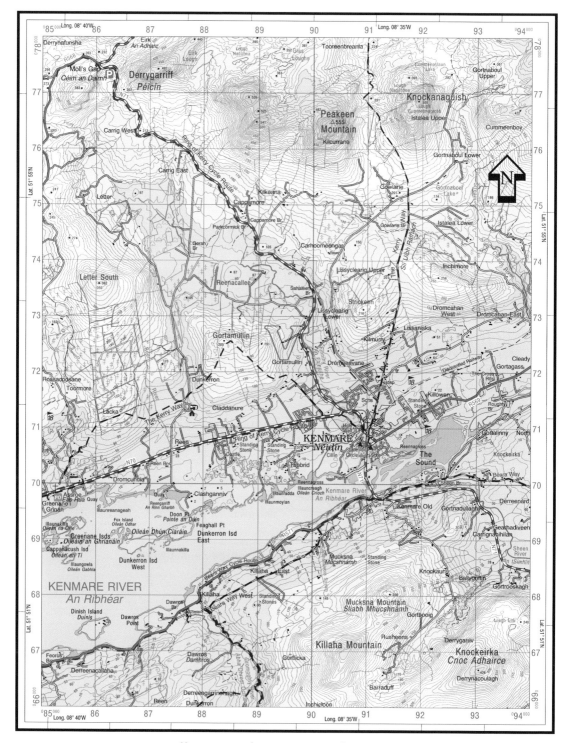

Kenmare region map extract (not to scale)

Case study 2: Dungarvan region (2014)

Sample question:

Examine the 1:50000 Ordnance Survey map of the Dungarvan region on page 76. Draw a sketch map of the area shown to half scale. On it, correctly show and label each of the following:

- The complete course of the Colligan River
- Locate a gorge on the Colligan River and mark it with an X on the sketch map
- The Cunnigar sand spit
- An area of land above 300 metres. (20 marks)

Marking scheme:

- Sketch outline – 4 marks
- Four features @ 4 marks each – 3 marks (graded 3/1/0)
- Named – 1 mark

Notes:

1. If sketch is traced or only a section of the map is drawn, lose 4 marks for sketch outline and lose 3 marks for showing per item. Allow naming marks only.
2. The sketch must have four sides drawn.

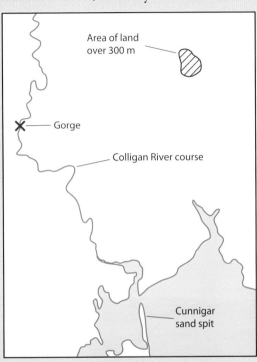

Sketch map of the Dungarvan region

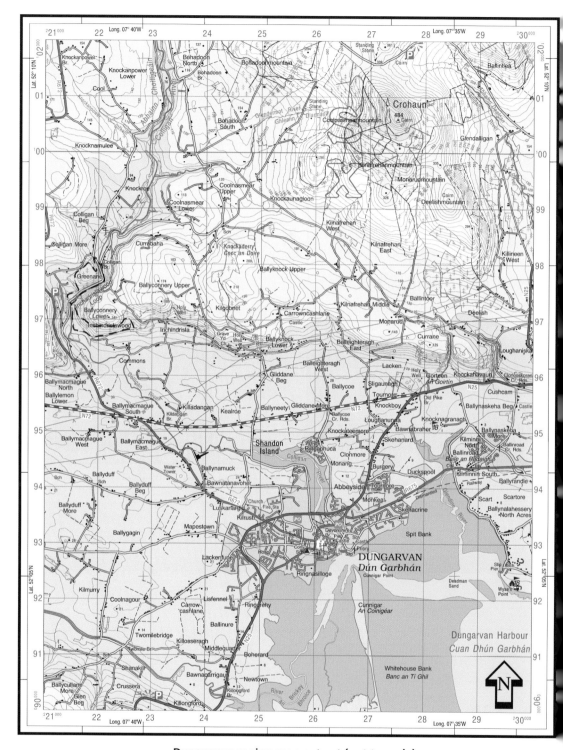

Dungarvan region map extract (not to scale)

Case study 3: Enniscorthy region (2013)

Sample question:

Examine the 1:50000 Ordnance Survey map of the Enniscorthy region on page 78. Draw a sketch map of the area shown to half scale. On it, correctly show and label each of the following:

- The complete course of the River Slaney
- The confluence of the River Slaney and Boro River (mark it with an X on the sketch map)
- An area of land above 170 metres
- An area of natural woodland. (20 marks)

Marking scheme:

- Sketch outline – 4 marks
- Four features @ 4 marks each – shown 3 marks (graded 3/1/0)
- Named – 1 mark

Note:

1. If sketch is traced or only a section of the map is drawn, lose 4 marks for sketch outline and lose 3 marks for showing per item.

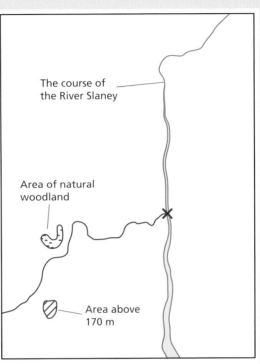

Sketch map of the Enniscorthy region

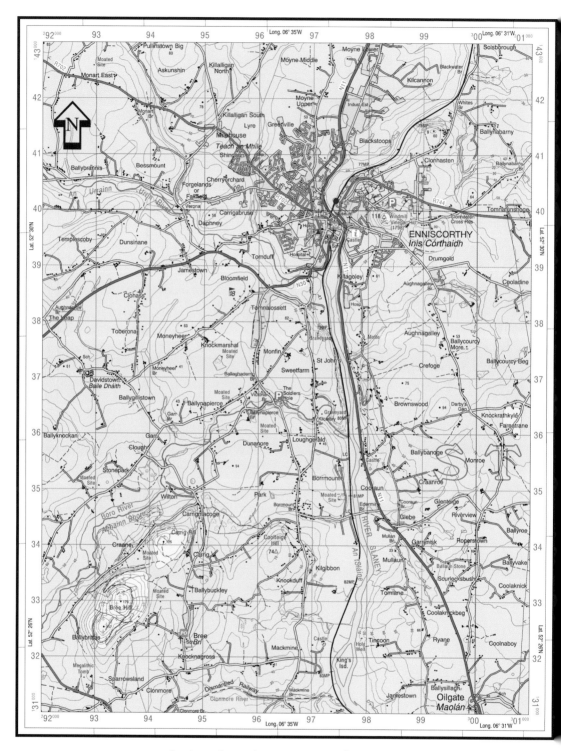

Enniscorthy region map extract (not to scale)

Drawing sketch maps from aerial photographs

1. Always draw a frame similar in shape to that of the map.
2. **Never trace a map. A sketch map must be drawn freehand.**
3. Draw the sketch to half scale (half the length and half the width).
4. Show and name only the features that you are specifically asked for.
5. Always outline your sketch with a soft pencil. This allows you to correct any errors you make.
6. Outline land-use zones with a heavy boundary line to limit the area.
7. Always mark and label each land-use area.
8. Use colour only if you have enough time.

Case study 4: Aerial photograph of Kenmare town (2015)

Sample question:

Examine the aerial photograph on page 80. Draw a sketch map of the aerial photograph, half the length and half the breadth. On it, correctly show and label each of the following:

- A car park
- The triangular street network in the middle ground of the aerial photograph
- A large commercial/ industrial building in the foreground of the aerial photograph
- An area of waste ground suitable for development. (20 marks)

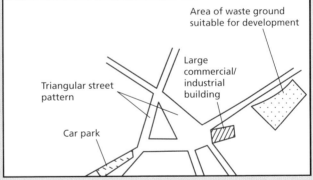

Sketch map of Kenmare town

Marking scheme:
- Sketch outline – 4 marks
- Four features @ 4 marks each – shown 3 marks (graded 3/1/0)
- Label – 1 mark

Notes:
1. Sketch outline means half the length and half the breadth.
2. If sketch is traced or a section of the aerial photograph is drawn, lose 4 marks for sketch outline and lose 3 marks per item for showing. Allow labelling marks only.
3. The measurement required is 14.2 cm × 9.25 cm, but allow 0.5 cm difference on each side.
4. If Ordnance Survey map is used instead of aerial photograph, 0 marks are given.

Aerial photograph of Kenmare town

Case study 5: Aerial photograph of Dungarvan harbour (2014)

Sample question:

Examine the aerial photograph on page 81. Draw a sketch map of the aerial photograph, half the length and half the breadth. On it, correctly show and label each of the following:

- A recreational area
- A large commercial/industrial building
- A bridge
- An area of waste ground suitable for development. (20 marks)

Marking scheme:

- Sketch outline – 4 marks
- Four features @ 4 marks each – shown 3 marks (graded 3/1/0)
- Named – 1 mark.

Notes:

1. If sketch is traced or a section of the aerial photograph is drawn, lose 4 marks for sketch outline and lose 3 marks per item for showing. Allow naming marks only.
2. The sketch must have four drawn sides.

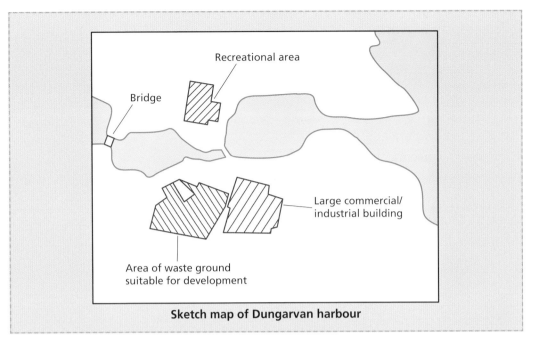

Sketch map of Dungarvan harbour

Aerial photograph of Dungarvan harbour

Case study 6: Aerial photograph of Enniscorthy (2013)

Sample question:

Examine the aerial photograph of Enniscorthy on page 83. Draw a sketch map of the aerial photograph, half the length and half the breadth. On it, correctly show and label each of the following:

- The railway bridge
- Two connecting streets
- The river
- The grain storage area in the centre of the aerial photograph. (20 marks)

Marking scheme:

- Sketch outline – 4 marks
- Four features @ 4 marks each – shown 3 marks (graded 3/1/0)
- Named – 1 mark.

Notes:

1. If sketch is traced or a section of the aerial photograph is drawn, lose 4 marks for sketch outline and lose 3 marks per item for showing.

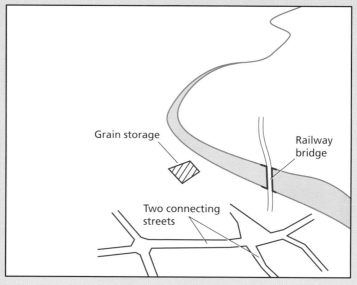

Sketch map of Enniscorthy

Aerial photograph of Enniscorthy

Drawing graphs from tables

Questions that ask you to draw a graph from information supplied in a table appear regularly in the elective section of the exam, so you need to know how to draw simple charts and graphs.

SAMPLE QUESTION AND ANSWER

The Environment (2015)

Question: Examine the data above showing the total waste generated by households and businesses in selected EU countries in 2004 and 2012.
Using graph paper, draw a suitable graph to illustrate this data. (20 marks)

Year	2004	2012
Ireland	24.5	20.0
Denmark	12.5	16.0
Czech Republic	29.0	23.0

Marking scheme:

	Bar chart, etc.	**Pie chart**
• Title	2 marks	2 marks
• Vertical axis named	1 mark	1 + 1 mark (circle and centred)
• Horizontal axis named	1 mark	
• 6 items illustrated	2 marks each graded	2 marks each graded

Notes:

1. Accept any suitable graph/chart.

2. Naming of graph/chart type not sufficient for title mark.

3. The title must have some reference to chart content and it can be written anywhere on the graph paper.

4. If graph paper is not used, deduct 2 marks from total.

5. For the bar chart, etc., both axes must be correctly plotted for 1 m + 1 m.

6. Apply the 2 marks graded (2/1/0) if the numbered spaces and the column widths are not plotted accurately.

7. Graph must be annotated to illustrate information regarding 2004 & 2012 and the named countries.

Answer:

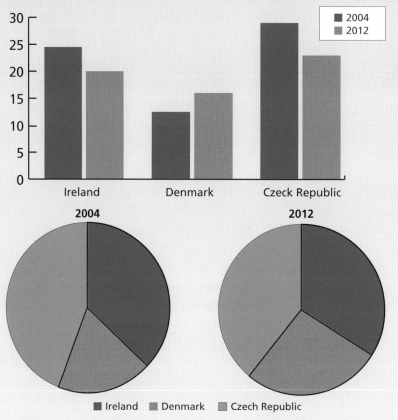

Total waste generated by households and businesses in selected EU countries in 2004 and 2012 (million tonnes)

exam focus

- Always draw your graph on the graph paper supplied in the exam.
- Use your **maths skills** to draw your chart/graph.

Types of graphs and charts

- **Bar charts:** The length of each bar represents the total or quantity of each factor. The bars can be simple, showing one single factor; or more complex, showing its component parts. Bar charts can also show gain or loss by showing bars above (gain) and below (loss) a central base line.
- **Pie charts** can show variations in size or composition of a feature/topic; for example the percentage share and total sales of cars in Ireland in a single year.
- **Line graphs** show change over time; increases or decreases; trends.
- **Scatter graphs** show relationships between two sets of data.
- **Flow charts** indicate at a glance occurring trends, e.g. numbers of migrants and their destinations.
- **Isoline charts/maps** show temperature (isotherms), rainfall (isohyets) or altitude (contours).
- **Choropleths** represent varying densities or population change.
- **Triangular graphs** are used to show information that can be divided into three variables, e.g. soil analysis; primary, secondary and tertiary industries.
- **Clock graphs** show activities/quantities of a recurring nature or pattern.

10 Types and Definitions of Regions

 aims You need to know about different types of region.

What is a region?

A region is an area of the earth's surface that has human and/or physical characteristics that give it an identity and make it different from all the areas that surround it.

What is a climate region?

A climate region is an area whose unique weather system, temperature, precipitation, seasons, soil and vegetation make it completely different from all the surrounding regions. *Example:* cool temperate oceanic climate region.

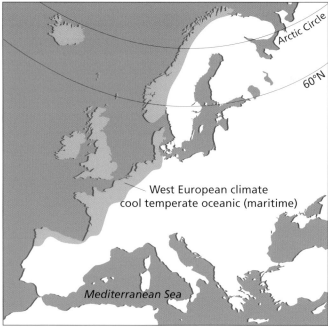

The western European coast has a cool temperate oceanic climate

What is a physical/geomorphological region?

Physical regions have unique surface characteristics, such as height, rock types, drainage patterns or internal rock structures, or a combination of these, that make them different from all surrounding areas. *Examples:* the Burren, Co. Clare; the Paris Basin.

The Burren, Co. Clare

What is an administrative region?

Governments divide their national territory into a hierarchy of local and regional areas that allows them to administer development more effectively. *Examples:* County Limerick, Waterford City, Border, Midland and Western (BMW) region.

— county boundary
— regional authority area
▩ Border, Midland and Western (BMW) region
☐ Southern and Eastern (S&E) region

Ireland's regional authority regions

exam focus

Definitions such as these may be required for the short-answer questions.

What is an urban region?

This is an area that includes a **town or city and its hinterland**. The hinterland that surrounds a human settlement is linked to it by interactions such as shopping, journeys to work, supplying farm produce. *Example*: the Paris Region.

What is a cultural region?

A cultural region is an area that has its own **unique identity** based on **human** rather than physical factors that are different from all surrounding areas. *Examples*: the Islamic World; Gaeltacht regions; the Walloon region, Belgium; Northern Ireland (a region of religious conflict).

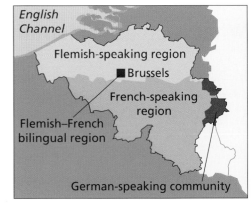

Belgium is divided into two main cultural regions

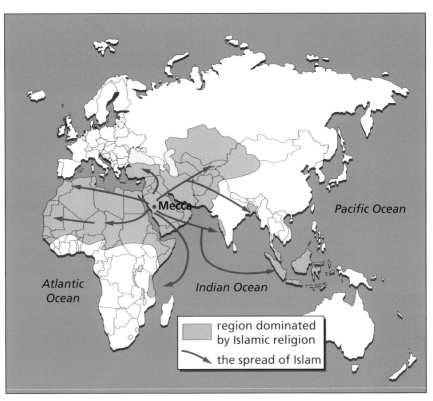

The Islamic faith spread from Saudi Arabia to other regions across Europe, Asia and Africa

What is a socio-economic region?

A socio-economic region is based on its **level of economic development**, defined by a combination of factors such as local supply of raw materials or local resources, strategic location for trade, or economic decline. There are three types of socio-economic region:

- less developed and peripheral regions, e.g. the West in Ireland, the Mezzogiorno in Italy
- core regions, e.g. Dublin, Paris
- regions of industrial decline, e.g. Sambre-Meuse region, Cork region.

This unit examines the following regions in detail:
Well-developed core regions:
- the **Greater Dublin Area** (pages 99–106)
- the **Paris Basin** (pages 111–116).

Less-developed/peripheral regions:
- the **West of Ireland** (pages 92–99)
- the **Mezzogiorno** in Italy (pages 106–111).

Core regions

Core regions are generally **centrally located** and **wealthy urban-industrial areas**.

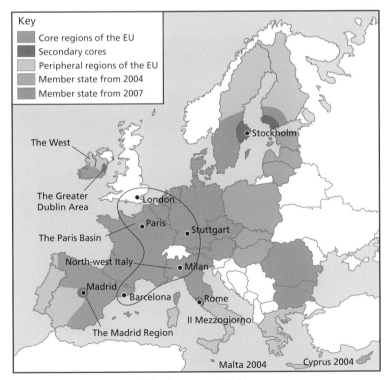

Key
- Core regions of the EU
- Secondary cores
- Peripheral regions of the EU
- Member state from 2004
- Member state from 2007

The West
Stockholm
The Greater Dublin Area
London
The Paris Basin
Paris
Stuttgart
North-west Italy
Milan
Madrid
Barcelona
Rome
Il Mezzogiorno
The Madrid Region
Malta 2004
Cyprus 2004

The European Union

Characteristics of core regions:
- highly developed, centrally located and prosperous urban-industrial areas
- an excellent range of services and job opportunities
- centres of decision-making
- a highly urbanised society, with 80 per cent or more of the population living in cities
- a wide range of resources, e.g. excellent agricultural land; and deep, sheltered port facilities.

Most national cores are centred on capital cities and have a historic as well as a present-day role as core regions. *Examples:* Dublin, Paris.

Some national cores have evolved away from their capital cities. *Examples:* Northern Italy (Milan, Turin and Genoa).

International core regions
- Western Europe has an international core region where a number of national core regions have combined.
- It is called 'The European Dogleg' or 'The Hot Banana'.
- It includes the following core centres: Stuttgart, Milan, Lyons, Barcelona.
- These core centres are also called the 'Four Motors of Europe'.

Peripheral regions
Peripheral regions are the opposite to core regions. They are on the edges of the EU, far from wealthy core regions.

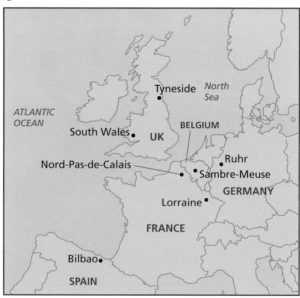

Principal European regions of industrial decline

- Many are mountain regions. *Examples:* the West of Ireland, the Mezzogiorno.
- They have a higher dependency on agriculture than core regions.
- They have poor transport networks and services.
- They suffer from out-migration and have low inward investment.
- They have high unemployment rates and a poor transport network.
- They are mostly rural regions with an average income of less than 75 per cent of the EU average wage.

Regions of industrial decline

Coal-mining regions

- These were once wealthy industrial regions based on coal mining and heavy industries, such as iron and steel manufacture. *Example:* the Nord-Pas-de-Calais in north-west France, the Sambre-Meuse region in Belgium.
- From 1750 onwards these regions experienced huge growth rates. Coalfields became the locations for manufacturing industry.
- From the 1950s onwards, regions of industrial decline became areas of severe unemployment because:
  - the best coal seams were used up
  - steel and textile industries could not compete with foreign manufacturing countries, e.g. Brazil, China and Korea
  - automation replaced workers.

Modern region of industrial decline in Ireland

- The Cork region suffered from industrial decline in the 1980s.
- Dunlop, Ford and Irish Steel closed their factories.
- New industries were attracted to create new sources of employment.

11 The Dynamics of Regions: Contrasting Regions in Ireland and Europe

 You need to be able to:

- show how economic, human, and physical processes interact in a particular region
- explain how two factors influence primary, secondary or tertiary activities.

 **You should study:**

- Two contrasting Irish regions, e.g. the West and the Greater Dublin Area (the GDA)
- Two contrasting European regions, e.g. the Paris Basin **and** the Mezzogiorno
- One continental/subcontinental region, e.g. India or Brazil.

You need to be able to:

- Draw sketch maps of:
  1. Two contrasting Irish regions
  2. Two contrasting European regions
  3. One continental/subcontinental region.
- Explain how two factors influence primary, secondary and tertiary activities in these regions.

The West of Ireland

Factors that created the environment

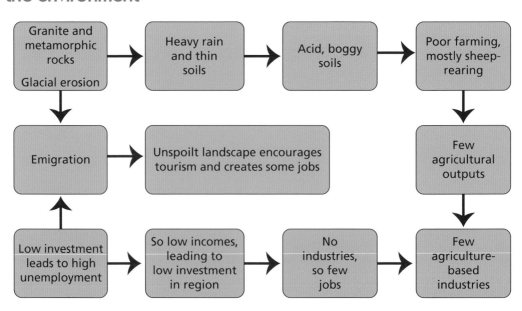

Practise drawing two contrasting Irish regions, e.g. the West of Ireland and the GDA, and mark in:

- 2 main uplands
- 2 main rivers
- 2 main lakes
- 2 main towns
- 2 main routes
- a surrounding box.

Practise doing these sketch maps in two minutes. Use a pencil – colour is not necessary. Drawing sketch maps is an important skill that's examined regularly in 20-mark questions.

The interaction of physical landscape, climate and human processes has made the West of Ireland an economically disadvantaged region.

SAMPLE EXAM QUESTION AND ANSWER

Question: Examine the factors that influence primary activities in one Irish region that you have studied.

Marking scheme:

- Named economic activity – 2 marks
- Two factors identified – 2 marks + 2 marks
- Region named – 2 marks
- Examination of 11 SRPs – 11 × 2 marks
- Give credit for examples (maximum 2 × SRP).

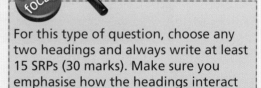

For this type of question, choose any two headings and always write at least 15 SRPs (30 marks). Make sure you emphasise how the headings interact with the economic activities.

The West of Ireland

Answer:

The West of Ireland is a peripheral underdeveloped region.

Relief and soils

- Much of the West has **bleak, rugged upland** areas, especially along the coastal edge. Some of these uplands include the Connemara mountains (or the Twelve Bens), the Maamturk Mountains, Croagh Patrick and the Nephin Beg Range.
- Many of these mountains were formed during the **Caledonian Foldings about 400 million years ago,** when the North American and Eurasian plates collided. They were heavily glaciated and only very thin soils cover their slopes. These thin soils negatively affect farming, and sheep-grazing is the only viable farming activity.
- Impeded drainage leads to water logging between drumlins, making the land infertile and unsuitable to tillage farming.

The thin, stony and poor soils of the West support only extensive farming methods

- The lowland areas have **boulder clay deposits**. In some places the boulder clay has been moulded into swarms of drumlins that form 'basket of eggs' scenery such as in western Clew Bay and along the shores of Lough Corrib.
- The bedrock of much of Western Galway and Mayo is either granite or metamorphic rock that forms infertile acid soils. Many of these rocks are impervious, which causes waterlogging of the soil. This leads to the creation of marsh and **peat** over large areas of the West that negatively affect farming.
- Many areas have podzol soils. These soils are heavily leached due to the heavy rainfall. Leaching leads to the formation of hardpans that prevent drainage. These leached soils have few minerals and lack nutritional value for animal rearing. Sheep numbers must be kept low as the sheep must roam over large areas to find sufficient food supply for fattening.
- These rain-drenched mountains, such as the Twelve Bens, are mainly covered with peaty soils. These soils are infertile because they are shallow, have low mineral content and are frequently waterlogged. These conditions limit farm production.

Climate

- The West of Ireland has a cool temperate oceanic climate with most rain falling in the winter months. Rainfall totals up to 2,000 mm annually in the high upland regions of the West.

- **Frontal depressions** are forced to rise over the Western mountains causing heavy rainfall. Many places have over 250 wet days each year. The prevailing winds of the region are the **south-west anti-trades** that blow from the Atlantic Ocean. They are rain-bearing on-shore winds. The heavy rain often causes mass movement, mud flows and bog-bursts that have a negative effect on agriculture.

- Winter temperatures average about 5°C; summer temperatures rarely average above 15°C. The low summer temperatures and heavy rainfall restricts the variety of crops that can be grown. Farming mostly involves the extensive rearing of sheep and cattle. The cattle are kept only for a short period before selling on for fattening in the better grazing lands of the east due to lack of good pasture.

- There is just one major farming co-operative company, Aurivo Co-op in Sligo, which caters for farming in the West. This has helped farmers to market their products in Ireland and abroad.

- The age profile of farmers in the West is older than the national average, and few young farmers are willing to devote their lives to earning the low income available to them in the West. Alternative work opportunities are limited in the area and so many young people emigrate overseas or migrate to the cities, e.g. Galway or Dublin.

- Traditional farming provides only low incomes to most farmers. Average farm income is only 50 per cent of that of the eastern region. Most farms are also small: the average farm size in Co. Mayo is only 22 hectares. Because farms are small, most farmers depend on **direct payments from the EU** to support their farms.

Farms in the West of Ireland are generally small and support a small herd of grazing animals, such as sheep and calves

Forestry

- Some **marginal land** is set aside for **forestry**. Forestry forms part of the **National Development Plan**, which aims to increase forestry cover to 15 per cent of total land use. Coillte, Ireland's state forestry company, has planted more than 30,000 hectares of conifers in the West. Large areas have been forested, e.g. near Lough Corrib, Lough Mask and Lough Conn.

- There are many natural advantages for fishing in national waters. However, due to **overfishing** by EU members such as Spain, the EU has imposed quotas on fish catches to protect stocks. So, only about 2,000 people are fully engaged in this activity. **Aquaculture** (fish farming) of salmon, sea trout and shellfish are produced in places such as Clew Bay, Killary Harbour and smaller centres.

exam focus

Exam questions regularly allow you to describe the **development** of either primary, secondary or tertiary industry in an Irish or European region (not in Ireland) of your own choice. For example, agriculture in an Irish region or agriculture in a European region (not in Ireland).

Marking scheme:
- Identify at least two examples
- Explain the **development** of that activity. This explanation is crucial to gain maximum marks
- Name the specific region that you have chosen
- Give a total of 15 SRPs
- Two examples may be credited as SRPs.

Secondary activities (manufacturing)

Manufacturing employs only about 28 per cent of all workers. The factors that hinder manufacturing in the West are:

- The region has only a small market locally. Towns are small and Galway is just a medium-sized city. This limits local labour supply and markets.
- The Western region is peripheral on the western edge of **Ireland** and away from the large urban centres of Dublin, Britain and the EU. This increases transport costs of raw materials and finished products.

Manufacturing may be examined under the following headings:

- **Resource-based manufacturing: this includes meat processing of local beef cattle in Ballyhaunis,** Gort and Oughterard. Small **fish-processing plants** are located in coastal sites, such as Rossaveal in Connemara.

Rossaveal provides this region with secondary jobs

- **Consumer-based industries** such as bakeries and confectionaries still survive but face increasing competition from supermarket chains that often source their products outside the region.
- Industrial estates and small industrial unit developments help small light engineering and start-up companies to establish themselves and to create a nice market for their products.

Government support

- Government support has allowed Shell Petroleum to develop a natural gas field, and gas is now piped ashore to an island refinery at **Bellanaboy in Co. Mayo.** This gas is now available for purchase to Bord Gáis (now called Ervia) for distribution throughout Ireland and may in time contribute to industries based on this natural resource supply.
- Larger industrial estates, such as that at Ballybrit/Parkmore in Co. Galway have well-established facilities and networks that offer multinational companies special government-based financial benefits. Up to 70 **US multinationals** that operate there include healthcare companies and the manufacturers of medical devices.
- **Boston Scientific** manufactures medical devices and researches medical device solutions. Graduates from NUIG, GMIT and Athlone Institute of Technology provide a steady supply of skilled personnel for Boston Scientific and other high-tech companies, such as Cisco Systems.
- Boston Scientific's Product Development Centre employs 150 people which helps the company remain a global leader in its field of expertise, such as the manufacture of **stents** for cardiovascular surgery and other less invasive medical devices.
- Boston Scientific, with more than 2,500 workers, is the largest employer in the West of Ireland.
- Galway was chosen as an urban gateway as part of Ireland's National Development Plan. It was hoped that Galway would act as a growth centre as an alternative to Dublin to help reduce congestion in the east, while also helping to develop the West.
- Galway is a major transport hub. It has a port, an airport, a railway station, and is located at the convergence of the M6 to Dublin, N17 to Sligo and N18 to Limerick. A new motorway to Galway from Limerick will be completed in 2018. These are very important factors in the movement of raw materials, finished products and personnel.
- There has been a constant movement of people from rural areas to the urban centres in the West and a steady decline of the total population in the West. This is a consequence of lack of amenities available in rural villages, the draw of larger centres to attract young people and the absence of sufficient basic services, such as post offices and food outlets.
- There are large areas with few people, as the area is mountainous with poor farming potential. Settlement activity centres around tourism related activities.

Tertiary activities

- Tourism is very important to the economy of the West. Ireland's tourist board, Fáilte Ireland, promotes the West under the banner '**The Wild Atlantic Way**'. This title has been very successful in targeting 'floating web users' that are seeking new destinations for their holidays. This helps develop new ways to offer tourists more varied and interesting facilities that fill niche markets.

- The loss of the transatlantic flight stop-off rule means that 90 per cent of passengers now enter the Republic of Ireland in Dublin. This increases holiday costs for tourists who wish to visit the West.

- Fast road access is restricted as only one motorway, the M6, connects Galway to Dublin and other urban centres. The N18 to Galway from Limerick is being extended and will be completed by 2018. This motorway will eventually be extended to Donegal, creating a western corridor.

- The rich cultural environment of the West, the natural rugged landscape of Connemara and Mayo, the Knock shrine and the Irish-speaking Gaeltacht areas attract thousands of tourists each year. However, tourism is seasonal and most visit during July and August.

- Expensive hotels during the high tourist season can make the West uncompetitive with other European destinations such as Spain. The lack of a year-round co-ordinated transport system makes car hire essential. Continental European competitors offer alternative, more efficient and cheaper transport.

- The natural amenities, such as hill walking trails and cycling route facilities are developing but only at a slow pace.

- Cycling, for instance, is popular with European visitors but most roads in Connemara are winding, uneven and narrow, making them unsafe for cycling. The **Great Western Greenway** is a new safe and scenic walking and cycle route on a disused railway from Westport to Achill. It has proved to be a very popular and economically successful development. It has sparked a number of cycle provider businesses that support this enterprise.

- Walking trails in the West are mostly along roads. Again, this is unsafe as Irish rural speed limits are high and roads are narrow, which discourages the potential for development. Most European walking trails are safe off-road trails. Efficient promotion of these on the Wild Atlantic Way could lead to the development of café stops and hostels along the routes.

- Surfing schools at beaches and fishing facilities are well developed in some areas. There are many surf schools in Achill, and fishing is catered for on the River Moy, Lough Corrib, Lough Mask and Lough Conn.

Human processes

- The population of the West varies greatly. Many rural regions continue to show a decline, while the urban areas increase steadily. Apart from Galway City, only two towns, Castlebar and Ballina, exceed 10,000 people. Castlebar and Ballina act as hubs as part of Ireland's development plan. They are administrative centres for their hinterlands.

- Towns generally provide market services for their hinterlands, and some have specific functions. Westport is the largest town in Mayo and is a tourist centre. Knock is a religious centre.

- Gort is still an important town due to the inward migration of Brazilians who have an established community in the town since the Celtic Tiger years. They work mostly in meat processing. Unfavourable weather, language difficulties, loneliness and now unemployment since 2008 are difficulties that face these migrants.

- The West has a population of about 450,000 people, just over half of the pre-Famine population. Population density is only 30 people per square kilometre. This is only half of the average density for the Republic of Ireland, which is very low by European standards.

- Galway has grown rapidly since the 1960s. It has become a major manufacturing centre. The role of the IDA, NUIG and regional colleges of technology have played a large part in this progress. The development of Galway airport, the M6 to Dublin and the new western corridor motorway will encourage increased growth.

- Galway is an important tourist centre. The city has many cultural attractions and tourist centres. The central city location of NUIG adds to the overall attractiveness of the city's nightlife.

exam focus

Using well-developed and explained SRPs, describe and explain the population distribution of the West. In your answer, refer to population numbers in various towns and villages from census statistics.

The Greater Dublin Area (GDA)

The Greater Dublin Area is a prosperous core region; it is also Ireland's core economic region. It is the most developed and richest region in Ireland. With Dublin at its centre, it is Ireland's most urbanised region.

The factors that influence agriculture in the GDA

Climate

- The climate is **cool temperate oceanic**, with warm summers (average 17°C) and mild winters (average 5°C). These temperatures encourage growth for eight months of the year. Little stall feeding is necessary.

- The land is low-lying and it is in the rain shadow of the western mountains. This results in much lower rainfall levels than the West: about in **750 mm in most areas**, which is less than half the rainfall in the mountain areas of the West.

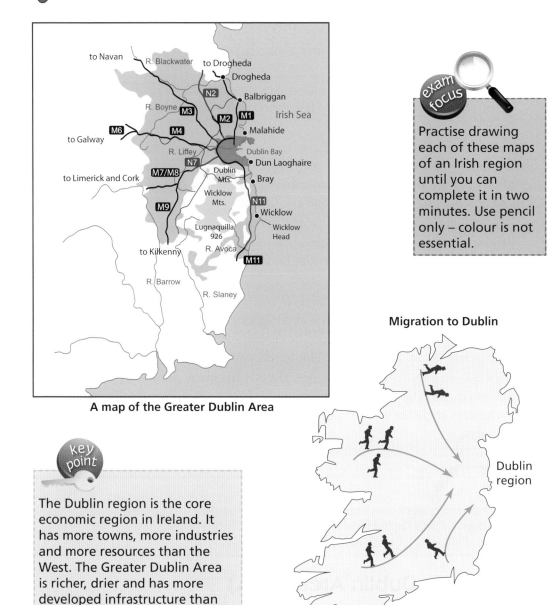

A map of the Greater Dublin Area

Migration to Dublin

The Dublin region is a prosperous/core Irish region

- Rainfall is better distributed throughout the year than in the West. The prevailing south-westerly winds are mild due to the presence of trees and hedgerows that are largely absent along the West coast.
- Winter temperatures are somewhat lower than in the West due to distance from the Atlantic, but summer temperatures are a little higher than in the West. The increased sunshine (about twice as many sunshine hours than the West) helps ripen grain crops and provides drier land for tillage.

The GDA is a prosperous farming region with incomes here
at least 40 per cent greater than in other western areas

Soils

- Fertile brown earths cover most of the GDA lowland region. This soil was originally formed beneath deciduous forests in prehistoric times. Much of the topsoil formed from weathered limestone is rich in calcium and is suited to the development of strong, healthy bones in cattle and horses.
- Soils are well drained with a balance of essential ingredients such as humus and sand that makes them particularly suited to tillage and market gardening.

Commercial factors

- Farms are larger than in the West, and they are managed by young innovative farmers who are willing to invest in modern commercial farm production methods and techniques. Land costs are high, so farming is intensive and specialised, creating higher income levels and better prospects for rural communities. Average farm income is 40 per cent above the national average.
- Market gardening around north Dublin produces fresh produce for a large urban market of 1.3 million people. The area has specialist potato, fruit, vegetable and flower farms.

North Co. Dublin is a region devoted to intensive
market gardening

- The soil here is sandier than the surrounding region, which makes it ideal for early vegetables and it has a long, frost-free growing season. There are many greenhouses near to the towns of Rush and Lusk that are heated in winter to help plants grow for intensive off-season production.
- The risk of late spring frost is lower because the area is so close to the sea. This is important for fruit crops and early potatoes.
- Market gardening or horticulture is labour intensive. During the boom years (1995–2008), foreign workers from Eastern Europe filled labour shortages. Many continue to work in Dublin market gardens. These farm workers are highly motivated and make the Dublin region very competitive for Irish and overseas markets.
- County Kildare is world famous for its bloodstock thoroughbred horses. Many important stud farms, such as the National Stud, are located here. Goffs sales near Naas sells these horses to international buyers for large sums of money.
- Because most lowland is used for farming, only upland slopes are forested. The most forested county is Wicklow. Wicklow has acid soils due to the weathering of its igneous and metamorphic rock. This primary activity of forestry is a positive way to use marginal land such as mountain slopes for long-term production.
- The fishing ports of Howth and Skerries provide a steady supply of fresh fish for the large Dublin market. A relatively small number of fishing vessels are actively involved in this commercial activity.

Relief

- The **Wicklow mountains** form the only highland area in the GDA. These mountains were formed during the **Caledonian Foldings** about **400 million years ago**, when the North American and Eurasian plates collided. The mountains are formed of granite, which is surrounded by slate and shale. Small areas of quartzite form pointed sugar-loaf peaks due to frost action during the ice ages.
- Most of the remaining region is flat or undulating, which is ideally suited to cattle-rearing.
- Landforms of marine deposition such as beaches such as at Laytown, in Co. Meath, and sand spits such as at Portmarnock form smooth a smooth coastline. Some of this sand has been blown by coastal winds over nearby lowland and has contributed to the loamy nature of the soil, which suits horticultural production.

Secondary activities in the GDA

- Dublin is the **single largest manufacturing centre** in Ireland. **One quarter of all manufacturing plants** in the country is located here. Traditional consumer industries, such as brewing and distilling, food processing, baking and confectionary are located in the region.
- **Diagio is the owner of the Guinness Brewery**, which is the oldest manufacturing facility in Ireland, beginning 255 years ago. Guinness is the biggest stout brewery in the world and is located at St James's Gate in the Liberties area in Dublin. It recently invested 169 million in updating its facility. It has 1,100 manufacturing employees and supports many thousands indirectly throughout Ireland.

- **Dublin is a world leader in ICT software** and is home to nine of the top 10 global software companies (IDA Ireland, 2017). IBM is located in the Technology Campus in Mulhuddart in Dublin and it manages services, manufacturing, research and software development for the world market. It also has a European Sales and Services Support centre based in Blanchardstown for the European market.
- **Microsoft** first opened its offices in 1985 and had a small manufacturing unit that employed just over 100 people. Today it has over 1,200 full-time employees and 700 full-time contract staff at its campus in Sandyford near the M50 in Dublin.
- **Eaton Corp** is a power management company. Eaton produces energy-efficient solutions that help its customers effectively manage electrical, hydraulic and mechanical power more efficiently. It has 100 employees.
- **Ingersoll-Rand** is an industrial technology firm that manufactures climate control systems. It is located in Ballybane Industrial estate in Dublin.
- **Smurfitt-Kappa** is one of the leading producers of paper-based packaging in the world. Its products include containerboard, corrugated and solid board packaging. This company is located in Clonskeagh in Dublin.
- **Greencore** is an international manufacturer of convenience foods, such as chilled, frozen and ambient foods that it supplies to retail, manufacturing and foodservice customers in Ireland, the UK and Europe. It is located in Santry.
- **Glen Dimplex** is the world's largest manufacturer of electrical heating products, and holds a significant global market position in domestic appliances, cooling, ventilation and renewable energy solutions. One of its manufacturing plants is located in Dunleer in Louth.
- The **pharmaceutical industry** is also well established in the GDA. **Pfizer's Biotechnology Campus** is located at Clondalkin. The company manufactures medicines and vaccines and employs 1,200 people. The biotech campus is one of the largest in the world. Other companies include **Glaxo SmithKline** and **Wyeth BioPharma**.
- The government-sponsored **Industrial Development Authority** has invested heavily in setting up specialised purpose-built industrial estates in new towns in west Dublin, such as Tallaght, Lucan, Clondalkin and Blanchardstown. Many small manufacturing companies and service and publishing companies are established in these centres that provide thousands of jobs.

Tertiary activities in the GDA

- The population of the GDA is relatively young, with more than 40 per cent of its people under 25 years of age. **Dublin's major universities**, such as Trinity College, UCD, and DCU and Smurfit Business School and the Institute of Technology in Tallaght, as well as other third-level colleges produce skilled graduates, such as engineers, business executives and pharmacists, that attract multinational companies to the region.

- **Google, Facebook and LinkedIn** have established their European headquarters in Dublin. So, Dublin has established itself as a world hub for technology companies and continues to attract international companies.
- Dublin is the focus of all **national road and rail networks**. The national routes M1 to M11 from all parts of the country connect into the M50, the semi-circular ring motorway around Dublin. This ring motorway also feeds into the numerous commuter towns that have grown around the capital city. This modern road network feeds all the manufacturing, service and industrial areas of the GDA, bringing thousands of workers to and from work each day.
- The **National Transport Authority manages transportation within Dublin.** Dublin's transit system currently uses electrified suburban trains, e.g. the DART, diesel commuter rail, trams and an extensive bus network to provide service to the population of the Greater Dublin Area. This system is based on the use of prepaid electronic cards, called Leap Cards. This transport system has become so successful that some of its routes suffer from extreme overcrowding due to cutbacks as a consequence of the Celtic Tiger crash in 2008.
- Plans have been designed for further development as part of the Transport 21 plan that includes the Dublin Metro, which is a two-line rapid transit underground system that will service Dublin Airport and other commuter belt cities such as Tallaght, Clondalkin and Finglas.
- **Dublin's port and docks** is Ireland's most important import and export centre. Its volume of imports and exports continue to grow annually by about 7 per cent, and its operating profit increased to €43 million in 2015. It has started the first stage of its master plan of 2015–2040, the Alexandra Basin project, by deepening and rebuilding and extending quay walls, creating more quayside, and deepening the navigational channel to accommodate larger vessels. This will also involve the relocation of cruise vessels to the newly built multi-purpose berths at the North Wall Quay extension, which will bring them closer to the city centre. This will bring extra tourist traffic to Dublin City, which is already a major international tourist centre.
- The **International Financial and Services Centre (IFSC)** is located in Dublin's north inner city in the former docklands area. It was established to create jobs for graduates at home and to launch a world-class financial centre in Dublin. There are **450 international companies** in the IFSC, and many additional companies such as law and accountancy firms that support them. Total employment in the IFSC is about **38,000 people**, a growth of about 7.4 per cent in 2015. This earns about **1 billion euro** in corporate taxes and another 1 billion in exchequer payroll taxes. Ireland's low rate of corporation tax at 12.5 per cent is a great attraction for major international companies.

Tourism in the GDA

- Overseas visitors to Ireland grew to record levels in 2016 with almost 8.3 million tourists. This represents an increase of 12 per cent over 2015 figures. Dublin attracts 27 per cent of all visitors to the country.

- Dublin's City Council decided to **pedestrianise** the city centre's main shopping streets to make them more attractive to visitors and retailers, e.g. Grafton Street, South King Street and Henry Street. Grafton Street is the most attractive for foreign visitors and has many important retail stores, such as Brown Thomas and Marks and Spencer, Karen Millen and Tommy Hilfiger, as well as numerous high street stores.
- **Dublin Bikes is a public bicycle rental** scheme that has been in operation since 2009. This system follows other similar rental bike schemes that operate in European cities such as Paris and Copenhagen. This facility helps tourists to tour the city alone or in groups, and makes a visit to Dublin more memorable for them.
- **Dublin Airport's** passenger traffic continues to grow annually. In 2016, passenger numbers increased by 11 per cent to a record 28 million. This was an increase of 2.8 million over 2015 figures. Nineteen new air routes were introduced during 2016 and three new airlines started operations last year. Over 1.2 million passengers used Dublin as a gateway between Europe and North America. It is now the fifth-largest airport in Europe for North America connectivity after Heathrow, Paris, Frankfurt and Amsterdam.
- **The Guinness Storehouse** and Visitors' Centre in the Liberties, one of the oldest parts of the city, is Ireland's leading tourist attraction. It explains the history of Guinness Brewery. This centre won the World's Travel Awards trophy by attracting 1.5 million visitors in 2015.
- **Trinity College** at St Stephen's Green hosts the Book of Kells which is Ireland's most richly decorated manuscript of the Four Gospels written by Early Christian Monks in about 800 AD. It attracts about 500,000 visitors to the library to view its pages.
- Other major tourist attractions include the **National Botanic Gardens** which attracts over 550,000 visitors annually; **The National Gallery of Ireland** on Clare Street, and the National Museum, which attracts 450,000 visitors. Other attractions include **The Chester Beatty Library** near Dublin Castle and the Irish Museum of Modern Art, which attracts over 480,000 visitors.
- **St Patrick's Cathedral**, founded in 1191, is the National Cathedral of the Church of Ireland. It was built where St Patrick is supposed to have baptised converts after he arrived in Ireland in 432 AD. It attracts over 500,000 visitors each year.
- **Dublin is a literary tourist centre**, as many of Ireland's famous writers and poets lived there. Oscar Wilde, Patrick Kavanagh and Brendan Behan are just some of the writers that are celebrated and remembered during literary festivals in the city each year. Also, **theatres** such as the **Abbey Theatre**, the Gate, Bord Gáis Energy theatre, the 3Arena, **The National Concert Hall** and other venues hold a variety of dramas and entertainment shows weekly that attract large numbers of visitors.
- Some specific visitor attractions, including the Ha'penny bridge, St Stephen's Green, Dublin Zoo, and the Phoenix Park together make Dublin one of Europe's most outstanding cities to visit.
- **Ireland's National Stud** and Japanese Gardens are located in Kildare. It is the national symbol of Ireland's thoroughbred equine industry. Famous horses, such as

Beef or Salmon, Hardy Eustace, Hurricane Fly and Kicking King can all be viewed there. The Japanese Gardens that are within these grounds also attract thousands of visitors each year.

- **St Kevin's Oratory**, located in the Glendalough glaciated valley in the Wicklow mountains, has a well-developed tourist centre. Another nearby attraction is **Powerscourt House and Gardens** in Co. Wicklow, which was voted No. 3 of the World's top 10 gardens by *The National Geographic*. Its walled gardens and Italian and Japanese gardens are visited by over 230,000 visitors each year.

- There are many major **sporting venues** built in Dublin. **Croke Park** has the largest stadium in Ireland that can cater for 80,000 spectators. It is the GAA headquarters where most All-Ireland semi-finals and finals are held. Many **open-air concerts** are held in Croke Park each year. The Aviva Stadium hosts all rugby and soccer international matches. Each of these stadiums are located in the city centre.

- **Numerous golf courses** have been developed on the coastal sand dunes along the north Dublin coastline. Such developments are located at Portmarnock, Malahide and near Laytown. This coastal stretch offers wind surfing, wave surfing and bird watching facilities that are availed of by many tourists. Many other golf courses are located inland such as the K Club in Kildare, Druids Glen in Wicklow and many other places. The K Club was the venue for the Ryder Cup, which is an important international event that drew thousands of visitors to Ireland. This venue continues to draw golfers from all parts of the world to play on its courses.

A European region (not Ireland)

When a question asks you to write about 'a European region (not Ireland)', it refers to a region of a country on the **continental landmass of Europe**, e.g. the Paris Basin or the Mezzogiorno.

The Mezzogiorno in Italy

The Mezzogiorno has many villages perched on high ground to avoid the wastage of precious farmland

The Mezzogiorno in southern Italy has suffered from out-migration for over a century

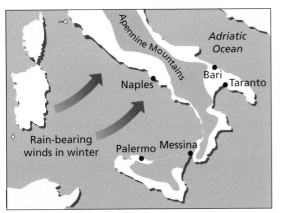

The Mezzogiorno receives rain-bearing winds in winter

key point

The Mezzogiorno is a peripheral/disadvantaged region in Europe.

exam focus

Practise drawing these sketch maps, marking their names and features in two minutes. Colour is not necessary. Drawing sketch maps is an important skill that's examined regularly in 20-mark questions.

Physical factors: Relief and soils

- The Mezzogiorno in southern Italy is dominated by the steep slopes of the **Apennine mountains**, which stretch 1,500 km along the spine of the peninsula from Rome to Sicily.
- The **rich, fertile, alluvial (river) and volcanic soils** from weathered lava are mostly located in **valley flood plains** or **narrow coastal plains**.
- Calabria, in the toe of Italy, is mostly made up of granite plateaus with poor, thin soils, and very steep slopes.
- The Apennines were formed from the **collision and subduction of small tectonic plates**.
- The Tiber is the largest river and enters the sea south of Rome. The remaining rivers are small, fast-flowing streams from the Apennines.
- Much of the **bedrock is porous limestone** that allows little surface drainage.
- The high Apennines are **karst** landscapes, where limestone bedrock is exposed over large regions. Villages are perched on hilltops or high ground to avoid using level land that is needed for farming.

Climate

- The Mezzogiorno has a **Mediterranean** climate and high pressure dominates in summer. **Winds are hot and dry** and blow outwards as north-easterly winds from the continent of Europe.
- Summer rains fall as **intense downpours** accompanied by thunderstorms. These create rapid runoff and erosion, often leading to landslides and mudslides.
- Summer temperatures are high, with an average of 29°C. Regular cloudless summer days increase temperatures.
- Winters are mild, about 17°C, and moist. South-west winds bring cyclonic rain. Rainfall amounts range from 500 mm to 900 mm annually.
- The lowest rainfall occurs along the Adriatic coast, because it is in the rain shadow of the Apennines.

Primary activities

Human factors

- The Mezzorgiorno contains 21 million people, or about one-third of the population of Italy. The region's overall population density, 140 persons per square kilometre, is 30 per cent less than that of Italy as a whole.
- Until the 1950s, the majority of the working population was employed in farming and fishing. The people were poor and incomes were low.
- The system of land ownership was called **latifundia**: most of the best land was owned by absentee landlords. A lot of land was farmed but yields were low. It was an **inefficient** system and farmers were poor.
- Peasant farmers lived in hilltop villages and travelled daily to work on the latifundia. Only one-quarter of the farmers owned their own land.
- By 1950, 70 per cent of these farmers' land holdings were smaller than three hectares. To support their families they overworked the land, leading to overgrazing, overcultivation and eventually soil erosion. This system was called **minifundia**.
- Most of the original pine woodland cover was cut down for agriculture, leaving the steep Apennine slopes without vegetation, the roots of which had bound soil particles together. This deforestation has caused severe soil erosion on the hillsides.

- The most fertile soils are found close to volcanoes, where volcanic soils developed. The plain of Campania, near Vesuvius, is very fertile and has these rich, volcanic soils.
- High temperatures favour the growth of citrus fruit crops, such as lemons, limes and oranges. Because of its high temperatures, Sicily produces 60 per cent of all Italian citrus fruits.

Government influence

- From 1950 onwards, most of the estates were bought by the state; the land was redistributed to the landless labourers by land reform agencies called Enti di Reforma, and holdings of 5–50 hectares were created.
- The development fund was called the Cassa per il Mezzogiorno. This fund transferred about 10 per cent of the Mezzogiorno's land from landlord to peasant ownership.
- Farmers were trained to work their newly family-owned land efficiently, growing a mix of crops such as cereals, citrus fruit and traditional crops of olives and vines.
- Three related factors were put in place to support this new farming system:
  - an irrigation network to promote growth in summer
  - improved transport systems, such as **autostradas**, to get high-value, perishable crops to market quickly
  - new villages and towns were built with all the important services such as schools, healthcare centres and leisure facilities.
- Today, only one in 10 of the region's workforce is involved in farming. The move to more intensive farming by fewer farmers has also increased rural prosperity. The Mezzogiorno is now a leading supplier of **citrus fruits**, vegetables and **olives** to European markets.
- The most successful farming areas are on coastal lowlands and river valleys where irrigation water is available. The **Metapontino** is a coastal strip in the Gulf of Taranto. It was once a malarial swamp, but was drained as part of the land reform programme.
- Using the waters of the five rivers that cross the plain, irrigation produces cash crops such as citrus fruits, peaches, table grapes, strawberries, flowers and salad crops.

Secondary activities

Government influence

- By the 1950s, only 17 per cent of Italy's workforce was located in the Mezzogiorno. Just as with agriculture, industrial development here has had its successes and failures.
- **Government help** was needed to encourage industrial development. This help included:

- ○ generous grants and tax relief
- ○ state-controlled companies had to make 80 per cent of new investment in the south
- ○ a number of key industrial development areas were created to act as a basis for regional growth.

Some results of the reforms

- Between 1960 and 2000 the region's industrial workforce almost tripled, to 1.4 million, and over 300,000 new jobs were created. This has reduced dependence on agriculture and increased the prosperity of the people.
- Almost 75 per cent of all new jobs have been in heavy industries such as steel, chemicals and engineering. Because the heavy industries are located on the coast, the inland rural areas have remained depressed.
- The most successful region is the **Bari–Brindisi–Taranto** triangle, where oil refining, chemicals and steel form the basis of this major industrial zone.
- The construction of a new deep-water port at Taranto was vital in the selection of this site for the country's largest iron and steel mill.
- **Latina–Fronsione** is the fastest growing industrial area in the South. Over 250 new factories, including a car plant, employ over 16,000 workers.
- **Catania–Augusta–Siracusa** is one of the largest oil-refining, chemical and petrochemical complexes in Western Europe. Local deposits of potash, oil, natural gas and sulphur favour this type of industry.

New industry

- The Naples area has a tradition of jewellery manufacturing as a craft industry. The EU, through the TARI Project in 1990, has helped fund skill trading and installation of new equipment. Now, over 1,500 skilled craftworkers produce jewellery for a worldwide market, e.g. China.

Transport infrastructure

- Major improvements in roads, autostradas, and **modernisation of ports** such as Naples and Taranto.
- Major investments were made to **improve transport systems**. The backbone of the system is the **Autostrada del Sole**, which runs from the Swiss border in the north of Italy to the 'toe' of Italy in Calabria. Another motorway runs along the east coast.
- Bridges were built over deep gorges and valleys; tunnels were drilled through steep mountain spurs to shorten journey time to this peripheral region.
- The supply of fresh food in winter and early spring, such as early vegetables, fruit and fish, to the much colder northern region (e.g. the Plain of Lombardy) was made possible and viable by this investment in 1,000 km of road way.
- Port developments have improved access to the south, and these regions have become core industrial centres.

Tertiary activities

Tourism

- The long, hot, dry summers, dramatic coastal scenery, extensive beaches, and historic cities have much to offer the tourist. The south also tends to be cheaper and less crowded than other Italian regions.
- Hotels have been improved to cater for the 12 million tourists who visit the south annually. More than 9 million of these tourists come from other parts of Italy.
- Sorrento, near Naples, is a major tourist centre. Located near **Mount Vesuvius**, **Herculaneum** and **Pompeii**, it is a busy coastal resort on cliffs that overlook the old town's fishing village and the Isle of Capri, another major tourist resort even in Roman times.
- Many of the towns and villages of southern Italy hold open-air processions on Catholic feast days of local saints. These are unique to each area; they are very colourful and are tied to local communities, often carried out in memory of family members.

Human processes

- Migration within Italy is a major factor, influencing population patterns in the country. Between 1951 and 1971 over 4 million migrants left the south because of unemployment and poverty. Most of those who left were attracted to the cities of Milan, Turin and Genoa, or to the USA.
- Over 1 million people left the Mezzogiorno in the 1980s, and this **out-migration** trend continued into the 1990s.
- Since the 1990s, increasing numbers of migrants from other countries, such as Albania and the former Yugoslavia, have been attracted to Italy.

The Paris Basin

How relief, climate and soils affect Primary activities in the Paris Basin

- The Paris Basin is a rolling/undulating lowland region located at about 48° North in mid-latitude. It has two climate areas that suit agricultural production. Along the English Channel coastal area it experiences a **maritime climate** with south-west prevailing winds that bring moisture-laden air and cyclonic rain that is well distributed throughout the year. These moist, warm winds keep the climate mild (5°C in January) in winter and cool (15°C in July) in summer.
- Further inland the basin has more of a **continental-style climate**. Winter temperatures are a little colder and average 2.5°C in January, and **summer temperatures are warmer**, averaging 24°C in July. These are nearly perfect temperatures for strong growth. The rainfall, which is at its maximum in summer, boosts crop growth, which is ideal for grain production.

The Paris Basin is a large, prosperous core region in northern France. The city of Paris lies at its centre.

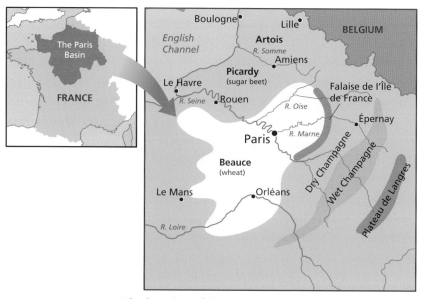

The location of the Paris Basin

- In the centre of the basin are layers of permeable sandstones and limestones, which allow excellent drainage for crop growing and harvesting. The **continental influence** raises ground and air temperatures, encouraging the growth of crops and helping to dry the grain in July and August. This helps boost yields and the quality of the grain for storage.
- The Paris Basin has a covering of **limon**, which is a **wind-blown soil**. Limon soils are level, fine-grained and rich in minerals. Dense dust storms at the end of the Ice Age dropped this soil, and thick layers built up that smoothened the ground and formed **wide open plains**. These soils are excellent for the growth of cereal crops like wheat, maize and barley.

France produces about 6 per cent of the world's wheat crop, and the Paris Basin produces a substantial proportion of this crop

- Erosion has exposed the **sedimentary rocks** that form a landscape of alternate **scarps** (Côte de Meuse) and **vales** (Dry and Wet Champagne). Dry Champagne has stony soils that suit vine-growing. **Champagne** has established itself as a **high-class wine-making region** that can command high prices for its sparkling white wines. Épernay and Reims are market centres for the wine industry. Wet Champagne is a lake-dotted region of damp soil with grassland suited to cattle-grazing and beef production. Brie cheese is the most famous soft cheese from the Paris Basin.

- Many farms **exceed 80 hectares (200 acres)** and have large fields where a high degree of mechanisation is achieved. The area is called the granary of France, which is about one-quarter the size of France itself. Intensive wheat production in the centre of the Paris Basin allows France to produce about 6 per cent of the world's wheat crop.

- The Paris Basin is **well drained by the River Seine and its tributaries**, the Oise, Marne, Aube and the Yonne and their tributaries. These rivers carry excess moisture off the land and away to the sea, which ensures that farms can be easily tilled during the autumn months for the replanting of winter wheat and barley. This ensures **farm production is maximised** throughout the year.

- Intensive market gardening is widely practised close to the cities that are scattered throughout the Paris Basin and in the vicinity of Paris itself. This combined urban population of 12 million people creates a huge demand for fresh vegetables, fruit and flowers. Year-round market demand creates steady employment for a large workforce that is specialised in specific product production.

A village farm in the Paris Basin

Secondary activities (manufacturing industry)

- Paris is a major port city and has heavy industry that includes the manufacture of railway engines, carriages and wagons. This is facilitated because heavy components can be brought to Paris by river transport. Heavy industry has established itself all along the River Seine from Le Havre to Paris, where deep water allows for the import and export of raw materials and finished products.

- Chemical companies and oil refining provide huge industrial centres on river bank sites that are many kilometres long and line the banks of the Seine from Le Havre to Rouen. Their **hydrocarbon by-products** are used in the manufacture of lubricant oil and grease, brake oil, paraffin wax, electrical insulation and fuel oils that are all used as raw materials and support products for the automobile industries around Paris and throughout the world.

- **Car assembly companies**, such as Peugeot and Citroën, have moved manufacturing plants away from Paris to other towns in the region due to the restriction of limited space for expansion and Greenfield sites for new enterprises. This is called **deindustrialisation** and is a positive indication that car manufacture intends to expand its manufacturing capability into the future.

Car assembly has established itself over many decades as a successful manufacturing enterprise

- The Paris region has established itself as a **centre for excellence in aircraft and equipment manufacturing**. Its locally based higher education institutions currently offer 128 courses in this field that includes universities and third-level technology engineering schools and associated institutions. The Paris region hosts the 30 per cent of the national workforce in aircraft and equipment manufacturing.

- Over 100,000 workers are employed by **four of the world's global leaders in the aircraft industry**. These companies included Airbus Defence and Space, Dassault Aviation (manufactures military aircraft), Safran (manufactures jet engines and components and Airbus helicopters), Zodiac Aerospace (manufactures seats, cabin interiors, power distribution, lighting, fuel and fluid systems and safety equipment) and Lisi Aerospace (manufactures specialist fasteners and structural components used for the airframe as well as the engine of the aircraft).

- Many newer industries such as electronics, telecommunications and healthcare have located in the hundreds of industrial estates and technology parks in the outer suburbs of Paris, or in new towns such as Évry and Marne-la-Vallée where workers live locally in self-supporting urban centres.

- Paris has been a long-established **international centre of the fashion industry**. Fashion workshops are located close to the city centre along the banks of the Seine. Famous fashion houses and manufacturers such as Dior, Chanel, Yves Saint Laurent, Louis Vuitton and Cartier are located in the city. More than 80 per cent of their products are exported.
- **Paris is the centre of the publishing industry**. Editions du Centre Pompidou has a worldwide reputation for its publications in the field of modern and contemporary art. It publishes about 40 new titles each year and has more than 300 listed in its catalogue. Larousse, a major publisher of dictionaries and encyclopaedias, has specialised dictionaries and books on astronomy and gardening. Cairn publishes journals in social sciences. WAN-IFRA is part of the World Association of Newspapers and News Publishers and publishes *World Press Trends*, which covers hundreds of countries.

Tertiary activities

- Transport systems within Paris create thousands of jobs. Paris is the centre of the French transport system. All autoroutes (motorways) and rail networks meet in Paris. Paris is the hub of the TGV rail system, a high-speed train network (bullet trains) on which trains can reach 300 km per hour. Paris is also connected by the TGV system to London, via the Channel Tunnel, and to Brussels. There are about 350 TGV trains in operation, making it a very efficient system.
- **The Metro** is the underground rail system in the city. The Metro is connected to the national network, the SNCF, and the Réseau Express Régional, an underground rail system that extends into the suburbs. This allows industrial and service sector workers great mobility in movement throughout the Metropolitan region of Paris. This adds to the attraction of Paris as a manufacturing centre.
- **Five new towns** have been developed on the fringes of Paris to house overspill population from the city and to control urban sprawl. These new towns include Évry and Marne-la-Vallée and contain more than 100,000 people. Each town has large office blocks, business parks and shopping centres that form self-contained urban centres. These cities have been built north and south of the Seine.
- Other human factors add a positive note to Paris as a thriving human community. A high proportion of its 22 million people are young. The birth rate is 15 per 1,000 and the death rate is only 7 per 1,000. So the Paris region has a fast-growing young population, which is an essential factor for the growth of the local workforce.
- Urban regeneration has helped renew decayed inner-city areas. Eight suburban nodes were chosen for development. One of the most successful developments in Paris has been at La Défense, to the west of the city centre. Thousands of jobs have been provided in the tertiary sector. Poor-quality old housing in Paris has been demolished and replaced with modern high-rise apartments in urban renewal projects, e.g. near Montparnasse.

- France is the world's most visited country, with over 85 million visitors. **Paris is the third most visited city** in the world and about 30 million people visit the region annually. Its wide boulevards that meet at the **Arc de Triomphe**, its ornate buildings that are uniquely French, the **Eiffel Tower** and street attractions such as the artists that work and display their work at Montmartre on Sundays, all add character to the city.

- **Notre Dame Cathedral** is a centre of attraction with its Gothic design and stained-glass windows attracting several bus-loads of visitors each day. The **Trocadero** has wonderful views of the **Eiffel Tower** and its gardens offer visitors a recreation space for families and places for children to play. **The Louvre** is a famous museum and art gallery located in the heart of Paris. The **Tuileries gardens**, once the playground of Queen Marie Antoinette, attract many people. Nearby is the Orangery Gallery that houses many of Monet's water-lily oil paintings, as well as the works of other famous artists.

- **The Palace of Versailles**, close to Paris, was the home of the Royal Family of King Louis XVI and Queen Marie Antoinette. It is a very famous tourist venue. Tours of the palace's famous rooms and gardens are taken by thousands of visitors each day. Also near Paris is the home of the **artist Claude Monet** at Giverny, who painted his famous water lilies that he grew in his ponds specifically for this purpose. His house and its gardens are a major tourist site.

12 The Dynamics of Regions: A Subcontinental Region (India or Brazil)

aims You need to be able to:

- Study **one** continental/subcontinental region only: **either** India (pages 117–130) **or** Brazil (pages 130–140).
- If you have not studied either of these regions, use this chapter as a guide on how to lay out your notes.
- Make sure you know everything about your chosen region under the headings in the chapter. *Note:* culture appears regularly in exam questions.

The Indian subcontinent

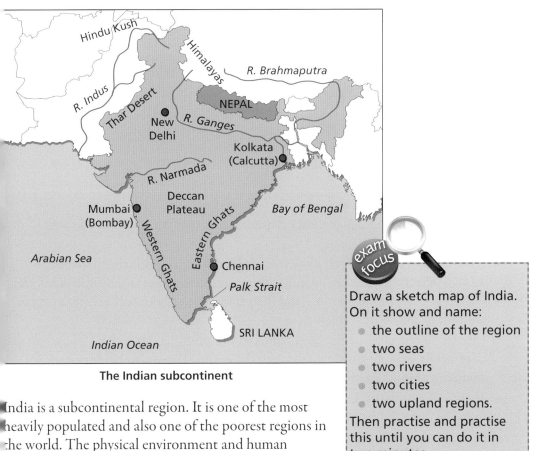

The Indian subcontinent

India is a subcontinental region. It is one of the most heavily populated and also one of the poorest regions in the world. The physical environment and human activities have a profound effect on each other.

exam focus

Draw a sketch map of India. On it show and name:
- the outline of the region
- two seas
- two rivers
- two cities
- two upland regions.

Then practise and practise this until you can do it in two minutes.

Primary activities

Physical factors: Relief, drainage and soils

There are three main physical regions in India:

- Northern Mountains
- Indus–Ganges Plain
- Southern Plateaux.

Northern mountains

- The world's highest highest mountains, the Himalayas, in the north of the country, separate India from its neighbours.
- They extend from the **Hindu Kush** in the north-west, through the **Himalayan range** to the extreme north-east of the country.
- Mount Everest, the highest mountain on earth, and the next 23 highest peaks are all in this range.
- They were formed by the **collision** of two of the earth's **crustal plates**, the Eurasian plate and the Indian plate.
- This collision compressed the earth's crust and buckled it upwards to form these fold mountains.

Always choose two headings/factors when writing about primary, secondary or tertiary industries. The marking scheme normally specifies:

- two secondary activities identified – 2 marks
- two factors named – 2 marks + 2 marks
- examination – 10–15 × SRPs @ 2 marks each.

Focus on how the physical landscape and climate affects agriculture. This shows an examiner that you understand the interaction between these forces.

Indus–Ganges Plain

- The Indus–Ganges Plain is a **huge depression** or syncline that formed south of the mountain chain.
- It is covered with thousands of metres of **alluvial (river) soils** that have been washed into the depression by India's three most important rivers – the Indus, the Ganges and the Brahmaputra – and their tributaries. About half of India's people, one billion, live in this region.
- Laterite, or red soils, are the most common soils in India. Heavy rain leaches almost all minerals, except iron, down through these soils. The remaining iron particles oxidise (rust) and give the soil a reddish colour.
- The rivers are swollen in summer by melt-waters from glaciers and monsoon rains from the surrounding mountains.
- Extensive areas of lowland are flooded by these waters, which deposit highly fertile soils on their flood plains.

Southern plateaus

- Southern India is made up of a number of plateaus. The **Deccan plateau**, the largest, is tilted from west to east. Its basaltic black soils retain moisture and are suited to growing cereals.
- Two mountain ranges, the **Western Ghats** and **Eastern Ghats**, border narrow coastal lowlands. Both of these increase rainfall amounts for peninsular India.

exam focus

Always give at least 15 SRPs in a 30-mark answer and explain the relationship or interaction between the statements you make.

Climate

- The climate of India is **tropical continental monsoon**. Most of India is in the tropics. Only the mountains of the north and north-west have frost. Temperatures are high year-round.
- India's climate can be divided into two main seasons: the dry monsoon and the wet monsoon.

The dry monsoon season

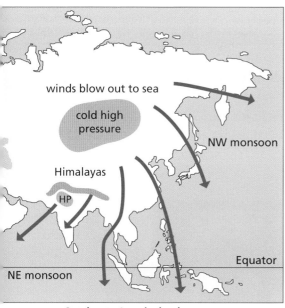

winds blow out to sea

cold high pressure

NW monsoon

Himalayas

HP

Equator

NE monsoon

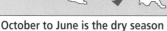

October to June is the dry season

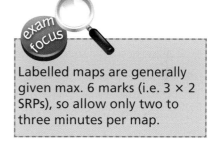

exam focus

Labelled maps are generally given max. 6 marks (i.e. 3 × 2 SRPs), so allow only two to three minutes per map.

- This occurs from **October to June**, when cold winds blow outwards from a high-pressure area in the centre of Asia. They are land winds, so they are dry. They bring freezing temperatures and snow to the mountains in the north.
- From March to June these winds become warmer, and by June temperatures can be as high as 49°C in the Ganges Valley.

The wet monsoon season

- From **mid-June to September,**
  warm ocean winds are sucked into a
  low-pressure area in the continent.
  One wind blows as a south-west
  monsoon from the Arabian Sea.
  Some of this air is forced to rise over
  the Western Ghats and intense rain
  falls. The second wind blows from
  the Bay of Bengal and veers north to
  blow along the Ganges and
  Brahmaputra Valleys. In some areas,
  up to **10,000 mm of rain** can fall in
  a six-week period.

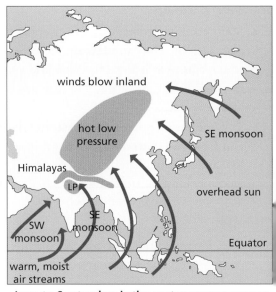

June to September is the wet monsoon season

- As the winds move west along the
  Ganges Valley, rainfall reduces.
  When they reach the extreme
  north-west, the winds have become
  dry, leading to desert conditions.

Exam questions often ask you
to explain how climate and
soils have influenced farming
in a continental or
subcontinental region.

- The monsoons bring essential water supplies
  to India's population. Some interior parts of
  India are not affected by monsoon rains. The
  Thar Desert area has little rainfall because by
  the time the summer monsoon winds reach the
  Thar, they have shed their moisture and are dry.
- The rains provide the ideal environment for the
  production of rice, which needs flooded fields
  in its early stages of growth.

Farming

India's farming output has increased substantially, but most of
its farms are tiny and output is low

- India's cultivated land is equal in area to the total cultivated land of the EU countries. Arable farming, especially cereals, is the main type of farming.
- Two-thirds of India's one billion people depend directly on the land for their living. Almost half of rural families have farms of less than 0.5 hectares, or no land at all.

key point

India's 'Green Revolution' is the government's aim to make India a net exporter of food to ensure political stability and security. The green revolution has led to India becoming a net food exporter.

- A quarter of India's agricultural land is owned by less than 5 per cent of farm families. Most family farms are broken up into tiny, scattered plots.
- Farming is mainly intensive subsistence. This means people depend on their own food supplies to feed themselves. Rice is the chief crop. Cereals such as wheat and millet are grown in drier areas.
- Almost all planting, weeding and harvesting is **done by hand**. Double cropping is practised: rice is grown in the wet season.
- The country's rapidly growing population places a huge demand on annual output. **Genetically modified**, high-yield varieties of rice and wheat have been introduced and are now grown. These varieties are resistant to many diseases and pests.
- Cash crops are often sold as exports to help India's balance of trade. Cash crops include tea, cotton, coffee, tobacco and sugarcane. Many of these are produced in commercial estates called plantations.
- India has the largest livestock population in the world. Many are in poor physical condition. The slaughter of cattle is illegal in many states because of the Hindu belief that the cow is a sacred animal.
- Most of the beef that is eaten comes from cattle that have died of old age. Many cattle are malnourished and old livestock are allowed to roam as strays or may be sent to special compounds until they die.

Mining

- India has **large reserves of iron ore and copper**. Other mineral ores are bauxite, from which aluminium is made, and zinc, gold and silver.
- Most of India's oil comes from Mumbai (Bombay) High Field in the Arabian Sea.
- The most important coal-producing regions are Bihar and West Bengal.

Secondary activities

Government influence

After independence in 1947, only 2 per cent of the labour force was employed in industry. Industry was concentrated in the major cities of Mumbai (Bombay), Kolkata (Calcutta) and Chennai (Madras).

Indian industry has three factors in its favour:

- a large home market
- a wide range of natural resources, such as coal and iron ore
- a cheap labour force.

The government has focused on new industries such as:

1. Agri-industries: the manufacture of fertilisers and machinery and food processing to benefit rural communities.
2. Consumer goods industries and small-scale, labour-intensive craft industries which can be competitive in export markets. These help reduce the migration from rural regions to cities.
3. Community-based developments and self-help schemes in rural regions: this was intended to create jobs in rural regions where over 70 per cent of the people lived.
4. High-tech industries: the growing educated workforce is attracting computer software companies to India. India produces more university graduates than the USA and Canada combined. Most of these new industries are located in urban regions such as Kolkata, Mumbai and Chennai and their hinterlands.

Planning programme in urban centres

- Following independence, national planning recognised the importance of urban centres for economic development.
- A new capital, New Delhi, was set up.
- Major urban growth centres were also established, based on existing cities.
  - **Mumbai:** Over the centuries Mumbai became a region of in-migration because it practised a policy of religious tolerance. Mumbai has attracted growth industries such as electronics and pharmaceuticals. It also has traditional industries, e.g. food processing and textiles.
  - **Chennai:** Chennai forms the core of the southern industrial zone. Textiles and light engineering are important industries. Many multinational computer software companies have set up here. The region is called **India's 'Silicon Valley'**.
  - **Kolkata:** Heavy industries such as iron and steel are long established, owing to local sources of coal and iron ore. The Indian-owned Tata Steel Limited is one of the largest in the world. Tata is involved with other companies in the manufacture of military armaments and aircraft.
- India is ranked 60th worldwide in manufacturing output, and the manufacturing industry employs 18 per cent of India's total workforce.
- India's iron and steel industries are based on large reserves of iron and copper ores in the north of the country.
- Government investment in education has driven India's increasing industrial production and services.

Tertiary activities

Services

India's service sector is underdeveloped. So many of India's population are poor and do not have the money for education, healthcare, or much else, even if these services were available. As with similar economies, there are two levels of services:

- One type caters for what are regarded as the rich; for them there is the full range of services.
- The other type caters for the poor, or underclass. It is similar to what you would find in any large city, and is the informal sector. There are the unlicensed street sellers such as shoeshine people and street vendors, alongside illegal activities such as prostitution and drug dealing.

Transport

Road transport is vital to India's economy. Huge investment is ongoing into road infrastructure. Concrete roads are gaining in popularity and new concrete technology has rendered it more attractive and eco-friendly than bitumen-based works. India's government plans to lay 19,000 km of new expressways by 2022. Many of these will be toll roads. Half of India's villages do not have access to tarred roads suitable for vehicles. These communities use dirt track roads and carts drawn by cattle.

Tourism in India

- Over 80 million foreign tourists visited India in 2015. In this year, tourism supported 37 million jobs and generated 6.5 per cent of GDP.
- India is ranked eighth out of 141 countries in price competitiveness, yet the nation has very few hotel rooms per capita by international comparison and low ATM facilities.
- Great efforts are being made to promote new forms of tourism such as rural, cruise and ecotourism.
- Despite its rich cultural and natural heritage, issues around female tourist safety is a major concern for the tourist industry.
- The rise in income for India's middle-income class allows for increasing amounts to spend on domestic holidays. The Indian government actively supports tourism and it offers tax breaks for Indian travel agents, hotel owners and private tour operators. 'Incredible India' is the banner that the Indian tourist board operates to promote holidays in India.
- Medical tourism is a growing niche market. Medical companies make arrangements through insurance companies for foreigners to receive medical treatment at affordable prices.

Human processes and culture

Population dynamics

- India's population is greater than **one billion people**. With a **natural increase of 1.6 per cent annually**, its population increases by 16 million people every year, and could reach 2 billion by 2040.
- The country has only recently **entered the third stage of the population cycle**.
- Even though healthcare has improved and the death rate has reduced, death rates are still high.
- Because rural families are large, it is **difficult to control population**. Large families are seen as a positive aspect of life, rather than as a burden to feed and clothe.
- Because India has a very young population, it will continue to have a large natural increase for the near future.
- India's population is very unevenly distributed. There are high population densities in the Ganges Valley, along coastal lowlands and in cities and their hinterlands. The interior regions have low population densities.
- India has many different cultural groups. A number of outside factors have complicated matters. These include:
  - ○ the migration of Europeans
  - ○ the spread of Islam
  - ○ British occupation.

A 30-mark question on culture regularly appears in the exam. The marking scheme in 2009 asked for the following.
- Aspect of culture identified – 2 marks
- Region named – 2 marks
- Examination – 13 × SRPs @ 2 marks each
- Other aspects of culture may be credited from SRPs.

A question asking you to explain cultural differences appears regularly in exam papers. Use any two headings (e.g. religion, language, customs, etc.) to structure your answer.

Make sure you can write at least 15 SRPs on culture in 12 minutes.

Languages

- The people of India speak many different languages: there are over **1,600 different languages and dialects**. Schools teach in 58 different languages.
- The constitution of India recognises 18 languages.
- National newspapers are published in 87 languages and radio programmes broadcast in 71 different languages. This creates difficulties and disunity between cultural groups.
- The two main language families in India are **Indo-European** (the largest language group) and **Dravidian**.

- **Hindi** is the official state language, but its position of importance is resented by other language groups. It is spoken by over 250 million people.
- Dravidian languages are spoken by 200 million people, mainly in the south of the country.
- English, which is spoken by about 2 per cent of the population, is a legacy of British colonialism.
- Language differences in India emphasise cultural divisions rather than unity within the state.

Clothing

- Many Indian people, especially in cities, wear Western-style clothes, but most Indians wear traditional clothes:
  - men wear a **dhoti**, a simple white garment wrapped between the legs, like loose trousers
  - women wear a **sari**, a straight piece of cloth draped loosely over the shoulders and head and around the body like a long dress. Wealthy women may wear saris of silk, with borders of gold thread.

Indian clothing is distinctive and colourful

- Indian men of the **Sikh** tradition wear a turban and a beard.
- Many women wear a **kumkum**, a round dot usually made with a red or black powder, in the middle of the forehead. The kumkum is considered a mark of beauty.

Religions

- Asoka, an ancient Indian ruler, converted to Buddhism and helped to spread it throughout India in the 4th century BC.
- Three other outside influences that affected India are: European migrations (Europeans moved to India, bringing their languages with them); the spread of Islam; and British colonisation.

Hinduism

- Hinduism is the dominant religion in India.
- In Hinduism there is a multi-layered society in which people are divided according to class or **caste**. At the top of society are the priests or Brahmins, and other

high-ranking people such as officials or professionals. At the bottom are the lowest castes (e.g. the **Dalits**), who do the menial or dirty work.

- Belonging to a caste is decided by birth and one cannot move up the system in a single lifetime. Caste members often only socialise or marry within their own group; but education has helped to change this perspective and today many educated Hindus of various castes mix freely, especially in urban regions.
- The castes help preserve and pass on various skills in the arts and crafts from generation to generation.
- Hindus are forbidden to kill cows or to eat their flesh, because cows are considered sacred.
- **Hindus** believe that all living creatures will have many lives on earth after they die. This philosophy is called **reincarnation**.

Every year, millions of Hindus gather at the steps in Varanasi to wash in the sacred River Ganges

While Hinduism is the main religion, other religions are also important.

Islam

- There are about 200 million Muslims in India. Islam was introduced through trade to India and it is most common in the Indus and Ganges basin. It is rare in peninsular India.
- Islam accepts all converts as equal and rejects the caste system, which is why it was attractive to many Indians.

Sikhism

Sikhism was founded in the 15th century. It does not have a caste system. The Sikhs are a powerful cultural group and are centred in the Punjab, an important farming region.

Buddhism and Christianity

Buddhism and Christianity are minority religions in India.

The political–religious divide in India (see pages 155–156)

- India was a **colony of Britain**. After **independence in 1947** it was **divided into two states**: India, a Hindu state, and Pakistan, an Islamic state. This division was based on religious grounds and caused many minority religious groups to remain within the Indian state.
- Large-scale migration resulted, due to fears of persecution. Over 15 million people moved home. Many Muslims left India for Pakistan, and many Hindus left Pakistan for India.
- Pakistan was initially divided into two parts: West Pakistan, in the Indus Valley; and East Pakistan, in the Ganges Valley. They were separated by a long distance, with northern India in between.
- In 1956 East Pakistan broke away from West Pakistan and became **Bangladesh**.
- Some territory is still in dispute between Pakistan and India; this disputed region is called **Kashmir**.

SAMPLE QUESTION AND ANSWER

Question: Account for the development of an urban region (not in Ireland) in a continental or sub-continental region.

Answer:
The growth and development of Mumbai

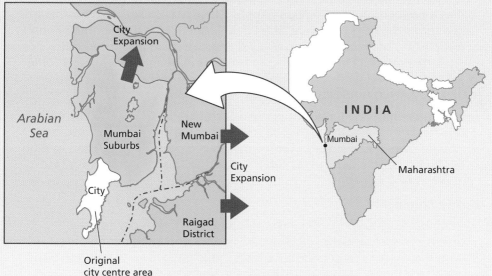

Map of Mumbai and its expansion

- Mumbai is the **most populated city in India** and is the financial capital of the country. Up until the 1980s, Mumbai owed its wealth to its historical colonial past, textile mills and its seaport. Since then it has diversified its industrial base, has most of India's specialised technical industries, has a modern industrial infrastructure and highly skilled human resources. Industries include aerospace, optical engineering, medical research, computers and electronic equipment of all kinds, as well as shipbuilding, salvaging and renewable energy.

- Mumbai is an **important economic hub** and contributes 10 per cent of all factory employment and 40 per cent of India's foreign trade. Many of India's numerous transnational corporations (Multinationals) are based in Mumbai. These include the State Bank of India, Tata Group, Godrej and Reliance companies. Most of India's major television and satellite networks, as well as its major publishing houses are located here. The centre of the Hindi film industry, Bollywood, produces the largest number of films per year in the world. The Oscar-winning movie *Slumdog Millionaire* was based there.

Growth from its origins to the 1970s

- Initially Mumbai was a fishing village that had a sheltered site and was protected from the strong winds and storms from the Arabian Sea. It was located on a peninsula on the southern tip Salsette Island, had access to the sea on two sides and, as a British colony until 1947, it grew into a major port. The British viewed Mumbai as the gateway to India. It was the closest port of entry to the subcontinent for travellers from Europe, through the Suez Canal. Areas around the port quickly became industrialised, processing goods for export and handling imports.

- After independence for India from Britain in 1947, Mumbai grew rapidly; by 1971 it had a population of 8 million people. Today, **greater Mumbai has a population of 21 million people**. The city has expanded northwards along the Salsette Peninsula. Slum dwellers make up an ever-increasing proportion of its population. Many mangrove swamps bordered the Salsette Peninsula initially. Most of these have been reclaimed but some of the marginal lands often form the location for the poorest people who live illegally in slums, called bustees.

- One such slum is Dharavi, India's and Mumbai's largest slum, which lies in the heart of Mumbai where one million people are crammed into one square mile (250 hectares). Some areas have population densities as high as 48,000 people per sq km. Yet, Mumbai has the highest literacy rate in India at 87.1 per cent.

Modern Mumbai

- Mumbai port supports the industries based on the import of raw materials, such as crude oil. The basic metals and engineering industries and the chemical and pharmaceutical industries are very important. The associated support industries are also major employers.

- **Mumbai is a global city**, and its employment structure has advanced accordingly. Manufacturing sector employment has reduced significantly, while the services employment figures have grown rapidly. The emergence of port and railway activities in Mumbai attracted huge numbers of migrants to the city. Initially the city had a flourishing textile industry but this ceased by the 1980s due to a very long strike by textile workers. The globalisation and liberalisation of government policies in the 1990s helped secure a change in employment.

- More than 60 per cent of workers are regular salaried employees in Mumbai, and about 33 per cent are self-employed. The majority of salaried employed females is higher in Mumbai than in other urban areas in India, but in recent years the numbers of casual workers is also increasing.

- The numbers of migrant workers from distant states in India to Mumbai has risen due to the pull factors associated with a demand for well-paid skilled workers. The **services sector is the largest provider of jobs for both male and female workers**. The average wage for workers in metropolitan Mumbai varies between 1.6 to 2 times higher than the State of Maharashtra as a whole.

- Nearly 2,000 slum settlements have been identified with a total population of 6.25 million people. This forms 54% of the total population of the city. Most of these slums are in the suburbs where boundaries are blurred between slums and the more developed areas. About 50 per cent have access to water from shared piped supplies. Only 5 per cent have individual taps. Sanitation is very poor and 73 per cent depend on community toilets. Only in 36 slums is there an organised system of collection and disposal of rubbish, and much is discarded in any convenient available space. Most slums have registered resident associations. Most settlements have a local politician or slum leader who is the final arbitrator of disputes. In several areas it is powerful women who play the role of mediators.

- The majority of slum dwellers identify themselves with the city rather than with their native place and plan to settle permanently in the city. In spite of poor conditions in slums, **most residents feel that life in a slum is tolerable and city life is certainly better than rural life**. All – irrespective of age, gender, wealth and education – express their high regard for education and aspire to upward mobility for their children by educating their offspring as much as possible.

- Because Mumbai is completely urban, just 1 per cent of employment is in the primary sector. The tertiary sector has increased its percentage of employment from 63 to 74 per cent, while manufacturing has decreased from 36 per cent to 25 per cent. This is a typical trend for employment structure in a region moving towards an advanced state of economic development.

- This growth of Mumbai is mainly because of increasing livelihood opportunities for workers and the possibility of living in neighbouring satellite cities and working in Mumbai. Mumbai remains a city of hope and aspiration.

Rapid urbanisation in India

- Approximately 70 per cent of India's population live in rural areas and about 30 per cent live in urban areas, with the urban population rapidly increasing. **India is in a rapid stage of urbanisation**; it has the second-largest urban population in the world after China. More than 70 per cent of migrants to Mumbai come from the state of Maharashtra itself where Mumbai is located rather than it being a focus for the whole of India.

Population growth rates have decreased in recent decades. Whatever growth Mumbai has experienced in the last 30 years has mostly **occurred in the suburbs.**

- These suburbs are not suburbs like we are familiar with, but really a city region that is newer than the core of Mumbai. In the period from 1990 to 2000, population growth rates were 2.3 per cent per annum. This dramatically decreased to 0.8 per cent during the decade 2001 to 2011. The **age/sex ratio has also improved**, with a greater percentage of females to males being recorded.

OR

Brazil: A subcontinental region

Key
- The Amazon Basin
- The Brazilian Highlands
- The North-East
- The South-East
- The South

- There are five main physical regions in Brazil: The Amazon Basin, the Brazilian Highlands, the North-East, the South-East and the South.
- The physical regions of Brazil are defined by a combination of climate and elevation.
- Most of Brazil's urban areas are located along the south-east coastline.

Key
- Equatorial
- Tropical
- Tropical Marine
- Subtropical

The climate of Brazil

Rivers, cities and surrounding countries of Brazil

Highlands and lowlands of Brazil

The factors that influence the development of primary activities

Agriculture

- Until the 1970s, agricultural practises in Brazil were traditional, **copying farming practises** in European regions in areas of temperate climates. Transferring these European practises to tropical and subtropical regions of Brazil failed badly, which caused mass destruction to ecosystems by soil erosion on a massive scale, as well as associated crop failure.
- Through the work of pioneering farmers such as **Herbert Bartz**, specialised modern farm technologies were used to counteract the potential for devastating environmental and economic devastation in these regions that are highly vulnerable to soil erosion. This is referred to as the **Green Revolution in Brazil**, which has led to the development of the principles of sustainable farming.
- **A company cannot be considered environmentally responsible if any of the links in its production chain – related to producers, suppliers, distributors or retailers – does not meet the standards of good practise.** Also, healthy links make a strong supply chain, offering better performance and competitive advantages.
- Good practises refine the traditional and current techniques for farmers that improve the conditions of workers and their families. Some of these modern techniques involve **satellite images** that are updated regularly, generating reports that analyse changes in land use, deforestation and any other changes that occur on farms. **Pilot projects** improve techniques of production and sustainability that can be replicated on hundreds of other farms within a two-year period after roundtable discussions.
- New farming practises in Brazil, such as **ZT/CA (Zero Tillage Conservation Agriculture)** has revolutionised the entire production chain of farming practises and products based on principles of sustainability mentioned above. Put simply, this ZT/CA is achieved by maintaining permanent soil cover while planting more productive specialised crop seed, fertilizer and weed control systems simultaneously using specialised machines. No soil areas are exposed to the torrential rains of the tropics that originally washed away the topsoil when traditional farming methods were used.
- The **Brazilian Highlands** is an elevated area that dips north-eastwards towards the Amazon. It is a region of cattle ranching and mixed cereal production. Its elevation has a controlling effect on summer temperatures within the tropics that create an ideal environment for agriculture with an average annual temperature of 22°C. Summer temperatures average 26°C, while winter monthly temperatures vary between 15°C and 24°C. Summer gets heavy rain when temperatures are highest. These climatic conditions are **ideal for crops such as cereals and soya.**
- **Soya needs a specialised management system** where seed variety and length of daylight are crucial to high production. High temperatures between 20°–30°C are

also important, so a sub-tropical region like the Brazilian highlands suits soya production well. Most soya farms are owned by agri-companies, and production has been moving northwards towards the edges of the Amazon rainforest.

- **Winter is the dry season** but still temperatures are warmer than in Irish summers. These ranges of temperature form an excellent basis for crop production. The **constant high temperatures** and the application of fertiliser to nourish grass production makes **beef production** one of Brazil's most important exports. The Brazilian Highland region produces most of Brazil's grains and oilseeds for export; their total value is in excess of $65 billion USD.

- The south-east region is mostly devoted to intensive plantation agriculture that produces coffee, sugar cane, rice and fruit. Brazil has been the world's largest producer of coffee for the last 150 years, and currently produces about **one-third of all coffee**. The generally warm temperatures and **terra rossa (red laterite) iron-rich soils** of the states of Minas Gerais, São Paulo and Paraná are ideal for coffee production. Most plantations are harvested in the dry seasons of June to September, usually in one huge annual crop when berries are ripe. The entire crop is placed in the sun to dry before being placed in bags for export. Two species, Arabica and Robusta, account for almost all coffee produced in Brazil.

- Today, **agribusiness** accounts for 26.5 per cent of Gross Domestic Product, which includes rural industry and trade, livestock and agriculture. Brazil itself has a huge market of over 200 million people. Brazil is the third-largest exporter of agricultural goods in the world after the United States and the European Union. The European Union and China are Brazil's largest markets for agricultural products.

- In general, **family farms** that employ mostly family members **provide the majority of Brazil's staple crops**, such as manioc, beans and corn. PRONAF (National Programme on Family Agriculture), which provides finance for family farms, has caused these small holdings to increase production by 75 per cent in recent years.

Mining

- Since 2006, Brazil has become self-sufficient in oil supplies. The Campos offshore field is the largest. Brazil now produces 2.5 million barrels per day. Natural gas supplies found close to oil wells are also exploited. Brazil itself has a population of 204 million, which creates a large home market for petroleum products.

- Iron ore is found in the State of Minas Gerais in the south-east, and in Carajás in the Amazon Basin. It forms from secondary enrichment through leaching and redeposition caused by the intense rainfall of the tropical climate. Brazil is a major exporter of iron ore to China, Japan, Korea and the USA. Some of the mountains are almost entirely iron ore, which led to extensive mining (in some places at the expense of the environment).

- Recent advances in environmental policy helped to put limits to mining. About 200 kilometres (120 miles) to the east of Belo Horizonte is the second metropolitan region of the state, Vale do Aço (steel valley), which has iron and steel processing companies along the course of the Rio Doce and its tributaries.

- Brazil has many other commercial mineral deposits such as **bauxite, pewter, gold and platinum**. Bauxite is the raw material in the manufacture of aluminium and is the result of a combination of intense weathering and leaching that leaves insoluble minerals at the surface. **Gold and diamond deposits** are the result of ancient igneous activity in the Brazilian Highlands and were mined originally at Minas Gerais (General Mines). Much if this gold has been concentrated due to weathering and erosion. Today it is mined at Eldorado do Juma in the Amazon Basin.

The factors that influenced the development of secondary activities

- **Brazil is the largest national economy in South America.** Its GDP per capita was US$15,000 in 2016. It has a labour force of over 107 million workers. It has an unemployment rate of about 5.5 per cent, down from 11.5 per cent in 2004.
- Brazil has a large internal market with an estimated population in 2016 of 204 million people, up from 73 million in 1960. Brazil's GDP per person was US$15,000 and is the fourth-largest car market in the world.
- Offshore oil and gas wells close to Rio de Janeiro have led to the development of oil refining and petrochemical industries that drive an expanding industrial region.
- Brazil's economy has been expanding in international financial and commodities markets. It is a **member of the BRICS economies**. These are rapidly expanding and industralising emerging economies that include Russia, India, China and South Africa. These countries are members of the G20 summits and represent over 3.5 billion people (equivalent to the entire world population in 1970).
- Brazil has developed **as a centre of excellence in aircraft and components** manufacture, and many of its products include business jet aircraft and pilot-training aircraft electrical equipment. Car manufacture, ethanol, textiles, iron ore and steel form the basis of much of these industries. The Brazilian steel industry, based on iron ore deposits nearby, is one of the most competitive in the world. It accounts for a trade balance surplus of US$4 billion, about 18 per cent of Brazil's total.
- The **steel industry employs 110 thousand people** and is committed to sustainable activities, based on economic, social and environmental pillars. Brazilian steelmakers continuously seek improvements in the co-efficiency of their processes and products. This expertise has led to the basis of large-scale manufacturing in the industrial triangle of Belo Horizonte, Rio de Janeiro and São Paulo.
- Large-scale production of HEP at **Itaipu Dam** on the **Paraná River** provides a plentiful supply of electricity for manufacturing. Brazil is one of the world's leading producers of hydroelectricity in the world. Brazil also has a number **of nuclear power plants** and it intends to build another 19 by the year 2020. This secures Brazil's future energy needs for the demands of the manufacturing industry.
- In 2011, an international company found that **27 million Brazilian adults aged between 18 and 64 had started or owned a business**, which meant that more

than one in four Brazilian adults were entrepreneurs. In comparison to 54 other countries studied, Brazil was the third highest in total number of entrepreneurs.

The factors that influenced the development of tertiary activities

- **Almost 70 per cent of Brazil's workforce is employed in the services sector**, and banking alone makes up about 16 per cent of GDP. However, because much of it is in the informal sector, figures are not exact.
- Brazil has a high number of foreign tourists and has the second-highest number of tourists in South America after Argentina. It had 5.7 million visitors in 2012, with Rio de Janeiro and São Paulo among the most popular destinations.
- The **Iguazu Falls** are now connected to major urban centres such as Rio de Janeiro and São Paulo. Each attracts more than one million visitors annually. Pristine beaches in the north-east and national parks in the interior have led to the development of luxury hotels in these neighbourhoods.
- Strong economic growth among the middle-income workers and rapid urbanisation has raised disposable income, which drives tourism. Domestic tourist volume has risen from 156 million in 2007 to 196 million in 2011. **Medical tourism is important** due to highly qualified medical professionals and advanced medical care.
- The density of transport infrastructure varies considerably throughout Brazil. The north-east and Amazonia are the least developed areas. Rail transport throughout Brazil is poorly developed and travel costs are high. Transport is highly dependent on its highway network. Sixty per cent of Brazil's total transport volume is handled by roads.
- São Paulo has spent vast amounts to extend its own metro network. New roads are being planned to link urban and industrial centres with its 36 deep-water and exporting ports. São Paulo State has invested in constructing new rail lines to its urban regions such as Santos and Jundiaí.
- **A new high-speed rail (up to 300 km per hour)** service linking Rio de Janeiro to São Paulo is already planned. Twelve thousand kilometres of new track is being built to serve areas of new mineral wealth and agricultural regions of production for the transport of crops for storage before distribution.

Human processes and urbanisation in Brazil

- Brazil's population was approximately **204 million people** in 2016, making it the fifth most populated country in the world. Thirty-three per cent of Brazilians are under 20 years of age. Its rate of natural increase is about 8.5 per cent and its total fertility rate is 1.86 children born/woman. So, Brazil has an expanding population although its rate of increase has slowed considerably in recent decades. This growth is slowing as the population becomes more educated, and as it urbanises and increases its wealth across all levels of society.
- Brazil has a **multi-ethnic population**. Its population mix is approximately 48 per cent white, 43 per cent Pardo (of tri-racial origins – European, Native American

and West African descent), 2 per cent Asian and 7 per cent Black Afro-American. The Japanese are the largest Asian group in Brazil, with 1.5 million Japanese-Brazilians.

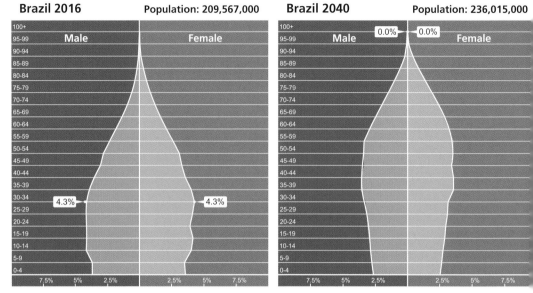

Brazil 2016   Population: 209,567,000   **Brazil 2040**   Population: 236,015,000

Male/female population of Brazil in 2016

Forecasted male/female population of Brazil in 2040

Questions: (a) explain the stage of development of Brazil's economy as indicated by the 2016 age/gender structure in Graph A; (b) explain the noticeable changes forecasted in the 2040 population pyramid when compared to those stated in your answer to part (a).

- Literacy rates in Brazil have risen in the age group 15–24 from 85 per cent in 1980 to **99.2 per cent in 2013**. Brazil has a well-educated young population, however, there has been a fall back to 85 per cent of teenagers attending secondary education.
- **The majority of Brazilians live within 300 km of the coast**, while the interior is almost empty by comparison. This concentration has historical origins as most ports and urban centres were established along the coast. Roads were initially built directly to plantation regions for the easy export of primary products to Portugal and other Portuguese colonies.

16–17th-century immigration from Europe and Africa

- European immigration to Brazil started in the 16th century, the vast majority coming from Portugal at a rate of about 500 people per year. The first region to be settled was north-east Brazil. Ports developed along the entire east coastline. These ports grew slowly at first and then very quickly after 1888, when slavery was abolished in Brazil. The Portuguese were not interested initially in developing the country economically. Rather, they were only interested in exporting raw materials for processing at home.
- The black people brought to Brazil were from different ethnic groups and from different African regions: the West African and the Bantu people. The **West**

African group were native to Guinea, Ghana and Nigerian regions. Some of these people spoke Arabic and many could read and write in this language. Many of these slaves were **better educated than their European masters** who could not even read or write in Portuguese. These slaves of Arab and Berber influence were largely sent to Bahia. Even today, the typical dress of the women from Bahia has clear **Muslim influences**, as the use of the Arabic turban on the head.

- Most of the slaves brought to Brazil came from the **Bantu regions of the Atlantic coast** of Africa where today Congo and Angola are located, and also from **Mozambique**. In general, these people lived in tribes. **The people from the Congo had developed agriculture**, raised livestock, domesticated animals such as goats, chickens, pigs and dogs, and produced sculptures in wood. Some groups from Angola were nomadic and did not know agriculture.

- The slave trade was a huge business that involved hundreds of ships and thousands of people in Brazil and Africa. There were officers on the coast of Africa that sold slaves to hundreds of small regional dealers in Brazil. **In 1812, half of the 30 richest merchants of Rio de Janeiro were slave traders.** Only 45 per cent of the Africans captured in Africa to become slaves survived. It is estimated that as many as **12 million Africans were captured to be brought to Brazil**. Today there are **14.5 million people of African descent** living in Brazil, who mostly live near the east coast in both urban and rural regions. Interior Brazil is settled mostly by people of Spanish European and Native American descent.

- As Brazil's economy started to develop, the original ports developed into export outlets for foodstuffs. Then came the exploitation of other products, such as brazilwood, gold and diamonds, which led to various waves of individual immigrants in search of work that was available when freed slaves fled to the cities. **Many immigrants also arrived in search of mineral riches, such as gold and diamonds.** These events led to the growth of these coastal ports and gradually developed into large cities.

- The **demand for labour in the laying of railroads** and urban infrastructure in Rio de Janeiro and São Paulo led to job creation in the late 1800s and early 1900s. Intense international migration during the first half of the 20th century led to rapid urbanisation up to 1950 when United Nations estimates indicate that 36 per cent of Brazilians lived in urban areas. As these cities grew into agro-commercials centres they added new functions, such as defence, for the new nation's needs.

20th-century urbanisation in Brazil

- The **1929 US stock market crash** and the drop in demand and prices for coffee led to two population flows in Brazil. The first was a progressive occupation of the interior of Brazil and the second was a concentration of populations in ever-larger cities. Declining mortality rates due to improved medicine and better housing and self-help urban schemes greatly increased these urban populations. Many immigrants who had come to Brazil as agricultural labourers subsequently turned their attention to industrial and service jobs.

- The need to integrate regional markets led to investments in ground transportation. **The state took a more active role in the economy** and in improving social conditions in urban areas. A crucial factor was the natural population increase as mortality levels declined due to improved sanitation and imported technologies to control infectious diseases. Brazil's total population grew from 33 million in 1930 to 70 million in 1960.

- To draw development away from the Rio de Janeiro-São Paulo coastal expansion, the regional development agency relocated **Brazil's national capital to Brasília** in 1960 which led to the construction of highways that linked it to the centre-south and to the underpopulated northern region. Today, Brasília is the fourth-largest city in Brazil.

- Various other incentives and ideas, such as **import substitution**, encouraged increased industrialisation and greater population concentration in industrial cities. Because Brazil lacked the expertise necessary to develop modern manufacturing industries, **multinational companies were encouraged to develop branch plants**, so Volkswagen, Ford and General Motors established manufacturing plants in Brazil. This early start allowed Brazil to establish itself as the main supplier of cars for the South American market, thus allowing it to become part of the global economy.

- Brazil had a **military government during the period 1960–1985**, which created huge national debt by completing big projects such as major dams and airport developments. This debt and high interest rates at the time caused the IMF (the International Monetary Fund) to impose **Structural Adjustment Programmes** to help Brazil repay its debt.

- New civilian government policies introduced **Green Revolution technologies** that modernised agricultural production through increased productivity. **Prior to 1960** there was little mechanisation involved in agricultural production. The Green Revolution changed all this and incentives helped farmers to invest in **new technologies** that led to rural depopulation and additional migration to urban regions.

- Then a turning point came in the 1980s when urban growth declined and natural fertility rates fell. This occurred in cities of all sizes. Cities remain huge but the quality of life in urban populations has improved substantially.

The 21st century

- The **fast rate of urban growth** was due because of **rural to urban migration** from the 1960s onwards. The Green Revolution released millions of agricultural workers who were replaced by highly sophisticated technology that revolutionised how crops were grown and harvested. These workers migrated to urban regions where they took up employment in services and in manufacturing industries that were expanding due to an influx of **multinational companies** that opened **branch plants** in the urban regions near the coast.

Case study: São Paulo in Brazil

Central São Paulo has a high population density of approximately 6,400 people per square kilometre

- São Paulo is Brazil's largest urban area and ranks among the top 10 most populous in the world. Between 1950 and 1975, São Paulo was also among the world's fastest growing urban areas. Today it is displaced from that position by the much faster growing Manila in the Philippines and Delhi in India.
- São Paulo is the capital of Brazil's largest state, also called São Paulo. Brazil's 2010 census counted more that 41 million people in the state.
- In 1900, São Paulo's population was 240,000 people. By 1950 its population was 2 million people; now it is approximately 20.2 million people. It is a megacity (see reasons for rapid urbanisation after the Green Revolution on page 138).

Location of São Paulo

exam focus

For homework, draw a simple labelled diagram that shows São Paulo and its surrounding urban centres. Write two or three labels that will get you extra marks in the exam. The information should be different than that in this text.

- São Paulo is sited on a low plateau 2,500 metres above sea level, which helps to make its climate more tolerable. São Paulo is the world's second-largest urban area not located on an ocean or sea coast. It is located 80 km from the seaport of Santos, which is an urban area of 1.7 million people.

- São Paulo is a dense urban region of 6,400 persons per square kilometre. It has close to double the population density of Paris and is about the size of the urban area of Washington DC. **São Paulo's urban area stretches nearly 100 km east to west and more than 50 km north to south** – it is not a compact city. The **fast rate of urban growth** was due to **rural to urban migration** from the 1960s onwards. **The Green Revolution** released millions of agricultural workers who were replaced by highly sophisticated technology that revolutionised how crops were grown and harvested. These workers migrated to urban regions where they took up employment in services and in manufacturing industries that were expanding due to an influx of **multinational companies** that opened **branch plants** in the urban regions near the coast.

- Over the past 10 years, the **central city of São Paulo has grown from 10.5 million to 11.2 million** people. This makes up approx 57 per cent of São Paulo's urban population. Over the same period, São Paulo's suburban population has grown from 6.7 million to 8.4 million people. **Consequently, São Paulo's traffic movement** in recent years has been **exceptionally congested**, mostly because until recently there was no dedicated freeway (motorway) for truck traffic travelling east-west or north-south from the surrounding affluent regions.

- The **Mario Covas Beltway** (São Paulo's metropolitan ring road) is a 177 km road that links 10 major highways that lead into and across São Paulo. The **Japan Bank for International Cooperation** has awarded a loan to finance the construction of this ring road. It was planned in four sections and is estimated to be completed in 2017. This development is part of the Brazilian government's **Growth Acceleration Programme**.

13 The Complexity of Regions 1

Case study 1: Northern Ireland

Historical background

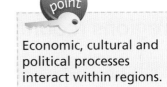

key point

Economic, cultural and political processes interact within regions.

- Scottish settlers were brought to the region during the Ulster Plantation.
- These settlers had a **different culture**, religion and traditions from the local Catholic population.
- In the 19th century, Ulster experienced the development of heavy industry based on coal supplies from Scotland.
- So when partition occurred in 1921 the Republic had an underdeveloped economy, while the north-east was a thriving industrial society.
- The majority of Irish people saw that political independence was essential for the economic and cultural development of the other three provinces, Connaught, Leinster and Munster.

See also Religious Conflict in Northern Ireland, pages 311–312 and 317–318.

Changing relationships on the island of Ireland

Economic trends

- Emigration was dominant throughout the decades up to 1960.
- Since then the Republic has attracted foreign multinationals to Ireland.
- Ireland has a developed, modern, industrial economy with high-tech industries. Some industries, however, have reduced their workforce to remain competitive in the recent recession.
- Northern Ireland, on the other hand, has a depressed economy. Its old textile and shipbuilding industries have gone, although modern green energy generators for wave power are manufactured here.
- Civil unrest and religious bitterness have discouraged foreign investors.

Political interaction

- Tensions between the Republic of Ireland and Northern Ireland faded somewhat between 1921 and the 1960s.
- The refusal of the British government to grant full civil rights to Catholics in the North led to a state of near civil war that persisted virtually continuously until the 1990s.
- The signing of the **Belfast Agreement** led to new political interactions based on the 'Strands'. These new political bodies are a new Northern Ireland Assembly, a North–South Ministerial Council and a British–Irish Inter-Government Conference.
- These bodies are designed to create inter-relationships and encourage co-operation rather than division.

The interaction of cultural groups within political regions (countries)

Some minority culture groups with a strong self-identity feel their interests are not represented by the larger host country in which they live; so the links that tie these regions together become weakened.

What emerges are nationalist groups that look for more powers of self-government.

This is called **autonomy** or **devolution**. A more extreme agenda would involve a new and separate state from the majority population.

exam focus

The syllabus requires you to study the interaction of cultural groups in Ireland and in Europe.

Case study 2: The Basques

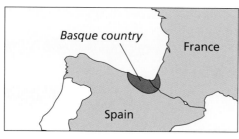

Basque country

France

Spain

Most of the Basque region is in Spain; the remainder is in France

exam focus

Always write your answers in paragraphs. The bullet points here are purely to help your revision.

exam focus

The Basques may be used as an example to answer a range of related questions on changes of political boundaries, cultural conflict and political conflict.

**The scenic landscape of the Basque region contributes to its
attraction for tourists**

A cultural group without nationality

- The Basque country is a region at the western end of the Pyrenees, the mountains
  that divide France from Spain.
- It is made up of seven districts, four of which are in Spain and form the largest
  section, while the other three are in France.
- Three of these historic Basque territories –
  Araba, Bizkaia and Gipuzkoa in the
  north of Spain – are grouped together
  to form a political unit, known as
  Euskadi, or the Autonomous
  Community of the Basque Country.
- Euskadi has a population of 2.1 million
  people. They have their own president
  and parliament but are represented
  internationally by Spain.
- Spain's other Basque district, Navarra, is
  its own region, separate from Euskadi
  and less troubled politically.

Who are the Basques and why are
they different?

- The Basques were living in the Pyrenees
  over 4,000 years ago, long before the
  Celtic tribes of central Europe moved
  west to Britain and Ireland.

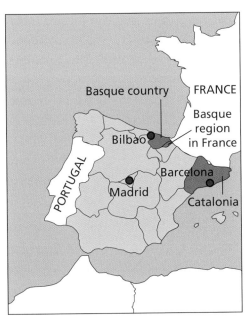

**Spain, showing the location of the
Basque country**

- Basque cuisine is based on seafood, especially cod and hake.
- Basque dishes are very popular throughout Spain and most major cities have Basque restaurants.
- The annual bull run has made **Pamplona**, a city in Navarra, famous.
- Every year, six bulls are allowed to run freely through Pamplona's streets before being killed later that day by matadors in a bullring.
- Many people run ahead of the bulls and some get hurt or killed.

The bull run in Pamplona is a well-known cultural event

Language

- The Basque language forms a crucial part of their unique identity. It is called **Euskara**, and it is spoken by about 520,000 people.
- It is one of the **oldest living languages** and is not known to be related to any other language.
- It was spoken in the Basque region in Neolithic or Stone Age times.
- The first written texts in Euskara date from the 10th century.
- The language was forbidden after the Spanish Civil War in the 1930s, when the dictator General Franco was in power.
- Basque schools, called **iskastolas** started in the 1930s in defiance of this policy.
- Because there were many dialects of Euskara, steps were taken in 1964 to create a unified Basque language.

Basque conflict with the Spanish government

- A small number of violent extremists are represented by **ETA** (in Euskara it stands for 'Basque Homeland and Freedom'), an **armed nationalist group**.
- They believe that complete independence from Spain and France can be achieved only by military means – similar to what the IRA believed about the reunification of Ireland.

- ETA was founded in 1958 because the Basque people were oppressed during the reign of the fascist dictator Franco in Spain.
- In the beginning they were a non-violent group, but their every move for independence was put down by force. This made them opt for armed resistance.
- Early in 2017, ETA announced that it was ending its armed conflict with the Spanish government.
- This disarmament is to be completed by the end of May 2017.
- Iñigo Urkullu, the head of the Basque regional government, said that he hoped it would be 'definitive, unilateral, irrevocable, complete and legal'.

The future of the European Union

New developments in the EU will influence trade, politics and sovereignty issues.

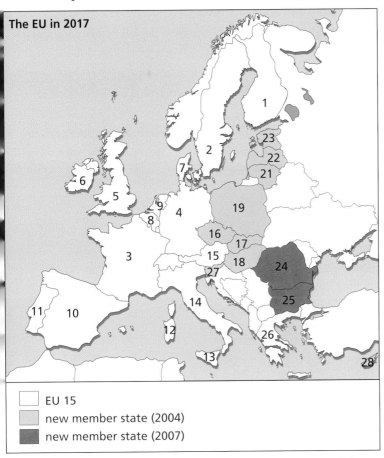

The EU in 2017

	EU 15
	new member state (2004)
	new member state (2007)

EU members at the time of writing. Name each country of the EU numbered 1–28

exam focus

Make sure you can name all 28 EU countries.

Recent treaties/agreements

- **Maastricht Treaty** (1992) – established the three 'pillars' of the EU (economic, political, social).
- **Single European Market** (SEM) (1993) – allowed for the free movement of goods, services and people within the Economic and Monetary Union (EMU).
- **Amsterdam Treaty** (1997) – placed employment and citizen rights at the heart of the EU.
- The **euro** – introduced in 2002.
- **Nice Treaty** (2002) – allowed for change in the institutions and voting systems so that the EU could be further enlarged.
- **The Lisbon Treaty (2009) made changes to the way the EU is run and how it makes decisions:**
  - Each member state will continue to nominate a Commissioner.
  - Many decisions on legislation are to be made by the Council of Ministers in co-operation with the European Parliament.
- A new post of President of the European Council was created.
- The European Parliament and the Council of Ministers to have joint decision-making powers over the entire EU budget.
- The European Parliament and the Council of Ministers to make co-decisions on agriculture, asylum and immigration.

Sovereignty

Each member had to give up some degree of independence or sovereignty, so four main political institutions were created to regulate the Union:

- European Commission in Brussels
- European Parliament in Strasbourg, Brussels and Luxembourg
- Council of the European Union (Council of Ministers)
- European Council.

Development and expansion of the EU

In 1957 the **Treaty of Rome** created the European Economic Community (EEC). Its purpose was to increase trade between six countries in the core of Europe. Since then there have been six enlargements:

- **1973**: Denmark, UK, Republic of Ireland
- **1986**: Spain and Portugal
- **1990**: East Germany became part of Germany
- **1995**: Austria, Sweden and Finland
- **2004**: a number of Eastern Bloc countries (Czech Republic, Estonia, Hungary, Latvia, Lithuania, Poland, Slovak Republic, Slovenia), plus Cyprus and Malta
- **2007**: Bulgaria and Romania.

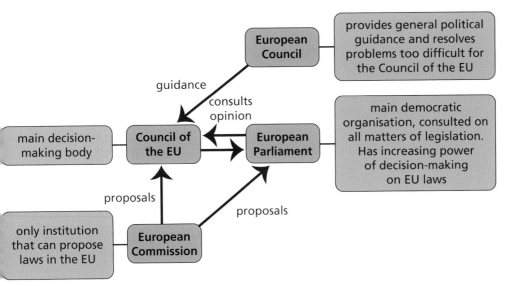

How decisions are made in the EU

SAMPLE EXAM QUESTION AND ANSWER

Question: Examine the impact of European Union expansion on Ireland's economy and/or culture **or** examine the impact of EU expansion on any one EU country.

Note: Use what you have learned in your Junior Cert CSPE course to develop these statements about the EU.

Answer:

- Ireland joined the European Union in 1973 and became one of nine members. Before 1973 the EU had only six members. This allowed greater access for Ireland to foreign markets.
- Ireland achieved Objective 1 status, which allowed access to Structural Funds for economic and social development.
- The Irish government invested large sums into the road network of the West, as well as funding a new airport in Knock to allow easier access to core regions for the western counties.
- Agriculture was the first Irish industry to benefit from EU expansion. Farms were modernised, improved breeds of cattle were introduced, and grants were given to farmers to improve their farms, e.g. milking parlours were built (the Guidance Fund).
- Rationalisation for the EU single market encouraged agricultural co-operatives to join and become some of the largest agri-based companies in the world.
- The Common Agricultural Policy created a **Guaranteed Fund** to maintain high prices for farm produce.

exam focus

Possible marking scheme:
- two impacts identified – 2 marks
- examination, 13 × SRPs @ 2 marks each
- discussion without reference to Ireland or EU country – 0 marks
- discussion without reference to enlargement – maximum 6 marks.

- Ireland became a major player for **foreign direct investment** (FDI) as industries that located in Ireland had direct access to the EU market.
- Ireland's new **branch plants** involved the processing or assembly of imported raw materials and component parts, e.g. Krupps in Limerick in the 1960s and more recently Dell Ireland in Limerick.
- The dependence on Britain as our main market for goods changed and mainland EU is now our major market area.
- Originally agricultural goods dominated Ireland's trade and this has been replaced by a range of manufactured goods, such as computers and computer parts.
- As almost all production by multinational companies (MNCs) is for export, membership of the EU has been and is crucial for the long-term success of Irish industries.
- Ireland has a **more diverse culture** as a consequence of migration from Eastern European countries such as Poland, as well as African-Europeans from former colonial powers such as Britain and France.

Disadvantages

- Membership of the EU allowed **foreign trawlers** access to Irish territorial waters: these caused overfishing in areas such as the Celtic Sea.
- While **farm income has increased**, the number of family farms and farmers has declined.
- Increased agricultural production has led to river, ground-water and lake **pollution**.
- The EU currently has 28 members. This will reduce to 27 when Britain leaves the EU.

The future of EU Expansion

Advantages

- As the EU becomes a larger region its increased population will provide a growing market for Irish products.
- The increasing area of the EU will provide a greater supply of raw materials that can be accessed by Ireland without extra import taxes being paid.
- The enlarged EU will provide new opportunities for highly skilled Irish graduates establishing new companies in these new states.

Disadvantages

- Newer member states have lower production costs and this encourages existing Irish companies to locate **replacement plants** in Central and Eastern Europe.
- New EU member states create **increased competition** for foreign direct investment (FDI).
- Higher levels of unemployment and lower living standards in **newer member states** encourages out-migration. This may have a negative effect if many people migrate to Ireland.
- The large new **eastern periphery** will take a large percentage of Structural Funds. This will lead to a reduced take for Ireland.

- Ireland has **lost its status** as a problem region, which has led to reduced support funds for roads and other developments.
- Difficulties arise as countries such as the UK leave the EU.

SAMPLE QUESTION AND ANSWER

Question: Examine the impact of the UK leaving the EU on Ireland.

Answer:

- **Ireland is the remaining EU country most exposed to Brexit.** When Britain joined the EEC in 1973, it was a foregone conclusion that Ireland would follow. Now Ireland's concern is about the consequences of a future in which the legal basis for the UK's economic relations with the EU – and hence with Ireland – is thrown into doubt.

- **Economic links** between Ireland and the UK have **declined over the past decades**. In the late 1930s, 94 per cent of Irish exports went to the UK. In the 1960s, this figure had reduced to 75 per cent, which was still a substantial figure. Today, the UK's share of Irish exports is less than 15 per cent. Account needs to be taken of the high import content of much of Ireland's other trade – the local content of Ireland's exports to the UK is relatively high. If the employment content was included, the UK share would be closer to a quarter. Half of Ireland's agricultural exports still go to the UK, and it is the biggest customer for the rapidly growing export of services.

- If **tariffs** were re-introduced in the agri-food sector, this is more **likely to happen for primary agricultural products** and the primary element in processed foods. This would add to the costs of trading those agricultural commodities, which could be prohibitive.

- Brexit could cause the **re-introduction of custom posts on the border** between Northern Ireland and the Republic of Ireland. Farm supports are mostly linked to farmland uses; other land uses or activities may not be recognised for subsidies. There is also much greater emphasis on animal identification and traceability, which would add to the difficulties of undocumented movement.

- Ireland's only physical **international electricity and gas connections** are with the UK. Ireland will no longer benefit from EU requirements for the UK to share its supplies in the event of a major disruption to EU gas supplies. This is a significant consideration given the high dependence of the Irish electricity system on gas.

- There is a universal reluctance to see the **re-introduction of physical border controls** on the island of Ireland. Their absence is an important symbol of the success of the peace process encapsulated in the Good Friday Agreement of 1998. Its significance should not be downplayed. New control and customs and design mechanisms should not have to rely on old-style physical border controls.

- Well over half of the tonnage of goods that are shipped from Irish and EU ports travel via the UK. **Logistical obstacles** will add costs to this merchandise.

Students should be aware of and add in other factors that become more obvious when this process gets into the mature stages.

14 The Complexity of Regions 2

aims You need to know:

- that the boundaries and size of regions may change over time
- how the size of some cultural regions has changed over time
- how one Irish urban region and one European urban region have expanded over time
- how cultural groups have been affected by changes to the political boundary of a country.

Changing boundaries in language regions

The size and shape of language regions can change over time.

The Irish language regions

The boundaries of Gaeltacht regions have reduced over the past century

- There were 1.5 million Irish speakers in 1851. Most of them lived in the western half of Ireland.
- From 1861 the number of Irish speakers declined to 544,000. This was due to:
  - large-scale emigration
  - the growing popularity of English.

From 1926 to the present

After independence, the Irish government was committed to supporting the Irish language:

- Irish became the official language of the state
- Irish was compulsory at school
- official Gaeltacht regions were identified.

The present

- About 1.5 million people can speak some Irish. However, few are fluent.
- The largest number of Irish speakers are in Leinster.
- The Gaeltacht boundaries have diminished to tiny pockets that are located on peninsulas in the West of Ireland.

Urban growth and city regions

World urban growth

- In 2004, half of the world's population of 6 billion people lived in cities.
- By 2025 about 80 per cent of people will live in cities.
- The growth rate of this trend is fastest in the developing world.

Urban growth in the EU

- About 80 per cent of the population lives in cities.
- Urban sprawl is a problem in every EU country.
- Rush hours create traffic jams in most city regions.

exam focus

You are expected to study urban growth and expansion of one city region in Ireland and Europe. Dublin and the Randstad are the examples chosen in this chapter.

SAMPLE EXAM QUESTION AND ANSWER

Question: 'The boundaries of city regions have expanded over time.'

Discuss this statement, with reference to **one** example you have studied.

Answer:

The Growth of Dublin – An Irish urban region

- Founded by the Vikings, **Dublin has become Ireland's largest city** with a population of 1.3 million people in the Greater Dublin region, 35 per cent of Ireland's total population.
- The original settlement of Dublin occupies a low-lying site on both banks of the Liffey where it enters Dublin Bay. This is the lowest bridging point on the River Liffey and so was a natural focus of coastal and inland routes.
- Dublin became the focus of the country's roads, rail and canal networks over the centuries. Today all national primary routes and rail routes meet in Dublin.
- Before World War II Dublin was a compact city. The built-up area did not extend more than 5 km from its centre.

1960s expansion

- Dublin underwent a period of **rapid expansion** during the 1960s. Most of this expansion occurred within 8 km of the centre of Dublin.
- Many inner-city communities were removed from decayed slum regions such as the Liberties and relocated in new housing estates and apartment complexes in places such as Tallaght and Ballymun.
- Dublin's expansion continued throughout the 1970s due to the development of three new towns: Blanchardstown, Clondalkin and Tallaght. About 40 per cent of Dublin's population now lives in this zone.

Recent expansion

- As competition for land and the cost of living continues to rise in Dublin, more and more people are encouraged to look farther from the city's edge. Many small towns and villages more than 16 km from the city centre have therefore increased in size.

- For people who live close to or on transport routes to the city, **long-distance travel to work** has become an accepted part of their daily lives. Dublin's hinterland has expanded, so many people commute from as far away as Arklow or Athlone.

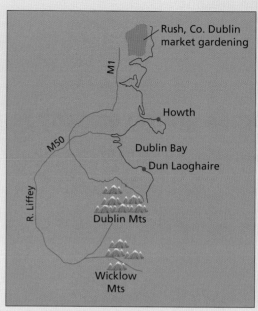

The urban area of Dublin has expanded dramatically over the past 20 years

Solving Dublin's urban problems

- Dublin is a **primate city** and it contains 10 times the population of our next largest city, Cork.
- The National Spatial Strategy formed part of the National Development Plan (2007–2013) with a fund of €184 billion to invest in new developments.
- The National Spatial Strategy proposed large-scale developments in a series of gateways and hubs to encourage the dispersal of population and employment out of the Dublin region.
  - **Gateways**, such as Limerick, Galway, Athlone and Mullingar offer the best prospects for countering the dominance of Dublin. These developments include:
    1. **Hubs**, such as Kilkenny, Castlebar and Monaghan. These are smaller urban centres that will help disperse development from gateways into their regions.
    2. **Strategic road corridors** that provide efficient links between gateways, hubs and Dublin.
  - Dun Laoghaire Corporation and Dublin County Council were abolished and three new counties – Fingal, South Dublin and Dun Laoghaire-Rathdown – were created to administer to the needs of Dublin's population.

SAMPLE EXAM QUESTION

Describe and explain the growth of one major urban area in a European region (not Ireland) that you have studied.

Marking scheme:
- region named – 2 marks
- urban area named – 2 marks
- examination – 13 × SRPs @ 2 marks each.

Case study: The Randstad

Growth of the Randstad

- The western part of the Netherlands is one of the **most urbanised** regions in Europe. It has a radius of approximately 50 km.
- Most of the country's major cities are in the Randstad: they include Amsterdam, Utrecht, Rotterdam and The Hague.
- The Randstad contains **40 per cent** (6 million) of the Dutch population living on only 17 per cent of the country's land area.
- The growth and expansion of the towns and cities of the Randstad have created a sprawling urban region which can be classed as a **megalopolis.** This means that many conurbations have grown towards each other.
- The Randstad is shaped like a horseshoe and is a **polycentric** city region. This means that it is made up of a number of major cities, with no single city being dominant.
- At its centre is an important agricultural and recreational area that contains small towns and villages. This is called the **Greenheart** of the Randstad.

exam focus

You could study **Paris** as an urban area within France/Europe instead.

The Randstad – urban region

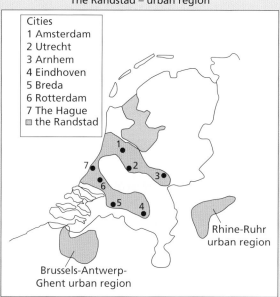

Cities
1 Amsterdam
2 Utrecht
3 Arnhem
4 Eindhoven
5 Breda
6 Rotterdam
7 The Hague
▢ the Randstad

Rhine-Ruhr urban region

Brussels-Antwerp-Ghent urban region

The Randstad is a horseshoe-shaped urban region in the Netherlands

- Since the end of World War II, the Randstad has grown rapidly. This has been due to the region's strategic location at the core of the EU, its excellent transport systems and Rotterdam, the EU's largest port.

- As this urban region developed, competition for land increased and caused urban sprawl to occur around the Randstad's cities. This in turn put huge pressure on the Greenheart.

Planning for the Randstad

New villages have been planned in circles around centrally placed towns on land recently reclaimed from the sea

- At the national level, **five regional centres** have been designated for major investment in infrastructure, such as transport and housing. Planners hope these will attract any new residential and economic developments.
- The greatest difficulty for the Randstad's planners is the **control of urban sprawl** and the prevention of urban growth in the Greenheart.
- Urban sprawl will be strongly controlled by **buffer zones** or **green belts** to prevent continuous urban sprawl and create areas of rural atmosphere in urban regions.
- New urban developments will also be encouraged along its eastern edge to close off its open end between Nijmegen and Eindhoven.
- New **overspill towns**, such as Almere on the south Flevoland polder, have been developed to cater for the overflow of people from Amsterdam and to control Amsterdam's outward expansion.

EU concerns for the Randstad

- If uncontrolled urban growth is allowed eastwards along the river Rhine, the Randstad could eventually join up with the expanding cities of the Rhine–Ruhr industrial region in Germany.
- To the south, unplanned expansion could link up with the **Brussels–Antwerp–Ghent growth zone** of Belgium.

Changing political boundaries and cultural groups

Changes in political boundaries can have an important effect on cultural groups. Some people, as a result of changes in a country's boundaries, find themselves living under a different government or political system.

Case study: The problem of Kashmir – a religious conflict

- Remember your study of how India, Pakistan and Bangladesh became independent countries as a consequence of partition in India after independence. Different religious beliefs was the main reason for this partition.

- Once independence was achieved, the ruler of each state had to decide whether to join India (if there was a Hindu majority) or Pakistan (if there was a Muslim majority).

- Violence broke out in the Kashmir Valley between the minority Hindu population, who looked to India for support, and the majority Muslim population, who looked to Pakistan for support.

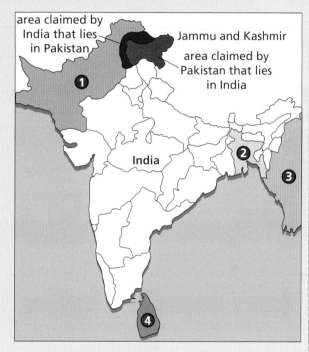

Name the countries 1–4 that surround India

- War broke out when the ruler opted to join India.

- Pakistan claimed Kashmir because there was a majority Muslim population. India claimed it because the ruler had decided to join India.

- Today the region is divided into two parts:
  - The part nearest India is under Indian control and has a Muslim majority who wish to be part of Pakistan.
  - The part nearest Pakistan is under Pakistani control and has a Hindu majority who wish to be part of India.

- The two areas are separated by a political boundary called the **line of control**. This boundary was agreed by both sides after the United Nations negotiated with the two nations.
- Regular clashes occur, as armies on both sides build up their arms in the face of a political threat. Relations between the two nations are sensitive because:
  - India controls 80 per cent of the Kashmiri population, where there is a majority of Muslims who want to be part of Pakistan.
  - The headstreams and many tributaries of the Indus river rise in the Indian-controlled part of Kashmir. The Indus is Pakistan's most important river and it depends on it for its water supply and for irrigation. It wants to gain control of this water source, which is vital for its future needs.
  - An increase in Muslim fundamentalism is creating unrest and fighting in the region.
  - Both India and Pakistan have **nuclear weapons** that could create massive damage and loss of life in a subcontinental region where one-sixth of the world's population lives.

Questions 20, 2011; 19, 2012; 20, 2014; 21, 2015; 20, 2016.

SECTION 2
Electives

All students must study **either**
Patterns and Processes in Economic
Activities (pages 158–191)
or
Patterns and Processes in the Human
Environment (pages 192–232)

Patterns in Economic
Development

 You need to be able to:

- explain the uneven patterns in the distribution of economic activities
- assess the accuracy/usefulness of varied indicators as measures of economic activity.

Economic activities and wealth are unevenly distributed over the world.

What does economic development mean?

Economic development refers to the total quality of life of a population. It includes the standard of its education, medical care and diet. The greater a country's economic development, the better the living standard of its people should be.

Measurement of economic development

Gross Domestic Product (GDP)

GDP is the total market value of all goods and services produced by that country's economic activities for one year.

Gross National Product (GNP)

- The GNP of a country is the total value of all goods and services (output) produced by that country's economic activities, **including any income from abroad**.
- It is measured in US dollars, so that relative comparisons can be made.
- For example, in Ethiopia US$1 will buy far more than in the USA.
- This is called **Purchasing Power Parity** (PPP).
- Purchasing Power Parity converts a national income to its equivalent in the USA.

SAMPLE QUESTION

Explain the difference between Gross Domestic Product and Gross National Product.

Human Development Index (HDI)

The Human Development Index has a range of values from 0.0 to 1.0. The closer a country's HDI is to 1.0, the higher the value of the HDI and the better the quality of life in that country.

Three factors are used as a way of measuring development:

- life expectancy
- GNP per person
- adult literacy rates.

Uneven economic development

- About one-fifth of the world's population lives on less than US$1 per day, and the world's richest 1 per cent of people receive as much income as the poorest 57 per cent.
- In general, people who live in the northern hemisphere have a high living standard, because of the development of industry and the gradual urbanisation of the population.
- The majority of people who are in poverty live in the southern hemisphere.

Regions differ in their levels of economic development.

Uneven patterns of agricultural and industrial activities

A country's wealth depends on its levels of:

- agricultural development
- industrial development.

The role of agriculture

Agriculture is more important in a developing economy than in an industrial economy because:

- there are few alternative employers
- it supports many people with the basic necessities, even though living standards are at subsistence level.

But agriculture does not improve living standards, as do industry and other occupations, because:

- only low levels of education are needed to improve output
- difficult conditions such as drought or flooding add to the problems of production
- there is often poor access to markets
- the price of cash crops is unstable and generally low.

In India, almost all planting, weeding and harvesting is done by hand, and all family members are involved.

The role of industry

In contrast to agriculture, the growth of industry improves living standards throughout a population because:

- once industry is established it encourages a wide range of services that provide well-paid jobs
- transport networks are improved
- a large home market for products is created by the high wages in industry
- industry educates its workforce by introducing new skills.

Uneven development in the EU

- Uneven economic development exists between the different EU member states. It also exists within member states.
- There is a core region in the EU where living standards are high. This region includes the Manchester–Milan axis.
- There are peripheral regions where living standards are lower. *Examples:* the West of Ireland, the Massif Central in France.
- There are rich and poor regions within individual countries. In Ireland, Dublin is a rich core region and the West of Ireland or BMW is a poor peripheral region.

1. Explain the global distribution of uneven economic development.
2. Examine the various methods of measuring economic development. Use examples where appropriate.

16 Changing Patterns in Economic Development

 aims You need to understand that:

- the economies of regions grow and change over time
- colonisation has had an impact on the level of economic development of a country.

Stages in economic development

Five changes are necessary for a country to improve economically.

1. *Change in structure.* Primary industries become less important. Industry and services improve.
2. *New technologies* are introduced.
3. Companies join together to create *larger companies*, to compete better at home and abroad.
4. Overall *quality of life* is improved. Better living standards prevail.
5. *Volume and value of trade increases.*

Fourteen of the 20 poorest countries in the world are located in sub-Saharan Africa. Their poverty is due to:

- political instability. Many are former colonies of European powers
- warfare and civil disturbances
- droughts, famines and diseases
- failure to attract industry
- a health crisis linked to AIDS.

Some countries have shown a measure of improvement. These are called **newly industrialising** countries: they include Hong Kong, South Korea, Singapore and Taiwan.

Case study 1: Changing patterns of economic development in France

Industrial development in the Nord-Pas-de-Calais was originally based on the coalmining districts near Lille. Coal was mined in these since the 1750s and the coal that remained was in thin seams of poor-quality coal. Many seams were folded and faulted (broken into short lengths and at different levels under the surface) that made their mining difficult and expensive. The Nord region fell into industrial decline because it could not compete with new steel industry locations that used oil-fired steel mills based on new uncluttered coastal sites.

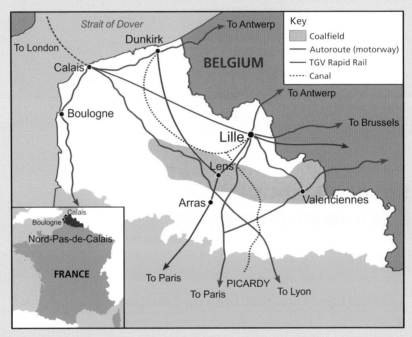

The Nord-Pas-de-Calais region of France

Industries closed, mines closed and mass unemployment resulted in the Nord region and in the nearby Sambre-Meuse region in Belgium.

The factors that brought about this change in industrial patterns were as follows:

- **New oil-burning engines** replaced steam engines in the 1950s, reducing the demand for coal.
- **New heavy industries** preferred coastal locations, where iron ore could be easily imported.
- **The quality coal seams** of the Nord were exhausted and the coal mines closed.
- **The rising costs of mining** made coal uncompetitive as a fuel.

The growth of the service sector created new wealth in the Nord region. Some heavy industry still remains, but today the region's economy is led by the service sector which employs 75 per cent of the working population, manufacturing 23 per cent and agriculture 2 per cent. The harbour is now a leading European seafood processing centre.

- The harbour at Boulogne-sur-Mer is the largest fishing port in terms of capacity, with 150 boats registered there.
- Manufacturing is now led by the automobile industry and employs some 55,000 people. The main car manufacturers in the region are Renault, PSA Peugeot

Citroën and car equipment manufacturers Faurecia. The new car manufacturing centres are now Valenciennes, Douai, Faurecia, and Lieu-Saint-Amand.

- The service sector is dominated by the Mulliez family who own superstore chains.
- Most of its population is urbanised and so the region has a dense and complex network of highways, railways, airports and seaports.
- The **Lille/Roubaix** urban region and the nearby towns region have a population of about two million people and include the two largest cities of the Nord which form one of the largest urban regions of Europe. Lille has many tourist attractions, which include the art gallery Musée des Beaux-Arts, the Opera house and an open-air market called Marché de Wazemmes.
- The centre of Lille has been redeveloped as Euralille, a new international business centre that caters for many involved in the services sector.

Colonialism led to the exploitation of a large number of countries in the interests of a few colonial powers.

Learn the effects of colonisation on one country that you have studied.

SAMPLE EXAM QUESTION AND ANSWER

Question: Discuss the impact of colonisation/colonialism on an economy in the developing world.

Answer:

- Brazil was a **Portuguese colony until 1822**. Like most colonies, its purpose was to supply Portuguese and European markets with unprocessed agricultural and mineral raw materials. Brazil exported sugar, raw cotton, coffee, beans, timber, rubber and precious metals to Portugal and other regions in Europe. During the earliest 300 years of Brazilian colonial history, the **economic exploitation** of the country was based first on Brazilwood extraction in the 16th century, sugar production in the 16th–18th centuries, and finally on gold and diamond mining in the 18th century.
- Brazil's colonial economy went through a series of **boom–bust economic cycles**. Brazilian cities were largely port cities and the administrative capital moved several times in response to the rise and fall of export products' importance. The Portuguese set up fortified trading where small commercial settlements anchored trade in a region. The initial costs of setting up these trading ports were borne by private investors, who, in return, received hereditary titles and commercial advantages. From the Portuguese crown's point of view, its realm was expanded with very little cost to itself. The **Treaty of Tordesillas** in 1494, which gave Brazil to the Portuguese, was the most decisive event in all Brazilian history.
- Slaves from Africa were imported to provide alternative cheap labour favoured by the colonists. These slaves settled on plantation lands that were

developed along the coast, creating the basis for Brazil's multiracial society. Commercial production and population were confined to a narrow coastal strip. All transport, roads, railways and port cities were developed to serve the need to export primary products to Europe and its colonies. The economic potential of the vast interior of rich farmland and mineral wealth was neglected until the 1960s.

Globalisation

- Due to the rise in oil prices, Brazil had to create an economy based on **indigenous industries**. But Brazil lacked the expertise necessary to develop modern manufacturing industries. Multinational companies were encouraged to develop branch plants and Volkswagen, Ford and General Motors established manufacturing plants in Brazil. This early start allowed Brazil to establish itself as the main supplier of cars for the South American market, thus allowing it to become part of the global economy.

- Brazil had a **military government** in the 1980s which created huge national debt by completing big projects such as major dams and airport developments. This debt and high interest rates at the time caused the IMF (International Monetary Fund) to impose Structural Adjustment Programmes to help Brazil repay its debt. Military rule ended and a **civilian government** implemented these new financial readjustment programmes. The Brazilian currency was devalued and increased exports, allowing Brazil to become a food superpower.

- Mercosul, the Common Market of the South, was established in 1991, which allows for the free movement of goods and services among member and associate member states in South America.

- Today, Brazil is a **major global player** and trades with all the major economic regions of the world, including China, South Korea, South-East Asia, the EU and USA.

An extra sample exam question and answer on the impact of colonisation and industrialisation on India can be found on moresuccess.ie.

17 Globalisation

You need to understand that:

- multinational companies play a central role in the development of a single global economy
- individual economies are linked in a global framework
- decisions and actions in one part of the world can have significant consequences in distant places.

Causes of globalisation

- Improvements in transport.
- Improved telecommunications.
- More multinational companies.
- Global banking.
- Free trade.

key point

The world is now a workplace where decisions made in one part of the world can have major effects on people living in another part.

Economic globalisation

The two key factors in understanding economic globalisation are: **multinational companies** (MNCs) and their **foreign investments**.

Multinational companies invest huge sums of money to set up factories or mines in many countries. This is called **foreign direct investment** (FDI).

Increased international trade

More and more goods and services are being traded worldwide than ever before.

The growth of multinationals

Some of the largest MNCs have sales that exceed the GNP even of some wealthy countries. Exxon-Mobil, an American MNC, has a business turnover equal to the GDP of a rich country such as Belgium. Other MNCs include Dell, Microsoft and Toyota.

Footloose locations

Multinational companies may move part or all of their production from one country to a new location in another country where they can manufacture their products more cheaply.

The product cycle and global assembly line

1. Initial research and development occurs in the major cities of a developed country.
2. Skilled graduates and a large market are needed for early product development and sales.

Pfizer in Newbridge is a multinational pharmaceutical manufacturing facility that exports to over 90 countries

3. As the product becomes simpler, less skilled workers and lower-cost labour become desirable.

4. As the product becomes more basic and easier to assemble, the branch plants are moved to less developed regions, such as India and South-East Asia, for cheaper production.

This pattern of location or production can be viewed as a global assembly line.

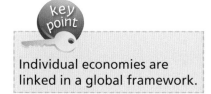

key point

Individual economies are linked in a global framework.

Location of MNCs

There are two main desired locations:

exam focus

Carefully look at the marking schemes that apply to questions in this elective.

1. major industrialised regions
2. peripheral regions.

Major industrialised regions – The Global Triad

About 70 per cent of all MNC investment is located in industrialised regions such as the USA, Japan and Western Europe. These are the **Global Triad**. They control 75 per cent of world trade today.

Peripheral regions

Some 25 per cent of world manufacturing production comes from branch plants located in developing countries. The most successful of these developing countries are called **newly industrialising countries** (NICs).

What are branch plants?

- Branch plants are factories of an MNC that are located in foreign countries, often developing countries.
- This is done to keep profits high and remain competitive.

Advantages and disadvantages of branch plants

Advantages

- They provide work for many people in each factory, e.g. Wyeth Nutrition in Askeaton in Co. Limerick has a workforce of approximately 600 people.
- People learn new skills and new technologies.
- They bring a lot of investment money from abroad.
- They increase exports.
- They create many types of factories and services that help an economy to modernise.

Disadvantages

- Wages can be low. *Example:* Nike was forced to change its wage rates after criticism of sweatshop tactics in Indonesia.
- MNCs may trade only with their branch plants abroad and may not create back-up services locally.
- Much profit is returned to the MNC's headquarters in its home country.
- If branch plants close, large numbers of people may become unemployed. *Example:* HP in Leixlip closed its print facility in February 2017, causing the loss of 500 jobs.
- Decision-making is generally done elsewhere and the host country has no control over these decisions.

The international division of labour

What is meant by the division of labour?

- All jobs or tasks need workers. If workers specialise in certain tasks they become more efficient at those tasks so costs fall.
- More profits can be achieved if different areas specialise in certain products or services.
- Infrastructures and land use are designed to suit this type of production.

What is meant by the international division of labour?

When a country specialises in producing certain goods or services for which it has an advantage over other regions, its productivity increases, its exports increase and its profits increase. This creates money for the country to import goods or services.

What is meant by comparative advantage?

Comparative advantage means that a region has some particular advantage that enables it to produce specific goods more cheaply than other regions. The advantage may be the presence of **raw materials**, a **specialised labour force** or some other advantage.

What has led to the development of the global economy?

There are two key factors:

1. multinational companies and the development and location of their branch plants
2. increased global trade.

Phases in the development of the global economy

Division of labour

1. The traditional international division of labour

During the Industrial Revolution colonies supplied raw materials to colonising countries, such as Britain. In turn, the colonial powers sold their manufactured goods back to the colonies. In this way the colonial powers became richer.

2. The newer international division of labour

From the 1990s onwards, a range of back-office services have been relocated from core countries to peripheral and developing countries. The developed countries then specialise increasingly in high-tech industries and higher-order services.

3. The most recent international division of labour

MNCs are subcontracting an increasing number of key functions from highly paid locations in core countries to peripheral regions where workforces are becoming well educated.

This prevents workers having to migrate for work to core countries and causing a brain drain at home.

Why do MNCs locate their branch plants and back-office services in peripheral regions?

- Labour costs are low.
- There are large workforces due to high birth rates.
- There is little union input, so workers can be exploited.
- Many developing countries have increasingly tried to educate their people so as to attract higher-value jobs.

MNCs in the EU and Ireland

Many foreign multinational companies have invested in factories in Ireland and in the EU.

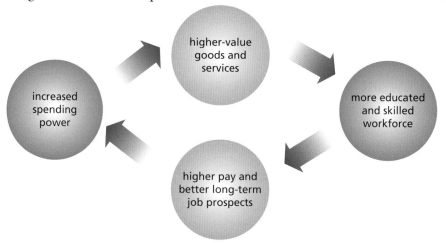

Advantages of the phases of the international division of labour for developing countries

European MNCs and their global investments

Multinational companies from the EU have been investing in branch plants in other regions for a long time.

Now the EU is the largest source region of MNC investment.

About 90 per cent of investment comes from the USA and Japanese companies, e.g. Toyota.

More and more MNC funds are used to set up branch plants and back-office services in newly industrialising countries (NICs) in South-East Asia and Latin America.

MNCs in Ireland

- MNCs laid the foundations of our industrial development in the 1960s in the Shannon Industrial Estate.
- Production is focused on high-value goods and services such as electronics, pharmaceuticals and internationally traded services.
- New plants were set up for key areas such as research and development.

Why do MNCs invest in Ireland today?

Because of:

- a large supply of well-educated, skilled young workers
- support from high-quality research facilities and universities
- low corporation tax rates of 12.5 per cent for companies
- direct access to the large EU market.

Why do MNCs leave Ireland?

- Uncompetitive because wages are high.
- Less expensive graduates are available in NICs
- Recession caused some MNCs to contract and close branch plants to protect their market share.
- Other countries offer better incentives to relocate.
- Corporation tax rates may increase.

SAMPLE EXAM QUESTION

Question: In the case of one multinational company (MNC) that you have studied, examine the global nature of its activities.
(30 marks)

Marking scheme:

- naming MNC – 2 marks
- naming two global locations – 2 marks + 2 marks
- examination – 12 × SRPs @ 2 marks each
- discussion with no obvious reference to global nature – maximum 6 × SRPs.

Write out a case study of one MNC that you have studied. Use the **Pfizer** or **Danone** case study on the following pages if you have not completed this exercise in school.

A case study on a multinational company

Marking scheme:

- MNC named – 2 marks
- Factors identified – 2 marks + 2 marks
- Explanation – 12 × SRPs
- All further factors require explanation
- Discussion without link to named MNC – 0 marks
- Max 2 × SRPs if merely a description of MNC without explanation of factors influencing its operations

Always refer to the **global nature of an MNC**. Name some branch plant locations.

Explain the factors that influence the operations of any one multinational company that you have studied.

Case study: Danone – a multinational company

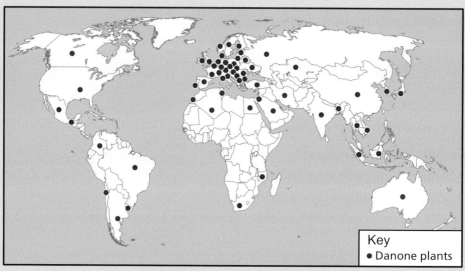

Danone worldwide distribution

- Company name: Danone
- Headquarters: Boulevard Haussmann, Paris, France
- Main products: Fresh dairy products, bottled water, baby nutrition and medical nutrition
- Global employment: 100,000 in 185 plants in 61 countries
- Sells in 130 markets worldwide.
- Annual sales: € 22.5 billion
- In 2015, fresh dairy products represented 50% of total sales, baby foods and nutrition 22%, bottled water 21% and medical nutrition 7%.

Danone was founded by Daniel Carasso who manufactured yoghurt in a small factory in Spain. The company was originally called Danone after Danon, the nickname of his son Daniel Carasso. Ten years later, the company moved to France, and its first French factory was built. During World War II, Daniel Carasso moved the company to New York to avoid persecution as a result of his Jewish faith. In the United States, he partnered with the Swiss-born Spaniard Juan Metzger and changed the brand name to Dannon to sound more American. In 1951, Daniel Carasso returned to France to manage the family's businesses in France and Spain. Later the American company was sold to Beatrice Foods in 1959 and was repurchased by Danone in 1981.

How did Danone become a multinational company?

Factor 1:

- Expansion from its origins in Spain and France was achieved by buying companies in the dairy and baby nutrition sectors, where its strengths and focus originated. It disposed of (sold) associated plants that were not part of its core businesses. For example, Danone bought the Dutch baby nutrition company Numico in 2007. This gave Danone ownership of Numico's Irish food processing plants in Macroom and Wexford.
- After the collapse of the Berlin Wall and the fall of Communism, Danone expanded into the former Eastern Bloc where it purchased other dairy and nutrition companies in Russia, Poland, the Czech Republic and other countries.

Factor 2:

- Over the past 20 years, Danone has expanded into Latin America, Asia and Africa. These are expanding economies, where **birth rates are high and standards of living** are rising. These conditions create a demand for all healthcare-based Danone products.
- By purchasing companies in these new regions, Danone is able to tap into local business expertise, as their business cultures are quite different from European culture. Local partners have the expertise to negotiate local company law, as well as dealing with marketing and language challenges.
- The location of branch plants in these different world markets ensures a competitive advantage in manufacturing costs and a constant market for Danone's products.
- It allows Danone to purchase and/or manufacture raw materials to market these products in shops and supermarkets, making them freely available to young mothers who are the prime carers for their children.
- This also allows its multinational company to be mobile and flexible in its international marketing strategy for the future.

Ethics and social awareness

- Danone has developed children's nutritional snacks at very affordable prices for Indian and other Asian and African markets where malnutrition is a serious problem.

- Danone has also increased its use of bio-plastics in packaging that are made from sugar cane waste.
- Baby food products go through many stages in processing where minerals and vitamins are added and the mix is evaporated and concentrated, then heated and dried into powder formula. Quality control is vital at all stages of the process, and the scientific expertise available to Danone by its large and broad base ensures that products are at the cutting edge of medicinal food science.

 An extra case study on Pzifer can be found on moresuccess.ie.

SAMPLE EXAM QUESTIONS

This is a popular question, so learn in detail about one MNC of your choice.

Sample questions:

With reference to one multinational company (MNC) which you have studied, examine how its distribution is influenced by global factors/the global nature of its activities. (30 marks)

or

Examine the factors that influence the global distribution of one multinational company that you have studied. (30 marks)

(2016, 2015, 2014, 2013)

The three developed regions of the EU, Japan and the USA (the Global Triad) control half the value of world merchandise trade. The EU is the most dominant of these three regions.

Patterns of world trade

World trade has increased hugely, especially between the EU, Japan and the USA (the Global Triad).

Two factors have been responsible for the increased volume and value of world trade:

1. the number and power of MNCs
2. improvements in transport and communications.

Merchandise trade (trade in products)

Trade is best developed in the developed world. Regions such as South Asia and sub-Saharan Africa trade little with developed regions because:

- they were colonies until recent times.
- they produce mainly low-value raw materials
- the prices of most raw materials have declined.

Patterns in the location of service industries

Globalisation has increased demand for a wide range of services, such as:

- legal and financial services
- marketing
- research and development
- back-office services.

1. Offshore financial centres

Many wealthy people use banks in island states, such as the Cayman Islands, to avoid taxation in their own countries.

2. Geographical centres of control

Major cities (London, New York, Tokyo) in the most developed regions attract the most service industries.

These cities and the global trading triad have used their power to increase their influence over poorer regions of world.

What has helped increase the trading power of the Global Triad?

- The USA has increased its influence throughout North and South America through **NAFTA** (the North American Free Trade Area).
- The EU is increasing its trading area through the eastern expansion of the EU and by creating closer ties with Russia.
- Japan is extending its influence throughout South-East Asia, Australia and New Zealand.

Questions 9B, 2012; 9C, 2013; 8B, 9B, 2014; 8B, 2015; 7B, 2016.

18 Ireland and the European Union

Trading patterns in the European Union

The EU accounts for 40 per cent of all trade in goods and services worldwide. Because a number of European countries were colonial powers, many of their former colonies are still major trading partners with the European Union. Forty per cent of the growing global trading patterns still focus on Western Europe.

Patterns of EU trade can be divided into two types:

1. **Internal-EU trade** – trade between member states
2. **External-EU trade** – EU trade with the rest of the world.

Internal-EU trade

Since World War II, the growth of trade between member states has grown rapidly because of:

- the **Treaty of Rome**, which created free trade between member states
- enlargements of the EU
- well-developed rail, road, pipeline and air routes
- the large size and wealth of the EU
- the creation of the **Single European Market** in 1993
- eastern expansion of the EU.

External-EU trade

1. **Colonial links** have created a web of trade routes with the EU.
2. **Japan and the USA** are the EU's most important trading partners, creating a Global Trading Triad.
3. The **Lomé Convention** in 1963 created trade links between countries in Africa, the Caribbean and the Pacific (ACP countries). Most of them were former colonies of EU countries.
4. There is increased trade between the EU and **MNC branch plants** in Asia and Latin America.

Ireland's trading patterns in the EU

- Before the 1960s, Ireland imposed a tariff or tax on imported goods to protect home industry from competition.
- Today it is part of a tax-free open market in which all EU countries export to each other without any additional tax.

> **key point**
>
> Ireland is a member of the EU and so is part of a major trading bloc within the global economy.

1. Ireland's changing pattern of trade

- Until the 1980s, Ireland was dependent on Britain for over 50 per cent of the value of its exports. Today it's 36 per cent.
- MNCs have created a global trading pattern with Ireland through their branch plants.

2. Changes in the make-up of Ireland's export trade

- Until the 1970s, food and live animals formed the largest part of our exports.
- EU membership and MNC operations, such as electronics and chemicals, increased industrial goods and services.
- Agricultural products now make up only 6 per cent of exports.
- Almost all MNC products are for export, and the EU market is hugely important to them.

EU policies and the Irish economy

The Common Agricultural Policy (CAP) and its impact on Ireland

It was introduced in 1962:

1. to increase production and productivity
2. to provide a fair living standard for all its farmers.

At that time farming made up 24 per cent of Irish jobs and 43 per cent by value of Irish exports.

What policies were needed to achieve these aims?

It was necessary to:

- introduce a **common tariff** (tax) on all imports from outside the EU, to protect farmers from cheaper imports
- establish a **Guarantee Fund** and a **Guidance Fund** to finance the CAP.

What did the guarantee fund do?

- It bought any surplus farm produce within the EU to maintain high prices that were fixed each year.
- It subsidised exports throughout the world and so reduced stored surpluses. These stored surpluses were called 'intervention'.

What did the guidance fund do?

It provided money to modernise farm buildings and machinery and to organise farms into single, larger farm units rather than scattered smaller ones.

Later changes to the CAP

1. A reduction in prices guaranteed to farmers.
2. Diversification of farm activities, so as to create more income for farmers, e.g. tourism, cheese-making.
3. Making farmers more competitive.
4. Creating more direct income support for small farmers.
5. Protection of the environment.

The Irish farming sector was given a guaranteed sale price by the EU for its products

Impact of the CAP in Ireland

Positive effects

- Farms were modernised and productivity was increased.
- Subsidies encouraged some farmers to change from dairying to sheep-rearing, especially in upland regions and the West.
- Farm incomes increased as their output increased.
- The number of small farms was reduced.
- Farm sizes increased and farms became more specialised.

Negative effects

- Greater inequality between small and large farmers.
- The number of farmers was reduced.
- Increased migration from rural areas.

The effects of CAP on the environment

Negative effects

- Increased use of fertilisers led to soil and water pollution.
- Hedgerows and stone walls were removed to increase field size.
- Habitat for wildlife such as plants and animals was reduced.
- Overstocking of the land led to overgrazing and soil erosion in hilly areas.

Positive effects

The Rural Environmental Protection Scheme programme (REPS) was introduced in 1994 to protect the environment.

The scheme's objectives:

- Establish farming practices and production methods to preserve the traditional landscape.
- Protect wildlife habitats and endangered species of flora and fauna.
- Produce quality food in an extensive and environmentally friendly manner.
- Produce a 5-year plan that protects the environment.

Find out more about the GLAS scheme, which will replace REPS, at www.farmersjournal.ie/tag/glas-scheme

---

The Common Fisheries Policy and its impact on Ireland

How has the Common Fisheries Policy (CFP) affected the Irish fishing industry?

- The Common Fisheries Policy was introduced in 1983, and Ireland was allocated only 5.8 per cent of the total allowable catch (TAC).
- Irish fishermen have exclusive access to waters within 19 km of the Irish coast only; they must surrender exclusive fishing rights to remaining territorial waters.
- This exclusive zone was kept to a minimum as a consequence of pressure from Spain, which has one of the largest fishing fleets in the EU.
- The Irish Conservation Box (ICB) has replaced the former Irish Box. The ICB is smaller than the previous box area but extends much farther south than before.

Negative effects

Ireland undervalued its rich fishing resources in return for getting a better deal from the CAP. This has restricted the development of the fishing industry in the following ways.

- It has exposed Irish waters to major fishing fleets of countries such as Spain.
- With 11 per cent of EU waters, Ireland has less than 6 per cent of the total allowable catch (TAC).
- Overfishing has almost wiped out many fish species, such as cod and herring.
- The number of days that Irish fishermen can operate at sea is currently 55 per year under the Common Fisheries Policy rules.
- Larger vessels have led to further overfishing.
- Fishing is concentrated out of a small number of major ports.

Positive effects

- The total value of fish landings has increased significantly.
- Killybegs port in Co. Donegal is now the largest seafood port in Europe.
- Some sea areas are closed off to protect spawning adult fish and help small juvenile fish reach adult size.
- Escape panels form part of trawl nets to reduce the catch of small fish.
- Reduction of fishing time at sea helps protect stocks.

The Common Regional Policy (CRP) of the EU and Ireland

When Ireland joined the EU it was the poorest of the member states. Since then, large transfers of **Structural Funds** have been responsible for Ireland's development.

Structural Funds of the common region

- **ERDF:** European Regional and Development Fund – to aid industrial development and upgrade roads.
- **ESF:** European Social Fund – to train/retrain workers who become unemployed in problem regions.
- **FIFG:** Financial Instrument of Fisheries Guidance – helps the fishing industry and fishing regions.
- **Guidance Section of the Agricultural Fund:** to improve farm structures.

The reformed CRP of 1989–99

This helped Ireland in the following ways:

- In 1989, Ireland was designated an Objective 1 region for guaranteed Structural Funds. Objective 1 regions are the least-developed regions and must have a GDP per person of less than 75 per cent of the EU average.
- Ireland had to submit National Development Plans to receive funds for:
  1. modernising high-tech industry
  2. improving transport and communications
  3. increasing labour skills for future challenges of change.
- Recently, structural funds were reduced because of Ireland's increased wealth.

The European Social Fund (ESF)

Through its National Development Plans, the ESF hopes to:

- reduce employment through training schemes
- provide affordable housing
- integrate minorities
- create gender equality in the workplace
- provide community support schemes for people in disadvantaged urban areas.

SAMPLE EXAM QUESTION AND ANSWER

Question: Examine how the European Union influences economic activity in Ireland.

or

Examine the impact of membership of the European Union on the Irish economy. (2013–2016)

Answer:

1. Enlarged market

- Ireland joined the EU in 1973. This gave it access to a market of 256 million people. Prior to 1973, Ireland was restricted to its own population of 3.5 million people.
- By joining the EU, Ireland immediately had **direct access to a vast market,** including the British market which it originally relied on for most of its exports.
- However, it was the signing of the **Single European Act (the SEA)** in 1986, which came into force in July 1987, that removed internal international borders and formed a single trading block that afforded Ireland the perfect vehicle for economic growth. This allowed ambitious companies and businesses within Ireland to **break free of the limited demand levels** of Ireland's tiny home market.
- As one of the lower-growth economies of the EU, it was the UK's geographical location and traditional linkages with Ireland, rather than its potential business opportunities, that had fostered this trade dependence.

2. Market deregulation

- The concept of the **Single Market** provided for the removal of international barriers and shattered national market protection. This had an immediate effect in Ireland, where, for the first time in its history, it was able to adjust to and benefit from such deregulation.
- The consequences were **increased levels of productivity and efficiency,** for example, the lowering of utility costs for domestic and multinational companies. Air, transport and telecommunications are all operating with a newfound level of competitive ability in this era of increased foreign competition.
- The creation of the IFSC, run by a relatively small workforce, and originally proposed by Charles Haughey, provides a financial oasis resulting in significant taxes for the Irish exchequer.

3. EMU (Economic and Monetary Union)

- The **Maastricht Treaty** led to the creation of the Euro.
- One of the obligations of the treaty for the members was to keep 'sound fiscal policies' with debt limited to 60 per cent of GDP. It also controlled allowable inflation rates, annual public sector borrowing and placed restrictions on currency devaluations.
- These factors have seriously affected our approach to national debt repayments as a consequence of the Celtic Tiger crash, and changed our attitude by being aware of and responsible for our economic programmes/philosophy by questioning political party promises during general election periods.
- The years following the crash have been demanding in Ireland, with salary cuts, a rise in unemployment and low wage demands. Generally, the EU has brought stability and responsibility to our own doorstep.

4. Foreign Direct Investment (FDI)

- The EU Single Market created the scenario whereby Ireland was able to market itself as a low-cost base to access the EU market efficiently.
- Market deregulation also lowered costs and reduced obligations for MNCs throughout the EU.
- Structural funding for transport development, e.g. motorways, and Regional Funds for areas with special needs have all contributed to our economic competitiveness.
- Through the implementation of programmes to tackle human resources, marketing and research and development (R & D) deficiencies, our economy has developed expertise at providing for new technical- and knowledge-based industries. Through 'learning by doing', Irish workers can now use technical expertise, much of which is in MNCs, to incubate their knowledge and transfer it to companies that they can start up themselves.
- Increased FDI into the Irish economy brought opportunities for Irish workers to seek highly paid employment in industrial jobs. Today, the EU is the world's largest trading block and the world's largest economy with a GDP per head of €25,000 for its 500 million consumers. Fuels excluded, the EU imports more from developing countries than the USA, Canada, Japan and China combined. More than 70 per cent of imports enter the EU at zero or reduced tariffs.

An extra sample exam question and answer on one EU policy (CAP) can be found on moresuccess.ie.

Questions 7C, 2012; 7C, 2013; 8C, 2014; 9C, 2016.

19 The Environmental Impact of Economic Development

 You need to understand that economic development, which sometimes involves the exploitation of natural resources, may have negative impacts on the environment.

Renewable and non-renewable resources:
- **Renewable resources** are those such as water that, when used wisely, can be used over and over again.
- **Non-renewable resources** are those such as oil and natural gas, which cannot be renewed.

Trends in energy resources in the EU

- Oil and natural gas have replaced coal as the main source of energy.
- Nuclear power use has increased rapidly for those countries that lack other energy resources.
- Owing to increasing affluence, almost half of EU energy demands must be met by imports.
- Most EU countries must import energy supplies to meet their needs.

Ireland's energy resources

- Bord na Móna provides low-grade fossil peat fuel for domestic use and for three peat-fired power stations.
- Six hydroelectric power stations.
- One coal-fired power station.
- Three oil-burning power stations.
- Three natural-gas power stations.
- Three gas fields: Mayo, Seven Heads and Kinsale.
- New wind turbine locations.
- Only 15 per cent of energy needs are met by home resources.

The environmental impact of burning fossil fuels

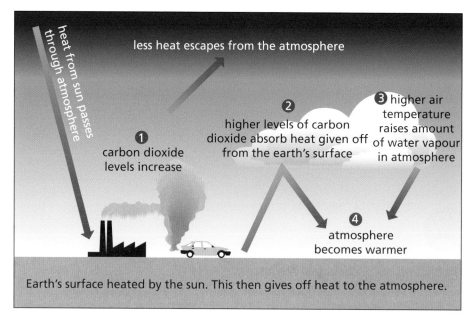

The effects of increased carbon dioxide in the atmosphere

Smog in urban areas

- Burning of fossil fuels, such as **coal and oil**, releases nitrous and sulphurous gases into the air.
- Smog is a yellowish-brown haze that forms when sunlight 'cooks' air pollutants to chemically react with each other.
- The main air pollutants that react together are **nitrogen oxides** and **sulphur dioxide**, produced by traffic and power stations.
- **Volatile organic compounds** (VOCs) from paint and solvent plants also add to the cocktail.
- The reaction of sunlight with these air pollutants causes lung/breathing difficulties (e.g. asthma) and reduces plant growth.
- Los Angeles and Athens are still affected by this problem.
- The biggest threat to air pollution in Ireland is now exhaust fumes from vehicles.
- These gases are also the cause of global warming.

exam focus

The marking scheme for any question on the impact on the environment of burning fossil fuels is likely to be:

Environmental impact named – 2 marks

Examples of two fossil fuels named – 2 marks + 2 marks

Discussion – 12 × SRPs @ 2 marks each

Discussion must refer to the environmental impact

Credit a max of 3 × SRPs for economic references.

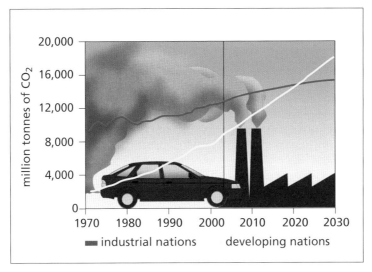

Carbon emissions from industrialised and developing countries 1970–2030

Some consequences of global warming

Note: global warming is also covered in Section 3, Option 1: Global Interdependence (see pages 240–242).

- Further information is available at www.microsoft.eu/environment.
- Play the DVD of *An Inconvenient Truth* and see the devastating potential of global warming.

Acid rain

The increased rain comes from two kinds of air pollutants: sulphur dioxide and nitrogen oxides. These gases are produced by fossil fuel power stations, cars, trucks and buses. They dissolve in rainwater to form sulphuric acid and nitric acid. These acids return to earth in rain and snow.

Effects of acid rain

- Forests are damaged:
  - tree growth is stunted
  - leaves are discoloured and fall early
  - bark splits and is affected by cold weather.
- Acid levels in rivers and lakes rise and kill aquatic life.
- Essential nutrients are leached from soils.
- Toxic minerals enter rivers and lakes.
- Buildings are damaged.
- Respiratory diseases such as asthma increase.

Renewable energy and the environment

Hydroelectric power

There are a number of difficulties in increasing the use of hydroelectric power supply:

- Most of the best sites are already developed.
- High costs of dam construction and reservoirs.
- Environmental problems such as adverse effects on wildlife habitats and fish migration.
- Local community disruption. People may have to be relocated and rehoused.
- Loss of land due to flooding behind the dam.
- Visual pollution from dam structures.

Wind energy in Ireland

Wind turbines are attractive features on the Irish landscape. Do you agree?

- Wind energy is the most preferred clean energy alternative in Ireland at present.
- Only 2 per cent of Ireland's energy was generated by wind in 2005. By 2015, this figure had grown to 23 per cent.
- Ireland is committed to produce at least 40 per cent of all energy consumed in Ireland by renewable rescources by 2020.
- If Ireland is to reach our renewable energy target, then wind farms must accelerate production to 250 MW per year by 2020.
- The most suitable sites for wind turbines are:

  1. large, uninhabited regions, or regions with a low population density, e.g. hill tops
  2. exposed coastal or inland sites with constant strong winds
  3. offshore shallow water banks such as the Arklow sand bank.

Disadvantages of wind farm development

- Noise caused by rotating turbine blades.
- Visual impact of turbines.
- Mass movement of surface material (e.g. peat) when disturbed for development.
- Damage to homes and life due to mass movement.

Wave energy

The world's first tidal turbine was installed and anchored to the seabed in Strangford Lough in Northern Ireland. Its 300-tonne turbine will generate enough electricity to power 1,000 homes. Due to its success, others are expected to be built in many rapid tidal currents worldwide.

Environmental pollution

Pollution at local and national levels

Waste disposal

As Ireland's prosperity has increased, so has its levels of pollution. There is an urgent need to find new ways to dispose of waste because:

key point

Pollution can occur at local, national, international and global levels.

- most existing waste-disposal sites are already near capacity levels
- most communities are opposed to new landfill sites nearby.

Ways of disposing of waste

Incineration

Advantages:

- takes up little space
- capable of huge volume of waste disposal
- generates heat for additional energy supply
- burning at high temperatures creates only limited pollution.

Disadvantages:

- increases air pollution
- releases dioxins into the air that may cause cancer
- toxic ash must be disposed of.

Six major incinerators, one for each of six regions, are planned to deal with waste in Ireland.

One at Poolbeg in Dublin could treat 25 per cent of the city's waste, and generate energy for 35,000 homes.

Most people are afraid that incinerators would damage the local environment and people's health.

Recycling
- Ireland's volume of waste is unsustainable for the future.
- Irish people are the least committed in the EU to recycling. We need to become more committed to recycling.

Sustainable economic development and environmental issues

Environmental impact studies in Ireland

These form a vital and integral part of national and county development plans.

They are carried out by independent researchers, who:
- assess and report on the state of the environment
- look at the costs and benefits of any new project
- estimate its possible impact on the environment.

key point

Sustainable economic development is a long-term plan that is vital for reducing the impact of people's activity on a region's natural resources.

The role of the EPA (Environment Protection Agency)

1. To promote and implement the highest practical standards of environmental protection and management for sustainable and balanced development.
2. To license and control all large-scale activities that could impact on the environment.
3. To ensure that all waste-disposal sites apply for a pollution-control licence to operate.
4. To record and monitor all industrial emissions from individual factories.

Irish fish stocks and sustainable development

Why have Irish fish stocks decreased?
- Irish fish landings have increased four-fold over a 30-year period.
- There has been an increase in the size and efficiency of fishing vessels.
- Unrestricted access has been granted to Irish waters by large EU fishing fleets.
- New research and monitoring of fish has provided details of shoal movements at various times of the year.

How can fish stocks be sustained?
- Allow spawning stock to reproduce at an effective level.
- Allow young fish to reach maturity so they can breed and multiply.
- Increase mesh sizes on nets.
- Make the use of all monofilament nets illegal.
- Reduce net sizes.
- Reduce the existing total allowable catch and national quotas for each fish species in EU waters.
- Create exclusion zones where fish can spawn.
- Provide protection vessels to control and enforce conservation measures.

Mining and environmental impact

Tara Mines has attempted to reduce the environmental effects of its mining operation on the local environment. Can you identify some of these efforts from evidence in the photograph?

Past mining operations created unsustainable development because:

- High-waste tip-heaps that encircled settling ponds were owned by the mines. These created visual pollution.
- Water used for treating mineral ores was released into nearby rivers.
- Exposed mining pits filled with polluted water once the mines closed.
- A high dust content was created in the air close to the mines.
- Local mining villages with a high unemployment rate depended on the mine for unskilled work (e.g. Silvermines village, Co. Tipperary) but created a spoiled landscape that discouraged new industry from coming to the area.

Case study: Tara Mines, Co. Meath

Tara Mines began operation in 1977 and is the largest zinc ore mine in the EU, and the world's ninth-largest zinc mine. Severe planning restrictions were applied to planning permission. The reasons for this were that the area:

- has a fertile farming region for fattening cattle
- is close to the Blackwater, a major fishing river
- is near large urban regions such as Navan town
- has a mining depth of 1,000 m.

Planning restrictions included:

- new tree plantations to screen the development from public view and reduce dust distribution
- noise and air pollution to be closely monitored
- water used in the mine to be purified before being released into the Blackwater
- large quantities of mining waste to be returned underground or contained in environmentally friendly settling ponds
- water from the tailings pond to be recycled in the mine.

Conflicts of interest due to resource development

Fish farming in Ireland

Reasons for the growth of fish farming

- The introduction of quotas on fishing fleets led to a shortage of fish supplies.
- Higher living standards led to a need for a balanced diet that includes fish products.
- Ideal conditions exist in Ireland for fish farming, including:
  - pollution-free waters off the west and south coasts
  - numerous sheltered bays and estuaries
  - regular tides that help flush out toxic waste from fish populations.

What negative visual effects do these fish cages have on the locality?

Economic advantages of fish farming

1. It creates employment for many coastal communities in the West of Ireland. Over 1,800 people are directly employed in fish farming.
2. Spin-off industries such as fish-cage manufacture, preparation of fish feed and fish processing add to employment numbers.
3. Generous government incentives are available for setting up fish farms.
4. There is local expertise in the fishing tradition.
5. Large quantities of fish can be reared in numerous coastal bays, e.g. Killary Harbour inlet.

Environmental objections to fish farming

1. Water quality declines owing to the addition of chemicals for flesh colour and prevention of fish diseases.
2. Toxic waste from excess chemicals, fish excrement and dead fish builds up directly under the fish cages.

3. Disease spreads to local natural fish populations: for example, the spread of fish lice to sea trout has almost wiped out this species in Irish waters.

4. Scenic locations can be visually polluted by fish cages.

5. Interbreeding of farmed salmon with wild salmon can interfere with the salmon's ability to survive as a species.

SAMPLE EXAM QUESTION AND ANSWER

Question: Conflict may develop between economic interests and environmental interests. Examine this conflict with reference to one example you have studied.

Marking scheme:

- Conflict identified – 2 marks
- Reference to one example – 2 marks
- Examination – 13 × SRPs @ 2 marks each
- Discussion on one side of the argument only – 6 SRPs maximum
- Example can refer to region/conflict.

Answer:

The Mayo gas terminal development: local/global interests

> **exam focus**
>
> Be aware of the marking scheme and time when preparing and answering the question. Remember, you have about 13 minutes for a 30-mark answer.

This development highlights the conflict between the development of a natural energy resource at sea by Royal Dutch Shell and the need to protect the safety of local people in north-west Mayo where the gas is brought ashore.

The gas project

- The Corrib gas field is located 80 km off the Belmullet coast in Co. Mayo and contains one trillion cubic feet of natural gas.
- It will supply 60 per cent of Ireland's gas needs for 20 years, so it will also reduce our gas import bill.
- Royal Dutch Shell, Statoil and Marathon have invested in the development of an off-shore gas terminal and pipeline to link the gas field to the Irish gas grid.
- The high-pressure gas pipeline surfaces near Rossport and continues to a terminal at Ballinaboy, where the gas is processed.

The cause of the conflict

Some local people fear:

- the danger of the **high-pressure pipeline** so close to people's homes
- the danger of the possibility of **bogbursts or landslides** in the local bogland environment during the development of the terminal
- the dangers to Carrowmore Lake and the local water supply posed by removing 500,000 tonnes of wet bog.

Some local people also wanted the gas processed in an off-shore terminal and then transported in a lower-pressure pipeline to the national grid.

Few benefits to local people or the state will accrue as a consequence of the development, e.g. no royalties are being extracted; no equity share taken; no windfall tax levied; companies are not obliged to employ Irish workers.

Royal Dutch Shell

The exploration company states that:

- there is **no threat** to the local community as a consequence of a high-pressure gas pipeline
- they have taken community interests on board by **adjusting the pipeline route** to cater for local concerns.

Consequences

- Campaigning by local people highlighted the method by which the government has granted exploration concessions over the past few decades.

exam focus

Research **one extra example** of a conflict of interest, e.g. the building of an incinerator for burning waste to generate electricity.

- Gas is now piped into the Gas Network Ireland (the National Grid) network from the Shell terminal at Bellanaboy, near Belmullet in Co. Mayo.
- More than 6,000 people worked on the development of the project, and more than €1.1 million was earned by the workforce.
- 175 people are permanently employed by the processing facility at Bellanaboy.

Development of Irish bogs

Conflict arises over the way Ireland's bogs should be used.

Economic advantages of bogland development

1. It creates employment in Ireland's Midland region, where few industrial jobs are available.
2. Peat is a major source of cheap fuel for many disadvantaged communities in the Midlands and West.
3. Energy is generated from peat-fired power stations, reducing the amount of imported fuels needed.
4. Many families depend on turf supplies for winter heating.

Environmental advantages of unspoilt bogs

1. They support a wide range of rare plants and animals.
2. They act as bird sanctuaries at night for many migratory birds, such as wild duck.
3. Many of Ireland's archaeological sites are preserved under their peat cover.
4. They are natural landscapes that attract many specialist tourists to study their flora and fauna.

Global environmental concerns

Deforestation

Economic advantages of deforestation

- Powerful logging companies have much profit to gain by this activity.
- Developing countries such as Brazil finance other development by exporting forest products.

- Large ranches are developed on cleared forest soil to graze cattle for low-cost meat for markets in the developed world.
- New farms can be supplied to poor, landless peasants.
- Consumers in the developed world provide a major market for tropical hardwood products.

Economic and environmental disadvantages of large-scale deforestation

- Large-scale loss of soil is caused by exposure to daily torrential tropical downpours. Upper soil layers are washed away.
- The absence of large quantities of tree litter leads to a quick loss of natural humus that enriched the soil through decomposing leaves.
- The felling of trees for agriculture leads to slash-and-burn activities, fast loss of soil fertility and, finally, abandonment of farms.
- There is a loss of vast quantities of plant, animal and human environments that were in balance with nature.
- There is also a loss of pharmaceutical products from plant life that could lead to medical cures for cancer and other diseases.
- Contact with modern society threatens the survival of ancient forest tribes who live in the rainforests.
- Tropical forests supply a large amount of oxygen to the atmosphere. They also absorb massive amounts of carbon dioxide from the atmosphere, so reducing global warming.
- Forests add a large quantity of water vapour to the atmosphere through the process of transpiration. An imbalance due to loss of forest cover could dramatically affect our human and wildlife habitat and even threaten our existence.

Policies for sustainable development

1. Promote the resources of the rainforests as a source of employment, health and wealth by selectively harvesting plants for medicinal needs and food supply.
2. Establish national parks so the natural landscape is preserved and for the development of high-income tourism.
3. Give financial incentives to countries that preserve their natural forests by offsetting debt against preservation.

Desertification

(See under Global Interdependence, pages 242–244.)

Questions 9C, 2012; 9C, 2014; 7B, 8C, 2015; 7C, 2016.

Elective 2: Patterns and Processes in the Human Environment

20 Population

aims You need to know how population statistics change over time and over regions of the world.

World population distribution and density

key point

Population density and population distribution change over time due to physical, social, political and economic factors.

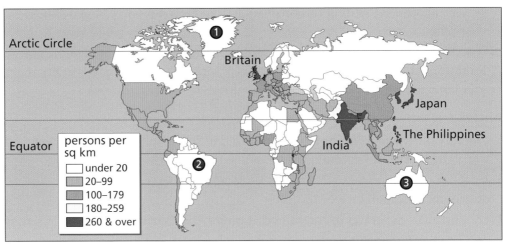

The patterns of world population density. Why do regions 1–3 have low population densities? In your answer refer to (a) climates and (b) vegetation.

SAMPLE EXAM QUESTION AND ANSWER

Question: Describe and explain, using examples which you have studied, the difference between the terms *population density* and *population distribution*.

(2008)

Marking scheme:
- Identify terms – 2 marks + 2 marks
- Two named examples – 2 marks + 2 marks
- Explanation – 11 × SRPs @ 2 marks each.

Answer:

Population density refers to the average number of people per square kilometre in a country or region.

- It is calculated **by dividing the population** of a country or region **by its land area**.
- Some regions have a low population density, e.g. Ireland (58 per square kilometre).
- Other regions have a high population density, such as the Island of Java in Indonesia, which has a density of 5,000 people per square kilometre. Some regions, such as hot desert areas, contain few or no people at all per square kilometre.
- Density per square kilometre may be misleading.

Population distribution describes where people are located in a country.

- It shows areas where lots of people live, as well as areas where few people live.
- In Ireland, for example, most people live in the east while few live in the west and north-west of the country.
- Population distribution may show the relationship between where people live and the height of the land. Mountain regions may have few or no people, while lowland regions have many people.

The world's surface is very unevenly populated. About 80 per cent of the world's population occupies about 10 per cent of the world's living space.

Four most populated regions of the world

1. Western and central Europe.
2. Eastern USA and south-eastern Canada.
3. The Indian subcontinent, including Pakistan, India, Sri Lanka and Bangladesh.
4. East and South-East Asia, including China, Korea, Japan, Malaysia, the Philippines and Indonesia.

Least populated regions of the world

1. The cold tundra of Northern Canada, Greenland, Siberia and Antarctica.
2. Mountainous lands such as the Rocky Mountains in the USA and Canada, and the Himalayas.
3. The plateau lands of Tibet and Central Asia.
4. Hot desert regions of Australia, the Sahara and the Arabian peninsula, and the deserts of Iran and Pakistan.
5. The equatorial rainforests of the Congo basin in Africa and the Amazon in South America. The Amazon basin includes much of Brazil and parts of Peru, Ecuador, Colombia and Venezuela.

Physiologic density refers to the ratio of people in a country per unit of area of agriculturally productive land.

The effects of urbanisation on world population distribution

- In 1950, 29 per cent of the world's population lived in urban areas.
- In 2000, 50 per cent lived in towns and cities.
- By 2030, more than 60 per cent of the world's population will live in urban areas.
- In 1960 there were two cities with a population in excess of 10 million people.
- A megacity is usually defined as an urban area with a total population in excess of 10 million people.
- In 2015 there were 36 megacities.
- All megacities lie within 500 kilometres of a coastline.

The growth of cities has changed population density and distribution on a world scale.

Some effects of migration on population distribution and density

1. Millions of Europeans migrated to the United States and Canada in the 18th, 19th and 20th centuries. This created a high density of population in eastern USA and south-eastern Canada.

The large-scale movements of people changes the density and distribution of world populations.

2. Over 6 million people from southern Italy have migrated to northern Italy over the past 50 years. This has had two effects:
   - it has increased the population of northern Italy
   - it has reduced the population of southern Italy.
3. Millions of people have migrated from Ireland since famine times. This has reduced the overall population and density especially in the west, north-west and Midlands regions.
4. Spanish and Portuguese colonisation of Latin America has led to:
   - a large density of people of European ancestry in this region
   - a low density of Native Americans in this region, due to the spread to the area of European diseases that wiped out native populations.

Patterns in the growth of population

Why did world population grow rapidly from 1750 onwards?

- New farming methods, such as selective breeding and creation of individual farm units, prevented the spread of animal diseases.

- Improved technology, such as seed drill machines, created increased output from farm units.
- The invention of the steam engine led to increased employment, affordable and better housing in urban regions and a corresponding rise in population.
- Hygiene improved and medical knowledge was gained.
- There was increased land supply in the New World.

> **key point**
>
> The world's population was low until 1750. Then large cities developed during the Industrial Revolution and numbers grew rapidly.

Why did world population grow rapidly in the 20th century?

- There were great improvements in medical care, such as antibiotics and the control of many diseases, e.g. tuberculosis.
- New high-yielding seed varieties increased food supplies.
- Increased clean water supplies and better sewage-disposal systems were developed, leading to control of infectious diseases.
- Lower death rates and increased life expectancy led to rapid population growth rates.

Why do population growth rates vary between regions of the world?

- Growth rates for developing countries such as India are high but declining quickly because they are in the late expanding phase of population growth.
- Birth rates are high, e.g. 1.5 per cent growth rate for Pakistan, which gives a fertility rate of 3.6 children per woman.
- Growth rates for developed regions such as the EU are stable. Growth rates for individual countries are declining, as in Germany. They are in the final or senile stage of the population cycle.

Changing population characteristics

Analyses of population pyramids

These are useful for the following reasons:

Birth rates indicate the potential:

- population of a country for many years ahead
- school-going population and the number of teachers required for the future
- paediatric care needed in hospitals and the number of doctors needed.

Death rates indicate:

- the standard of medical care, which reflects the wealth of a country
- the number of pensioners or elderly dependants
- the number of nurses, doctors and nursing homes needed for the future.

> **key point**
>
> Population pyramids display a population's structure in age groups. These statistics are used by governments to plan for future services and predict population trends.

Case study: The population of India

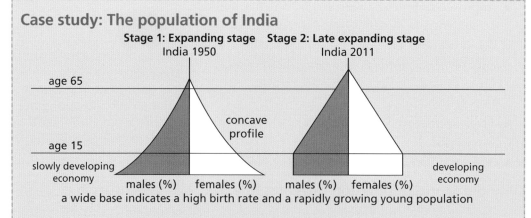

Stage 1: Expanding stage India 1950 — concave profile — a wide base indicates a high birth rate and a rapidly growing young population. slowly developing economy. males (%) females (%)

Stage 2: Late expanding stage India 2011 — developing economy. males (%) females (%)

age 65, age 15

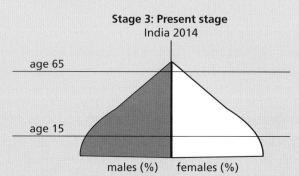

Stage 3: Present stage
India 2014

age 65, age 15

males (%)   females (%)

Age pyramids showing population of India from 1950 to today

Stage 1: Expanding stage

- Few old people. Death rates high in all age groups.
- No social welfare system.
- High birth rates and high death rates indicate a poor, undeveloped country. Few industries.

Stage 2: Late expanding stage

- More elderly surviving to older ages. Many reach in excess of 65 years of age.
- A fall in death rates causes a growth in the middle-age groups.
- A fast-growing population.
- High birth rates still occur.

Stage 3: Present stage

- Longer life expectancy – death rates are falling.
- Rapid fall in birth rates.
- Many new industries are being set up in expanding urban regions.
- In rural areas, many young men do not want to work in agriculture. Young women in rural areas are more motivated and are replacing the need and the desire for the sons to work in the fields.
- Wages for women are rising and education and mass media are raising their aspirations.
- Among the growing urban elite, many couples are content to have just one child, and have less of a preference for sons over daughters.

Population pyramids indicate:

- migration patterns reflecting movement into and out of the country
- dependent age groups and size of working population
- balance between males and females.

Dependency ratio:

- This ratio is the number of children under 15 and people over 65, relative to the working age group.
- In developed countries, the young dependency group rises as school- and college-going ages rise.
- The greater the number of the dependent age group relative to the workers, the larger the number of people being supported by a smaller number of workers.
- As populations grow older, so the cost of caring for the elderly in that country rises. This increases taxes on the workers in order to provide for them.

Patterns of population change in Ireland

Stages in Ireland's population growth pattern

1. Famine and emigration led to a rapid fall in Ireland's population in the 1800s.
2. Improved food supply and medicines slowed population fall. Many people continued to emigrate because of a lack of jobs.
3. A new economic policy and attraction of MNCs led to increased employment that halted emigration in the 1960s.
4. An economic depression in the 1980s forced many to emigrate, especially the young.
5. The Celtic Tiger economy attracted many foreign nationals and returning Irish from abroad. This led to a rapid rise in population.
6. The end of the Celtic Tiger has caused both Irish and foreign nationals to leave Ireland for work abroad.

key point

The Republic of Ireland's population declined from 6.5 million in 1841 to under 2.8 million in 1961. Since then, Ireland's population has grown to approximately 4.76 million people.

Age-structure changes

There are clear changes in the age structure of Ireland's population since 1961.

In 1961 there was a high dependency ratio

- A large number of children in the 0–14 category had to be supported by workers with low income.
- Huge numbers of young people emigrated to the United States, Australia and Britain once they reached working age. This left a great shortage of educated people of working age. The country suffered from a 'brain drain'.
- Ireland had a very high birth rate at this time. Few people went to third-level colleges.

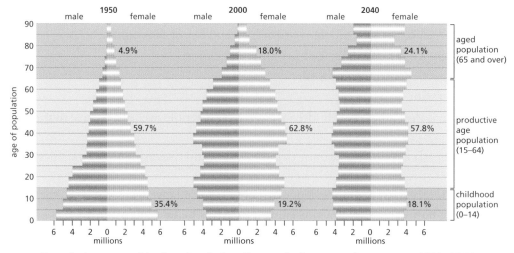

Population pyramids showing Ireland's population growth patterns, 1950–2040

In 2017, there is a lower dependency ratio

- There are more people in the 65+ category. Medical care is improving, resulting in fewer deaths.

- There is a very large educated workforce, but emigration has increased the dependency ratio.

- Ireland has become a multi-ethnic society for the first time.

These points provide background information on graphs and population pyramid-type questions.

- Many mothers work outside the home.

- The birth rate is low and stable, but still 2 per cent greater than in Japan, indicating an industrialising economy in Ireland.

Life expectancy for both males and females in Ireland remains low compared with many other EU countries.

Questions 12A, 12B, 2012; 11B, 12A, 2013; 11A, 12C, 2014; 11A, 12A, 2015; 10A, 10C, 2016.
Graph and chart exercises: graph, 2012; chart, 2013; chart and graph, 2014; graph, 2015; chart, 2016; 11B, 12A, 2013; 12A, 2014; 12A, 2015; 10A, 2016.

21 Overpopulation

aims You need to:

- understand the meaning of overpopulation
- study examples of overpopulation.

key point

Optimum population is the number of people working with all the available resources of that area, who will produce the highest standard of living and quality of life available to them.

Overpopulation occurs when there are too many people in an area for the resources of that area to maintain an adequate standard of living.

exam focus

Learn this definition of overpopulation: you could be asked for it in the exam. *Example:* the Sahel in Africa is overpopulated.

SAMPLE EXAM QUESTION

Question: Examine one cause and one effect of overpopulation, with reference to an example(s) you have studied.   (2006, 30 marks)

Marking scheme:
- Cause stated – 2 marks
- Effect stated – 2 marks
- Example – 2 marks
- Discussion – 10 SRPs
- Overall cohesion – 4 marks graded
- A second example may be credited from the SRPs
- If cause only or effect only – 0 marks.

When the waters of the Syr and Amu were reduced due to irrigation, the size of the Aral Sea was also reduced

Overpopulation in the Aral Sea region

The Aral Sea region is located in central Asia. Two large rivers, the Amu and Syr, flowed through a desert region to feed the Aral Sea with fresh water. This water supply was in perfect balance with the amount lost from the sea through natural evaporation. For thousands of years this ecosystem was in perfect harmony with the demands of the local population on its resources.

The main cause of creating overpopulation was the **overdevelopment of water supplies for irrigation**. Numerous canals were built to divert the water from two rivers, the Amu and Syr, to provide water for irrigation. Over seven million hectares of cotton, rice, and melon fields were irrigated to increase agricultural production for the markets of the former Soviet Union.

Consequences

Only tiny amounts of fresh water now reach the Aral Sea. This has had a 'domino' effect on every living creature in its environs. The ecosystem of a freshwater sea was destroyed because:

- Its fresh water gradually **changed to salt water** as water levels fell due to evaporation.
- As a result, fish life, delta farmland, forestry and swampland were destroyed.
- Coastal fishing communities were economically devastated as fish life disappeared from the sea.
- Much of the sea bed became dry land, and toxic sediments became airborne.
- Respiratory diseases and cancers increased, causing higher death rates.
- Migrants fled from towns that were once coastal settlements and are now 50 km from the sea.

Overpopulation has also occurred in the **Sahel** as a consequence of **desertification**, while in parts of India where population density is extremely high (e.g. Kolkata), other **social factors** as well as a **lack of infrastructure** play their part. See pages 242–244 on desertification.

The influence of society and culture on overpopulation

(a) Religious influence causes overpopulation

The combination of the following factors cause overpopulation:

- India's Hindu religion and traditions restrict it from

exam focus

Marking scheme:
- Cause identified – 2 marks
- Effect identified – 2 marks
- Examples – 2 + 2 marks
- Description – 11 SRPs @ 2 marks each.

creating extra food supplies and resources to employ more of its people and create more employment.

- Hindus are mostly vegetarians and prohibit the eating of pork. For Hindus, the cow is a sacred animal, so the slaughter of cattle is illegal.
- Many of India's cattle are poorly bred and undernourished. Old livestock are allowed to roam as strays.

(b) Cultural influence causes overpopulation

- Much of India's poverty is influenced by high fertility rates and the status of women. Many people in India live on less than $1 per day.
- In the past, rural females entered marriage in their teens with the prime task of producing children. For adults, literacy rates in rural areas are lower at 64 per cent than at 84 per cent in urban areas.
- Women are severely discriminated against and married women are often secluded from other males.

Examine two case studies of overpopulation:
1. The Aral Sea on the previous page
2. The Sahel in North Africa, on pages 242–244.

Low incomes cause overpopulation

- People who live in poor underdeveloped regions generally have large families. These high birth rates are generally driven by the need to ensure enough financial support for parents in their old age.
- In the past, large families in India and South-East Asia were seen as an economic advantage. In India, the northern states are the least educated and the poorest and they have the largest families. Its southern states, e.g. Kerala, are the richest and most educated and have the smallest families.
- Industries are poorly developed and a subsistence way of life is the norm. However, this is changing due to rural to urban migration.

The influence of technology on overpopulation

- The invention of the steam engine, however, provided vast numbers of jobs for Britain's population that was migrating to coalfields and factories at that time.
- Over the past 100 years, and especially the past 50 years, Japan has invested vast resources in developing a highly sophisticated technology-based society.
- Japan is an exporter of flawless computers, cars and electronic equipment, and these industries allow it to purchase all its material needs to maintain the highest living standard in the world.

- Genetically modified foods offer the prospect of a limitless world food supply, or at least an increased supply, for the most highly populated countries such as India and China.

Your knowledge of India from your regional geography studies should help you develop these points on its society and culture.

For questions on overpopulation you should refer to population numbers, resources and culture.

Questions 10C, 2012; 11C, 2013; 10C, 2015; 10C, 2016.

22 Migration

- changing migration patterns in Ireland
- migration policies in Ireland and the EU
- ethnic, racial and religious issues that arise from migration
- contrasting impacts of rural/urban migration.

Migration and changing migration patterns in Ireland

Migration patterns in Ireland

key point

Push factors force people to leave a region. They may include financial, religious, social or environmental reasons.

Pull factors attract people to a region. Again, they may be financial, religious, social or environmental.

exam focus

Ordinary level students should focus on two reasons why people migrate from their home in the West of Ireland and two problems caused by this migration for the Dublin region.

Higher level students should study two impacts, in detail, of rural to urban migration.

Marking scheme (2009):
- Two impacts named – 2 + 2 marks
- One migration named – 2 marks
- Examination – 12 × SRPs (6 × SRPs per impact) @ 2 marks each.

From west to east

- The Leinster region's population has increased each year since 1926.
- Connacht's population has fallen from 1.4 million people in 1841 to 433,000 today, a 70 per cent drop.

From rural to urban regions

- In 1926, 68 per cent lived in rural regions; 32 per cent lived in cities.
- In 1961, 54 per cent lived in rural regions; 46 per cent lived in cities.
- Today, approximately 60 per cent of Irish people live in urban areas.

Reasons why people leave the West of Ireland for Dublin

1. Farms in the West of Ireland are small and unprofitable. People leave for jobs in the cities.
2. Industry is reluctant to set up in an area where the workforce is limited. Therefore, jobs are few and people leave to find employment elsewhere.
3. Standards of living are lower in the west than the east of Ireland. Young people leave the west for better lifestyles in the east.
4. Many industrial estates and business parks offer high-income jobs in the Leinster region.
5. Many young people attend third-level colleges and remain in the Dublin region, as they become accustomed to the lifestyle.

Effects of migration on the West of Ireland

Loss of young population

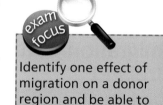

1. As young people leave the west, the services (e.g. schools, recreational centres and hospitals) close. The region becomes unattractive to live in, so even more people leave the area.

Identify one effect of migration on a donor region and be able to write about it in detail.

2. Many people between the ages of 18 and 30 migrate from the area, so marriage rates and birth rates are low.
3. Farms are left in the care of older people who often lack the energy to work them fully. Many farms become neglected or abandoned when the older people die.
4. Industry is reluctant to set up in an area of low population and out-migration, as the labour force is limited.
5. Community services and facilities decline as the population falls. This, in turn, reduces the attraction of the area for the young people.

Effects of migration on Dublin

Expansion of Dublin

1. The population of Dublin has increased. Large suburbs and dormitory towns have developed around the city to create a greater Dublin with a population of 1.3 million.

Identify one effect of migration on a receiver region and be able to write about it in detail.

2. Greater Dublin has expanded rapidly. Its commuter hinterland now reaches the Midlands to the west and Dundalk to Arklow in the east.
3. The cost of housing has risen massively, so many people are unable to purchase their own home.
4. Young educated people from the West of Ireland help to develop the city's economy, e.g. bringing new skills and differing social backgrounds.
5. Overcrowding may be the result in parts of the city. Great demand for accommodation raises prices and this may lead to overcrowding.

Post-1950 migration trends

Focus on any **two** positive and negative consequences of migration.

- Ireland was overpopulated during the 1950s because it was unable to provide sufficient jobs for its working population and so they had to emigrate to Britain, Australia and America.
- The Irish economy was developing and expanding from the 1960s onwards due to a new economic policy developed by T. K. Whitaker.
- The Irish economy collapsed in 2008. It caused mass unemployment and mass migration to the UK, USA and Australia.

Positive effects of in-migration

Cultural effects

- Foreign nationals make Ireland more outward-looking and cosmopolitan.
- People from China, Nigeria, the Balkans, India and the Philippines added a cultural diversity to an isolated, island nation.

Employment

- Many job vacancies are filled by people who are willing to work for lower wages, adding to the competitive nature of the job market.
- Foreign nationals bring new skills and ideas to the Irish workplace.

Ireland's influx of foreign nationals created a new and increased market for rental accommodation, housing and consumer goods. They played a major and vital role in the creation of the Irish Celtic Tiger economy.

Negative effects of in-migration

Repatriation of guest workers

- When foreign nationals are employed nowadays, it is generally on a fixed contract basis.
- New migrants become used to a higher living standard than they were accustomed to at home.
- When their contract expires they must return to the prospect of unemployment or lower wages at home.
- Political pressure is often put on governments to allow such people to stay, especially if some of their children were born in the host country.

Refugees

A high proportion of immigrants into some countries are refugees from wars or persecution. They occur generally in large numbers, and the cost of coping with their needs can be a severe financial burden on the host country.

SAMPLE EXAM QUESTION AND ANSWER

Question: Describe and explain changes in migration patterns to and from Ireland over time. (2010, 2013, 2016, 30 marks)

Marking scheme:
- Changing pattern to Ireland identified – 2 marks
- Changing pattern from Ireland identified – 2 marks
- Description/explanation – 13 × SRPs.

Answer:
All further changes in patterns require explanation.

Pattern 1: Out-migration (1922–61)
- From the foundation of the state in 1922 there was a steady increase in migration from Ireland to Britain and the USA. In 1958, annual migration reached 58,000 people and Ireland reached its lowest population level of 2.8 million people in 1961. The Irish government under the leadership of Éamon de Valera offered no vision and no future for its people. Then a change in leadership changed everything. Seán Lemass, under the guidance of T. K. Whitaker offered a new vision and new prospects for Ireland.

Pattern 2: In-migration (1960–80)
- Generally, the period between 1960 and 1980 was a time of economic expansion. Ireland's economic policy of investment in footloose industries was designed by Dr T. K. Whitaker and led by the Taoiseach, Seán Lemass.
- MNCs were attracted to invest in Ireland by offering generous grants and tax incentives to set up branch plants for manufacturing. Shannon Free Zone was one of the first industrial estates established in the country.
- Free education for all was introduced in 1966. Now great opportunities were opened up to a young, well-educated workforce and the need to

emigrate was reduced. Many returned from abroad, especially from Britain, to work in an expanding economy where new suburbs were being built on urban fringes in the 1970s throughout Ireland, especially in Dublin.

- Industrial estates were built on Greenfield sites to cater for expanding companies in urban suburbs adjacent to major transport routes. The MNC branch plants offered thousands of jobs to workers who now purchased suburban homes near to their place of work. Motor cars became commonplace and fuel was inexpensive to buy.
- Ireland joined the EEC (EU), the European Economic Community in 1973. This led to a surge in Ireland's economy, which helped provide jobs in companies that located in Ireland to access this large wealthy market.

Pattern 2: Out-migration (1980s)

- The 1980s in the Republic of Ireland was one of the bleakest times of the 20th century. An extremely **irresponsible budget** by the majority Fianna Fáil government in 1977, which included the abolition of car tax and increased borrowing to fund public spending, combined with some global economic problems to ruin the Irish economy for most of the 1980s.
- This was also a time of extreme **political corruption**. Many politicians, especially Fianna Fáil TDs and local government councillors accepted bribes to favour the rezoning of agricultural and greenbelt land for housing. In addition, trade union unrest and regular strikes listed Ireland as the 'Sick man of Europe', which had negative consequences for Foreign Direct Investment. These events caused high unemployment and mass emigration.
- The Charles Haughey and Garret Fitzgerald governments made this bad situation much worse, with more borrowing and tax rates as high as 60 per cent. Irish currency was also overvalued and much of the borrowing went towards propping up this overvalued currency. This situation continued until 1986 when the Irish currency was devalued.

Pattern 3: In-migration (1990s)

- In the 1990s, the Republic's economy began the Celtic Tiger phase. High Federal Direct Investment from MNCs, a low corporate tax rate of 12.5 per cent, better economic management and a new social partnership approach to industrial relations transformed the economy.
- Newly built third-level colleges such LIT, CIT, DIT and expanded universities offering new courses in IT, healthcare, business and engineering catered for a more diversely educated 21st-century workforce. Third-level student numbers soared as **further education** became the acceptable norm for teenagers and young graduates. These new graduates became a desired workforce for new MNCs who wanted more specialised and skilled personnel.
- The European Union invested over €10 billion into infrastructure. **By 2000, the Republic had become one of the world's wealthiest nations.** Migrants returned, unemployment fell to 4 per cent and income tax was almost half the 1980s levels. During this time, the Irish economy grew by 5 to 6 per cent annually, dramatically raising Irish incomes to equal – and eventually surpassing – those of many EU states.

- Foreign workers from low-wage economies in Eastern Europe, such as Poland, Latvia, Lithuania and other regions came into Ireland seeking employment in service industries and construction. These were highly motivated migrant workers eager to earn higher wages than they could in their home countries. They were readily accepted socially as they were hard workers eager to integrate fully into Irish society.

Pattern 4: Out-migration (2008–2016)

- The economic crash of the Celtic Tiger years began in 2008 and continues to affect Ireland. This crash brought economic and mental devastation to the Irish workforce and its households. Mass unemployment resulted and people, especially young adults, emigrated to places such as Australia and New Zealand, where job opportunities were available.

- **Irish banks became insolvent** and their share values collapsed. Many people's savings and investments were wiped out. Mortgage arrears and bankruptcy became commonplace for the purchasers of property during the Celtic Tiger, as property prices were overvalued at that time. Many companies and industries closed and workers were made redundant.

- **Government and civil servants' salaries and pensions** were cut in order to adjust to Ireland's new reality of overborrowing. Taxes increased and these events brought economic recession to Ireland with which it still struggles today.

Pattern 5: In-migration

- There appears to be the beginning of Ireland's newest trend of in-migration in 2017. New opportunities and confidence is returning to the Irish economy and some immigrants are returning home. The new skills developed by Irish migrants when working abroad allow them to seek employment in the new manufacturing and service industries at home.

Migration policies in the European Union and Ireland

Migration policy in the EU

- The EU allows for the free movement of workers among all EU countries.

- Its policy states, 'The mobility of workers must be one of the ways by which the worker is guaranteed the possibility of improving his living and working conditions and social advancement.'

- Migrant workers are entitled to remain in a country after working there. In principle this applies to refugees and EU citizens.

- The country that first accepts a refugee must take responsibility for awarding refugee status to that person.

key point

Changes in EU treaties, improvements in transport over the past 40 years and the reduced cost of travel have created a mobile workforce throughout the European Economic Area.

Ireland's immigration policy

The main components of Ireland's immigration policy include:

- Nationals from the European Economic Area (EEA) do not need a visa to live and work in Ireland. The EEA consists of the EU states plus Norway, Iceland and Liechtenstein. For all others, a visa is essential.
- Those who need a visa must apply for a work permit before they enter the state.
- Persons who claim asylum are given full-board accommodation while their claim is being processed.
- Those who do not require a visa include:
  1. Persons who have permission to remain in Ireland, such as people with special skills and foreign full-time students.
  2. Persons who have refugee status.
  3. Persons who have been granted permission to remain on humanitarian grounds.
  4. Persons who are claiming refugee status while their claim is being processed.

Ethnic, racial and religious issues created by migration

Race refers to biological inheritance: to DNA or the genes passed from parents to children. There is no such thing as a 'pure' race.

Ethnicity refers to minority groups with a particular self-identity, such as Cubans in America or Chinese in Ireland.

Minority groups may be defined by:
- place of birth
- language, e.g. Hispanics in an English-speaking country
- religion, e.g. Muslims in a Christian country.

Racial division

Apartheid in South Africa

- Apartheid was the racial separation of blacks from whites as a principle of society enforced by law.
- Under British law and after independence, segregation of blacks from whites was practised.
- In 1948 racial discrimination was justified and enforced by law.
- Nelson Mandela was imprisoned for protesting against this unjust law.
- Blacks were forced to live in poverty in 'homelands', the most deprived, almost uninhabitable regions of South Africa.

- All homelands people lost their right to citizenship of South Africa.
- Non-whites could not buy land.
- Apartheid ended in 1994.

For many decades, black South Africans were forcibly relocated into townships where they lost their entitlement to citizenship of South Africa

Ethnic cleansing

International migration often happens as a result of ethnic differences.

- This term was first used in the war that occurred during the break-up of Yugoslavia.
- It is a policy where ethnic groups are either slaughtered or expelled by force, threat or terror from the country in which they live.
- The deliberate attempt to eliminate the Muslim people from Bosnia–Herzegovina led to ethnic cleansing, e.g. the massacre in Srebrenica.

Religious conflict in India

(See pages 155–156.)

Rural-to-urban migration

Impacts of rural-to-urban migration in developing regions

Rapid urban growth

Why did cities grow in developing countries?

- The growth of cities in developing countries resulted from population growth and rural-to-urban migration before industrialisation occurred.
- So the cities came first; then industry developed later, over a period of only 60 years.
- Cities grew mainly because of rural 'push' forces, such as poverty and hunger.
- People moved to cities with the hope of employment and the prospect of access to schools, health services, a safe water supply and other services.

Urban problems

Dense population

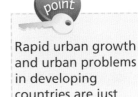

- There is an exceptionally high rate of population growth in cities, as most migrants are young adults of childbearing age.
- This young population accounts for over 60 per cent of urban population growth.
- Many cities have grown so large they are now called **megacities**.

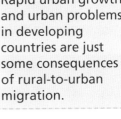

> **key point**
>
> Rapid urban growth and urban problems in developing countries are just some consequences of rural-to-urban migration.

- Squatter settlements, called **shanties**, or **bustees** in India and **favelas** in Brazil, have grown on the outskirts of cities.
- Males are the most likely to migrate to cities. This leaves an unbalanced male-to-female ratio in rural regions.

Unhygienic conditions cause disease in overcrowded slums

Over 50,000 one-roomed factories offer hope to many slum dwellers in Mumbai

Congestion

Developing world cities have chronic traffic congestion. This is especially true in the cities of India, where cars, motor bikes, buses, carts, elephants and cows may all compete for space. Dust, exhaust fumes and the unrelenting heat all combine to create a difficult living and working environment.

Congestion on urban streets is a constant problem in India

SAMPLE EXAM QUESTION AND ANSWER

Question: Problems can develop from the growth and expansion of urban centres. Discuss this statement with reference to one developing world city that you have studied. (30 marks)

or

Describe the causes and effects of overpopulation, with reference to examples you have studied. (30 marks)

or

Examine the impact of migration on a city in the developing world that you have studied. (30 marks)

Marking scheme:

- Example of developing world city – 2 marks
- Problems identified – 2 + 2 marks
- Discussion – 12 × SRPs
- All further problems require discussion
- Accept any valid example of a developing world city or part thereof, irrespective of size
- Discussion without reference to problems – max 2 × SRPs
- Discussion without reference to named world city – max 2 × SRPs
- Max 2 × SRPs for discussion on solutions.

Answer:

The bustees of Mumbai

Unhealthy living conditions

- Greater Mumbai has a population of about 21 million people. Its space is physically limited because it is located on a peninsula and can only grow in a northerly direction. Surrounding mangrove swamps also complicate issues and often form the location for the poorest people who live illegally in slums.

- **Slums house 40 to 60 per cent of Mumbai's urban residents.** With a population of 21 million people, that means that Mumbai's slum residents number between 8.5 and 12.5 million. One such slum is Dharavi, in the heart of Mumbai. In the slum people must live with many problems.

- An estimated one in 20 people in these slum settlements are compelled to perform daily ablutions and relieve themselves in streets or open areas. Children play among sewage waste and doctors deal with 4,000 daily cases of diphtheria and typhoid.

- Next to the open sewers are water pipes, which can crack and take in sewage. Dharavi slum is based around this water pipe built on an old rubbish tip. There are also **toxic wastes** in the slum, including very dangerous heavy metals.

Overcrowding

- Overcrowding is a fact of life. People live in very small dwellings, 10 m × 11 m, often with members of their extended families. The people have not planned this settlement and have **no legal rights to the land**. Within Dharavi, about one million people live within one square mile, making it the most populated area on earth. The slum is divided into communities by religion. There is an average of one toilet per 1,450 people.

- There are over 7,000 different businesses and 5,000 single-room factories within the slum, making it the most productive slum in the world. Some of these businesses generate million-dollar incomes.

- **Overcrowding** makes it virtually impossible to find even a toe-hold on some of Mumbai's suburban trains during morning and evening rush-hours. Commuters take a lot of risks by jumping into and out of moving trains, standing on windows or jumping onto the tracks to cross platforms. In 2016, almost 10 people were killed every working day while commuting on Mumbai's overcrowded suburban railway system.

Lack of a sufficient clean water supply

- These vast numbers mask the fact that these slums are **economically and socially diverse** – not all slum residents are poor. There is significant diversity with respect to age, legal status, degree and character of authorisation, nature of land ownership and environmental characteristics.

- Water is a big problem for Mumbai's population. In Kaula Bandar, a slum within Mumbai, water pipes are turned on for two hours as water is rationed.

- A 2011 study found that 76 per cent of household water in Mumbai was contaminated with coliform bacteria, and up to 43 per cent was contaminated with E. coli. Notably, almost all contamination happens within the household from people's hands and houseflies, because water is stored in unsafe, open-mouthed containers.
- Kaula Bandar residents pay as much as 200 times the price for water as the wealthier city residents. About 16 per cent of household income is spent on buying water in the summer season. Despite spending so much on water, nearly half of households use less than 20 litres per person per day, which is below the minimum water usage recommended even in disaster situations.

Migration and hope

- Mumbai is now a megacity of 21 million people. In 1981, the city of Mumbai and its suburbs had a population of 8.3 million people. It has an average population density of 5,000 persons per square kilometre, one of the highest in the world throughout the entire mega-urban area.

> **exam focus**
> Use your study of India in regional geography to develop your answer.

- **Birth rates have fallen** to 1.6 children per woman in recent years and the literacy rate in Mumbai is 83 per cent. Migrants constitute about 37 per cent of Mumbai's population. About 75 per cent of the migrants come from rural areas, compared to 23 per cent from other urban areas. There has been an increase in female migrants compared to male migrants.
- Social reasons such as marriage and accompanying the family constitute about 90 per cent of female migration. Most migrants come for job opportunities in the expanding industries and other areas. Even though life is very difficult, few, if any, would return to their original life outside the city because it offers employment, better prospects for all family members and hope for the future.
- Traditions are slow to change in developing countries, and **violence against women** has become increasingly viewed as a major obstacle to overcome throughout Indian society. Women find greater security in urban areas as they can flee the traditional family bonds that bind them to a certain way of life and the limited opportunities in rural areas. Traditional farming practises and few economic prospects also push young adults towards urban areas where there is opportunity and hope.

> **exam Q**
> Questions 10C, 2013; 10B, 10C, 11C, 2015; 9B, 11C, 2016.

23 Settlement

Site, situation and functions of Ireland's settlements

Prehistoric settlements

Ireland's first settlements

- The earliest Irish settlers were hunter-gatherers and belonged to the Middle Stone Age or Mesolithic Period.
- They came to Ireland about **9,000 years ago** (**7000 BC**).
- They lived close to rivers or lakes where fresh water supplies were available.
- Many settled temporarily on coastal sites where shells and animal and fish bones were dumped in heaps called **middens**.
- Middens appear on Ordnance Survey maps in a linear pattern near present high-tide levels along the coast.

Ireland's first farming settlements

- The first farmers belonged to the Neolithic or Young Stone Age and the Bronze Age.
- They buried their dead in stone tombs called **megaliths**, cairns, passage graves, wedges or dolmens.
- Their tombs form a dispersed pattern:
  - across the Burren in Co. Clare
  - in the drumlin lands of Sligo to Dundalk
  - in West Cork, where the people mined for copper.
- They chose upland areas and raised, dry or hilly lowland sites because the gritty soil was easier to till than the heavy clays of lowland areas.
- The Young Stone Age settlers came about **7,000 years ago** (**5000** BC).
- The Bronze Age settlers came about **4,000 years ago** (**2000–650** BC).
- Their works include **megaliths, stone circles, cairns, cist graves, standing stones, wedges and fulachta fiadh.**

Celtic settlements

- These farmers belonged to the Iron Age (650 BC to AD 250).
- They introduced iron working to Ireland.
- They built their ring forts in a dispersed pattern throughout farming lowlands.
- They divided the country into **tuaths**.
- They built (**Lis, Dun**) **hill forts**, (**Lis, Dun**) **ring forts, crannógs, cahers or cashels (stone forts) and promontory forts**, which were built on cliff edges for protection against attack.
- Elevated sites were generally chosen for the more important larger settlements.

Small monastery settlements

- Individual missionaries chose isolated sites in glaciated river valleys for their settlements.
- These sites are listed on maps as **ch**, printed in red. Local place names that include the word 'kill' often suggest such settlements.
- These settlements were near streams or lakes for a fresh water supply.

The historic development of Irish towns

Large early Christian settlements

1. These were sited:
   - at what were then route centres, e.g. Clonmacnoise, Co. Offaly
   - on fertile plains, e.g. Kells, Co. Meath.
2. They were centres of religion and education for people from Ireland, Britain and the European continent. At the centre was the monastery with its churches, round tower, monks' dwellings and graveyard.
3. The words Manister, Monaster, Kil, Cill or Ceall on Ordnance Survey maps all suggest that the town developed as a monastic centre.

Some Irish towns, such as Kells, Co. Meath, began as early
Christian settlements

Norman settlements

1. The Normans came to Ireland in 1169 and spread west and north, capturing the best farmland and building castles and towns to protect this captured land.
2. They built:
   - beside existing thriving monastery settlements, or
   - on new sites that were easily defended.
3. They chose:
   - bridging points inland and lowest bridging points on coastal estuaries, and
   - river loops, islands and elevated sites.
4. Unplanned towns developed around the castles, which were enclosed within high, defensive walls with guarded gateways for protection.
5. Abbeys, priories and friaries were generally built outside the town's walls.
6. Abbeys provided services such as education, accommodation for travellers, alms for the poor and hospitals for the sick.

Many towns and cities in Ireland, such as Limerick City,
began as Norman defence settlements

7. Norman towns were market centres, where fairs and markets were held at regular intervals.

8. **Cas, castle, motte, town wall, gate, town gate, abbey, friary, priory, grange, castle land:** all these indicate Norman origins and are printed in **red** on Ordnance Survey maps.

Planned plantation towns

- Planned towns were built as part of the plantation of Laois–Offaly, Munster or Ulster.
- All have parallel or evenly wide streets.
- Centrally placed Protestant churches introduced the new faith.
- The towns had central diamonds or squares where markets and fairs could be held.

Canal towns

- These towns include Newry, Mullingar, Tullamore and Athy.
- Rivers in the Midlands and east were widened and deepened.
- Canals were built during the 18th and 19th centuries to carry bulky goods from our largest cities and ports to inland towns.
- Canal barges carried people.
- Large grain stores and mills, warehouses and hotels were built alongside canals for easy access for barges.
- Mills for grain and flour, and for wool and linen were built in many towns on canal routes.

Canals, such as this one in New Ross, Co. Wexford, brought business to rural towns and created an economic revival

Railway towns

- Railways were first built in the 19th century.
- Hotels were built near railway stations to cater for long-distance travellers.
- Towns expanded as a consequence of this new business.
- Railway towns prospered at the expense of canal towns. Trains were quicker and cheaper than canal transport.

Seaside towns

- Seaside towns developed as railways were built to join them to nearby cities.
- Army camps were built for summer training of part-time military volunteers at seaside locations. This encouraged the development of golf courses nearby.
- Hotels developed near seaside beaches to cater for visitors.

18th- and 19th-century expansion

1. Most urban rebuilding and redevelopment took place during the 18th and 19th centuries.
2. This period of urban growth was called the **Georgian period**.
3. Wide streets formed a mesh with blocks of buildings in between, creating a grid pattern.
4. They formed the Georgian suburbs at the edge of the old, often unplanned, medieval towns.

New towns

- Towns such as Shannon New Town in Co. Clare, and Tallaght and Blanchardstown in Dublin, were built to cater for the many migrants who came from rural and inner-city regions.
- Shannon was a well-planned town with local services and an industrial estate to cater for workers' needs.

Rural settlement patterns

There are three categories of rural settlement pattern: dispersed, clustered and ribbon.

Dispersed or scattered pattern

- This is created by widely spaced homes.
- Dispersed or scattered housing is usually associated with farmhouses with outbuildings or sheds nearby. The pattern developed when farms were enclosed after commonage-type farming was abandoned.
- Farm buildings are widely scattered where farms are large, such as in the rich farmlands of counties Meath, Westmeath, Tipperary, Limerick and Clare.
- In more western regions, many farmhouses are located at the end of long passageways or on roadside sites.

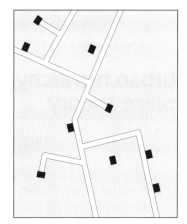

Scattered or dispersed housing is common in rural regions

Clustered settlement

- This pattern is created by groups of houses.
- Dwellings that are grouped together are generally farm dwellings of the 18th, 19th and 20th centuries. In isolated cases they may be remnants of the **clochán** system of the West of Ireland.

- Farmhouses were built in clusters in counties Kilkenny and Waterford as part of the division of land in the 18th and 19th centuries.
- Some clusters were built at road junctions where shops and a post office, and maybe a filling station, have developed over time.

Ribbon settlement

- This is a recent pattern development. It is generally composed of individual, one-off houses that developed in a line along a roadway.
- Local planning authorities were lenient as regards planning permission, and there were no overall planning controls for such housing from the 1960s until 2000.
- The presence of telephone cables, electricity lines and piped local authority or private water schemes also encouraged this kind of development.
- Landowners could increase their income from sales of individual roadside sites.
- Suburban arterial routes (main roads) were the preferred choice for filling stations, bed and breakfast accommodation and buildings for local people.
- County and national development plans no longer encourage ribbon development. It is **unsustainable development**.

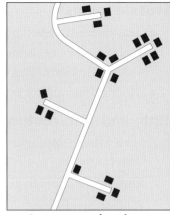

In some rural regions, buildings – especially farmhouses – are arranged in a cluster

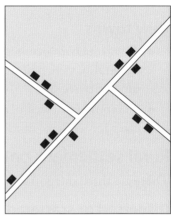

Buildings along a roadside form a linear or ribbon settlement pattern

Urban hierarchy, hinterland and central place theory

- Settlements can be classified according to size, function and population density.
- A major function of all settlements is to provide services for their inhabitants and the people who live in their **hinterlands** (surrounding areas).
- **Central Place Theory** means that the arrangement of towns is determined by the hinterlands that they serve.

Three basic concepts of central place theory

1. The **range of goods and services** is divided into three categories: high-order, medium-order and low-order goods.
2. **Frequency of demand** refers to the level of demand for goods and services, e.g. daily needs, weekly needs, monthly needs or annual needs.

3. **Threshold** refers to a certain threshold, or minimum number of people, required by each shop/service to be viable. For example, the threshold for a supermarket will be greater than that for a local shop.

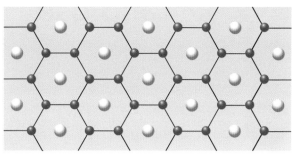

Hexagonal areas
This produces no competition and leaves no area unserved, so it is the best model.

● first-order (lowest) settlement, e.g. village
◔ second-order settlement, e.g. town

Model of hexagonal areas

Hinterland or trade area

- Every city, town or village has its own hinterland or area from where people travel to do their shopping. Cities have large hinterlands and villages have small ones.
- Hinterlands may be affected by physical features such as unbridged rivers, mountains or high upland, bogland or areas liable to flooding, which may distort and reduce their almost ideal circular shape.
- Hinterland size also varies according to density of population. Villages in isolated regions, such as in the West of Ireland, may have large hinterlands to remain as viable communities; whereas in high-density lowlands a number of villages may each be viable in a similar-sized region.

How modern changes affect the number of functions

- Modern transport, such as cars, allows people to travel further and buy in bulk. This affects the range of services that are viable in rural villages.
- Deep freezes and convenience foods reduce the need to make daily trips to local shops.
- Larger settlements can be more competitive and, by charging lower prices, can attract more customers.
- Villages may no longer have sufficient populations to support their traditional functions, leading to the closure of many of these service outlets.

Some criticisms of central place theory

- It was designed to work on a featureless plain that does not really exist in nature.
- Modern transport systems have undermined the original concept, as they favour some centres more than others.
- Population is not evenly dispersed.
- Settlements compete with each other to enlarge their hinterlands.

exam Q

Questions 10B, 10C, 12B, 2013; 10B, 2014; 11B, 12C, 2015; 10B, 2016.

24 Land Use

 You need to understand changing land use patterns and associated planning problems.

Planning strategies in rural areas: Sustainable development

This involves environmentally friendly planning that seeks an acceptable quality of life for present and future generations. It is the careful management of economic activities so that local environments and people's activities are interdependent.

Planners try to promote orderly development to:

- ensure the land is used for the common good (the good of everybody)
- meet the needs of society for housing, food and materials, employment and leisure
- support policies concerned with regional development, social integration, urban renewal and the maintenance of strong rural communities
- balance competing needs and protect the environment as much as possible.

Careful planning can help to achieve these objectives in a number of ways:

- controlling the development of transport, natural resources and the efficient use of energy
- the careful location of industry, houses and business/shops/services
- controlling the shape, size and structure of settlements
- effectively using already developed areas
- protecting and supporting our natural environment and wildlife habitats, including areas and features of outstanding beauty
- accommodating new developments in an environmentally sustainable and sensitive manner
- strengthening villages and towns, both socially and economically, in order to improve their potential as growth centres.

The role of county councils

County councils are legally obliged to:

1. determine a policy for proper planning and development

2. implement the National Development Plan by:
- controlling planning and enforcing planning decisions
- creating sustainable development in rural areas that respects nature, natural systems, natural habitats and species and protects the environment
- making good-quality decisions and encouraging public participation, openness and proper enforcement
- being responsive to change and reviewing development through compulsory five-year reviews.

Environmental issues

Urban-generated housing in rural areas is regarded by the National Development Plan as being unsustainable because these houses:
- are isolated and away from central services
- are serviced by septic tanks that may pollute ground water
- create suburban development.

Some people disagree because they believe that new rural housing has the advantages of:
- a healthier rural environment than cities for family life
- sustaining rural community life and support services.

Environmental Impact Assessment (EIA)

This involves compulsory environmental impact assessments for:
- major developments such as new roads, and large forestry projects that exceed 70 hectares
- the location of waste material disposal sites
- projects that do not reach acceptable levels of agreement or standards, if it is believed that the project would affect the local environment negatively.

Strategic Environmental Assessment (SEA) examines the policies, plans and programmes of environmental impact assessment.

Changing urban land use patterns

Land use zones and land values in cities of the developed world

- A city's land uses may be divided into concentric zones. The oldest is at the centre and the youngest is at the city's edge.
- The oldest parts at the centre are often the present-day commercial downtown districts.
- The city centre is surrounded by a band of old housing with some old light industrial sites that may now be derelict sites or renewed structures.

- These old housing regions may house ghetto communities.
- A band of newer housing or pockets of high-income housing may surround the old housing.
- The newest housing is in the suburbs, on housing estates.
- Heavy manufacturing is now located in industrial estates on major routes.
- Many office services and wholesale outlets are located in business parks.
- Shopping complexes and hospitals create growth centres in certain locations on city boundaries.
- Some wholesale and light manufacturing land uses form wedges or sectors along major routes, increasing with distance from the centre.

Central Business District (CBD)

- This is the heart of the city, with department stores and specialist shops.
- It has the highest land values and tallest buildings.
- There are multi-storey buildings, offices and apartment blocks.
- Financial and commercial land uses are the most common.

Industrial zones

- The first industries in urban centres were located close to the city centres, because the towns were small. Almost all of these are now closed, and their sites are taken by new apartments, shopping or office complexes.
- New industries are located in industrial estates on the outskirts of towns and cities and on main routes.
- Heavy industries are located close to water routes for easy import and export of goods.
- Business, wholesale and science parks are also located on the edge of cities or towns.

New suburban downtowns

- A new type of growth area involves suburban downtowns in large urban regions.
- Offices, hotels, department stores, industrial parks, entertainment facilities and car parking are grouped together to create a growth centre.

Land use zones in developing world cities

Central Business District

This will have:

- the business, employment and entertainment centres
- a central square or plaza with government buildings
- a spine of commercial land use surrounded by high-class residential housing radiating out from the core or centre
- sectors of the best housing around the core
- sectors of modest housing and derelict sites surrounding the high-class housing
- shanty towns surrounding everything for many miles.

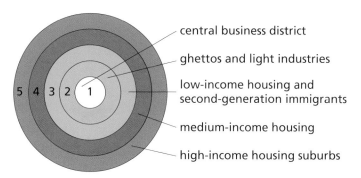

Burgess's Concentric Zone Theory

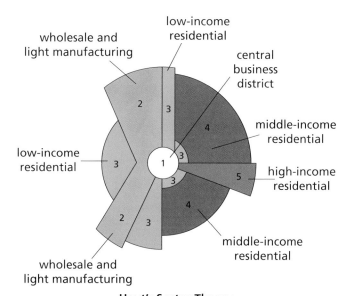

Hoyt's Sector Theory

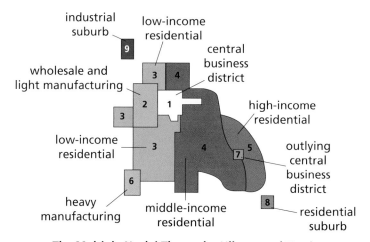

The Multiple Nuclei Theory by Ullman and Harris

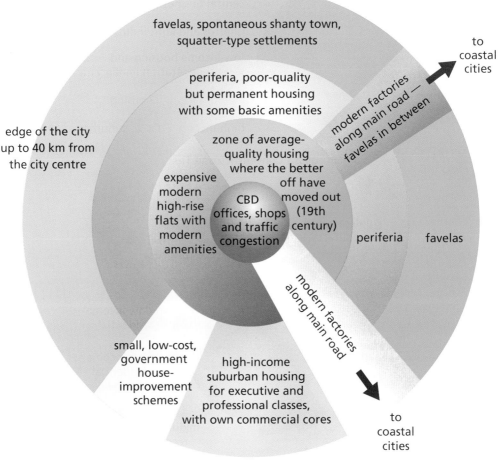

favelas, spontaneous shanty town, squatter-type settlements

to coastal cities

periferia, poor-quality but permanent housing with some basic amenities

modern factories along main road — favelas in between

edge of the city up to 40 km from the city centre

zone of average-quality housing where the better off have moved out

expensive modern high-rise flats with modern amenities

CBD offices, shops and traffic congestion

(19th century)

periferia   favelas

small, low-cost, government house-improvement schemes

high-income suburban housing for executive and professional classes, with own commercial cores

modern factories along main road

to coastal cities

(the colonial powers linked the cities to the coast for export of primary goods)

The functional zones of developing world cities

exam Q

Questions 10B, 11C, 2014; 11B, 2015; 10B, 2016.

25 Urban Problems

You need to know about the urban problems of developed and developing world cities.

Urban problems of developing world cities

 key point

Developing world cities are expanding so rapidly they have individual populations greater than many countries, as well as alarming social problems.

Bustees in India have many social and environmental problems

Revise the sections on Rapid Urban Growth, Urban Problems, and the sample question and answer on bustees in Mumbai in Chapter 22 (pages 213–214).

Urban problems of developed world cities

For a question asking about two problems in an urban centre, the marking scheme is likely to be:

- two problems identified – 2 marks
- named urban centre/region – 2 marks
- examination – 12 × SRPs (6 × SRPs per problem)
- both problems must be tied to same region chosen.

key point

Developed world cities have created problems such as residential segregation, urban sprawl, pollution and waste disposal. Other problems include urban decay, traffic congestion, and loss of green belts.

Residential areas and segregation within cities

- Certain environments attract a particular type of housing. Local authorities provide subsidised housing, either in flat complexes in inner-city areas, or in semi-detached or terraced housing estates.

key point

People with different incomes, cultural or racial backgrounds tend to cluster in separate parts of a city.

- Many housing estates, such as those that were built in the 1960s and 1970s, are unsuited to the modern demands of urban living. Some of these housing estates are being redeveloped with modern designs, leisure and social facilities, such as in Tallaght in Co. Dublin and Moyross in Limerick City.
- Residential groups sometimes interact with developers and planners to produce areas with compatible neighbours with whom they have most in common and live together for support.

Ghettos

- A **ghetto** is an area of a city that is settled by a minority racial, religious or national group with certain characteristics that distinguish them from the urban population as a whole.
- The term ghetto originally referred to sections of European cities where Jews settled or were forced to live.
- A ghetto today refers to areas where black and other minority groups live, e.g. Chinatown and Harlem in New York.
- A ghetto is a product of discrimination by society against a certain group of less well-off people.
- Cities that experience high immigration tend to be structured in a series of concentric zones of neighbourhoods of different ethnic groups.

Urban sprawl

- Urban sprawl is a 20th-century phenomenon. Until the 1960s, urban sprawl was mostly confined to advanced developed societies, such as the USA, Britain and the Netherlands.

> **key point**
>
> Urban sprawl is the expansion of urban regions out into the countryside.

- Since the 1960s, most urban expansion has occurred in developing countries where shanty town development has swallowed up vast expanses of rural land.
- As cities expand, they force surrounding rural areas and some inner-city areas to change their land use function from green areas to built-up, urban land uses.
- Suburban housing estates expand into the countryside, occupying vast tracts of once productive agricultural land.
- Urban traffic congestion increases as vehicles use new feeder roads and streets access arterial routes that lead into the city. This is especially severe during morning and evening rush hour.
- Neighbouring villages and towns are eventually absorbed into the larger urban regions, making them into conurbations. This has happened to create the Greater Dublin region.
- In Ireland, the corruption of planning officials, TDs and county councillors caused land to be rezoned, leading to loss of green belts and uncontrolled planning. This has led to the growth of one of the poorest planned capital city regions in Europe.
- When a cluster of large cities expand and join, they create a vast urban environment called a **megalopolis**.
- The Randstad is a megalopolis in the Netherlands that has endangered its Greenheart, an open green region of farmland with scattered small towns and villages.
- **Green belts** are open spaces of rural land use, parks or woodlands within towns or between towns. Green belts are designed to be permanent features to:
  1. prevent the development of vast urban regions
  2. prevent continuous urban environments
  3. provide recreation areas within urban centres.
- Local communities, as well as local government, should develop strategies together to protect and manage these areas successfully.

Atmospheric pollution

- Industry, people's homes and their cars produce vast quantities of greenhouse gases that trap the heat that rises through the atmosphere.
- This build-up is causing the atmosphere to overheat. That in turn is causing melting of the Arctic and Antarctic ice sheets and a rise in sea levels.

- Smog is a combination of smoke and fog that hangs over a densely built-up area under calm atmospheric conditions. Because there is no wind to blow it away, the fumes from chimneys and car exhausts build up in the air.
- Smog may conceal a range of dangerous chemicals, such as sulphur dioxide and nitrous oxides, as well as a variety of gases from industrial plants.
- Old people, young children and those who already have lung disease are the most vulnerable to respiratory complaints from smog.

Urban waste

The careful disposal of urban waste involves many environmental practices

- A report in 2015 found that of the 174 large urban areas in Ireland, 31 (or 18 per cent) did not meet EU standards of compliance. Twenty-seven of these were in Cork, Donegal and Galway, and were completely untreated and discharged waste directly into water regions.
- A capital investment of €1.6 billion was allocated between 2012 and 2016 for water services.
- In 2015, sewage received no treatment in 43 urban areas.
- Primary and secondary treatment plants have been developed in many urban areas over the past decade.

exam focus

Other urban problems include **urban decay** and **traffic congestion**.

This was necessary as ground water and many lakes had high nutrient levels, as well as pathogens (disease-carrying bacteria) caused by urban waste water disposal.

- However, waste water from some towns is still untreated and most towns and cities lack secondary and tertiary treatment facilities.

Solutions to urban problems

Improvements created by planning and renewal

- Old buildings and derelict sites have been renewed, creating a vibrant, young city area that attracts shoppers and nightlife.
- New streets create easier traffic flows.
- Parking zones and multi-storey car parks.
- The restoration of old buildings with architectural character.
- Pedestrianised streets and new pedestrian crossing places.
- Disc parking that contributes to improved traffic flow and revenue.
- Ring roads and bypasses.
- Tunnels under river estuaries and channels, e.g. the Jack Lynch Tunnel in Cork and the Dublin Port Tunnel.

The Dublin transport strategy

This plan involved:

- a vision statement to create a plan and vision for the future
- an integrated public transport system that everyone can reach within a 10-minute walk at most
- quality bus corridors
- a light rail system in Dublin
- cycle routes
- a National Roads Authority that has responsibility for the development and management of our roads. This includes PPPs (public–private partnerships) and toll charges.
- PPPs may involve toll charges on new developments over a 30-year period to recoup costs and maintenance charges for investors and obtain best value for money for the taxpayer.

The Luas has reduced street traffic in Dublin and cut down CO_2 emissions

Questions on urban growth: 12C, 2013; 10C, 2014; 10B, 10C, 11C, 2015; 11C, 2016.

SECTION 3
Options

NB: Study only ONE of these options.

Option 1: Global Interdependence

exam focus

You must write your answer in **paragraphs** or you may lose cohesion marks.

MARKING SCHEME

Choose three or four headings/aspects for your answer. The marking scheme will be as follows:

Number of aspects:

- 3 aspects @ 20 marks each **or** 4 aspects @ 15 marks each
- Identifying heading/aspect — 4 marks
- Discussion — 8 × SRPs **or** 6 × SRPs
- Overall coherence — 20 marks graded
- Select scheme according to number of headings/aspects discussed
- Allow credit for up to 3 examples from SRPs.
- Allow for 2 labelled illustrations to a max of 2 SRPs (different illustrations in different aspects).

Note: Some questions have alternative marking schemes, depending on the answers required.

26 Models of Development

The meaning of development

In the past, development referred to:
- the state of a country's economy, which was judged solely by the GNP of an individual, or
- the average wealth produced for an individual by the country in one year.

Today it is felt that real development must include sustainable economic, medical, spiritual and cultural aspects of a society.

Development, according to Abraham Maslow, includes a number of human needs that must eventually be reached before a society can be defined as developed. They include:
- basic needs, such as clean water, balanced diet, access to good healthcare
- security, such as personal protection from violence by any individual, groups or the state
- being valued by society, loved by family and friends
- self-respect, through secure employment, with adequate income
- personal growth through development of a person's talents.

The last few needs can be achieved only when basic needs are fulfilled: so there is a 'ladder' of human needs.

Third World images in First World countries

- The underdeveloped countries contain two-thirds of the world's population, but they receive only one-tenth of news time on Irish news bulletins.
- Most news from Third World regions focuses on wars, famines and disasters.
- Local people are stereotyped as inactive, helpless victims, rather than creative and willing participants.
- TV often focuses on trivial news items when larger, more important issues need to be aired.
- Few news programmes examine the real causes of underdevelopment, such as unfair prices or unfair trading practices.

- Few local people are interviewed on programmes that concern their countries.
- Images from NGO agencies appeal to people for charity. These images may have a reduced effect over time. They also tend to reinforce a stereotyped image of Third World people.

Examining world models and labels

The poorest regions of the world are referred to in a number of ways.

The Three-World Model

Until the 1980s the world was split into three divisions:

- the **First World** – the rich regions such as Western Europe, North America, Australia and Japan.
- the **Second World** – the communist countries of the USSR and Eastern Europe, such as Poland and Hungary. These people enjoyed adequate living standards.
- the **Third World** – the 75 per cent majority of the world's people who were poor.

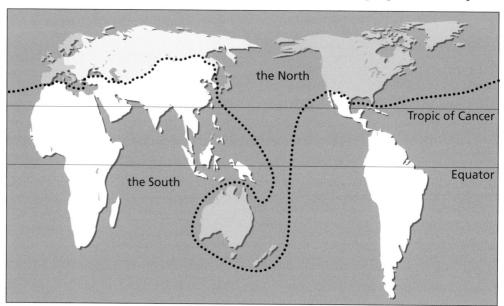

This map is called Peter's Projection. It shows the correct sizes but not the correct shapes of continents. How does this view of the world differ from that presented by most maps of the world that are used in Ireland?

Objections to the Three-World Model:

1. It was felt that this model created a three-tiered society with the rich countries at the top.
2. The Second World no longer exists, owing to the fall of the communist system in the former USSR.
3. The term Third World suggested a third-rate world. However, geographers use the term to suggest the lack of real political power enjoyed by these nations.

The Two-World Model

The Brandt Report in 1980 suggested the following division:

- **the North** – the rich and powerful countries. This includes the First and Second Worlds. However, not all of the countries are located in the northern hemisphere: for example, Australia is not.
- **the South** – the poor countries of the Third World. However, there are great differences in stages of development among these countries.

Other suggested models

- **Developed** countries – those where industry and services are well developed and people have a good living standard economically.
- **Quickly developing** countries – those where industrial development is quickly being established and is leading to improved living standards.
- **Slowly developing** countries – those that are still without any real industrial development and remain the poorest regions of the world.

Question 14, 2011; 13, 2014; 13, 2016.

27 The Impact of the Global Economy

aims You should:

- do one case study of the trading patterns of a multinational company – prepare your own example
- know about global environmental issues of deforestation, desertification and global warming
- know about the impact of social and political decisions on migration and human rights issues.

Modernisation and free trade

This model of development is designed to create a world economy (**globalisation**) where all barriers to trade are removed and private enterprise (**capitalism**) is unrestricted by governments or people.

Impact of multinational corporations (MNCs)

Multinational corporations are also called Transnational Corporations (TNCs). Multinationals:

- provide large sums for investment
- provide large numbers of jobs
- provide branch plants for manufacturing and research
- increase exports
- increase imports for manufacturing
- create global trading networks.

But they also:

- cause job losses when local firms close as they are unable to compete with large companies
- create jobs in one region at the expense of job losses in another
- cause branch plants to close because of decisions in another country
- work on the principle of profits first.

The power of some multinationals can undermine the rights of workers to form trade unions, or can undermine the government by threatening to withdraw all investment. Many multinationals are wealthier than some countries. Multinationals return millions of the profits they make in foreign countries back to their home country.

exam focus

Study Danone (pages 170–172), Pzifer (found on moresuccess.ie), or a multinational of your own choice.

Deforestation, global warming and desertification

key point

We live in an interdependent, global economy. Actions taken in one area have an impact on other areas.

Sample question and answer

Examine the impact of any **two** of the following environmental issues:
Deforestation, global warming, desertification. These are all either a cause or an effect of processes elsewhere
Use these points to prepare a sample answer.

Deforestation in the Amazon Basin

- Most of the Amazon Basin in Brazil is covered by forests called **selvas**.
- The region contains one-third of all the tropical forests on earth.
- Until the 1960s, this region was lightly populated with native American Indian tribes, who lived as hunter-gatherers in the forests.

Deforestation leads to increased levels of carbon dioxide in the atmosphere and to soil erosion

Why have the forest's resources been exploited?

- These selvas are viewed as a rich source of tropical wood.
- They are also seen as a wilderness region to be conquered to create profit.
- They have vast mineral deposits of iron ore, bauxite, gold, silver and tin, timber and oil.
- Most of the rich east coast farmland is owned by landlords.

- The Amazon Basin was seen as a way to give land to the poor, hungry, landless peasants without causing conflict with the powerful landowners.
- Large beef cattle ranches aided by government funds focus on producing low-cost meat for American fast food outlets.
- The World Bank supported large projects like that which was responsible for large-scale deforestation of the selvas in the state of Rondonia in Brazil.

The effects of deforestation

- Forest peoples are being forced from their natural environment by the cutting down of the forests.
- These tribes traditionally lived by hunting, fishing and subsistence.
- Constant contact by 'outsiders' is eroding their culture and bringing deadly diseases, such as measles, that their immune systems are unable to withstand.
- Traditional social life has been shattered. Many of the survivors are forced to live in squalid roadside conditions.
- One-quarter of all medicines owe their origins to rainforest plants, even though only one-tenth of these species have been studied.
- Selvas thrive in a very sensitive, balanced ecosystem. Deforestation upsets this balance and leads to a series of knock-on effects.
- Soils that are exposed to the heavy tropical rain are quickly washed away.
- **Global warming**: trees naturally absorb carbon dioxide from the atmosphere. When trees are cut down, less oxygen is reproduced.
- The amount of carbon dioxide increases and the balance of the atmosphere changes.
- Carbon dioxide traps heat and prevents it from escaping into outer space. This increases the atmospheric temperature near the earth's surface.
- **Desertification**: As a consequence of global warming, some desert regions such as the Sahara in North Africa are expanding.

Global warming

The earth's atmosphere is gradually getting warmer. Glaciers are melting in mountainous regions such as the Alps and the Andes. 1999 was the warmest year of the 20th century.

How the greenhouse effect works

1. The sun heats the earth's surface.
2. The earth's surface radiates this heat back into the atmosphere as long-wave radiation.
3. The normal amounts of greenhouse gases (e.g. carbon dioxide and methane) in the atmosphere trap some of this heat.
4. Increased greenhouse gases as a consequence of people's activities are trapping excess long-wave radiation and causing the atmosphere to overheat.

5. Some greenhouse gases are essential for humans to live on earth. But too much of them may cause drastic changes in climate that could lead to severe human and ecological consequences.

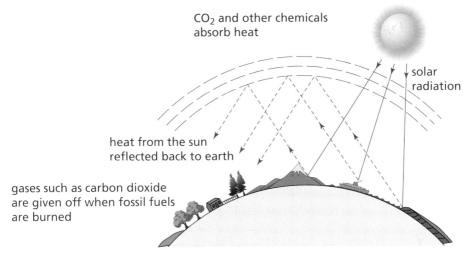

CO_2 and other chemicals absorb heat

solar radiation

heat from the sun reflected back to earth

gases such as carbon dioxide are given off when fossil fuels are burned

Increased carbon dioxide, methane and other gases are trapping excess heat and causing a rise in global temperatures

Some causes of global warming

- When fossil fuels such as coal, wood and oil are burned they release carbon dioxide into the air. Carbon dioxide traps heat and prevents it escaping into outer space.
- Increased industrialisation, intensive farming and vehicle usage all use vast amounts of fossil fuels.
- A greatly increased use of fertiliser, huge herds of cattle and large areas of paddy rice release extra methane gas.
- The use of chlorofluorocarbons (CFCs) in aerosols, fridges, foams and solvents causes about 14 per cent of global warming.
- America's population produces 25 per cent of the global emissions of carbon dioxide.
- India, with 16 per cent of the world's population, produces only 6.5 per cent of total carbon dioxide emissions.
- Deforestation is reducing the amount of forest cover worldwide.
- Deforestation reduces the amount of carbon dioxide that can be absorbed from the air, and so adds to global warming.
- In 1973 the world's population was 3.5 billion. Today it is 7.4 billion.
- This huge increase has led to a corresponding rise in the amount of fossil fuels that are burned.

Consequences of global warming

Negative effects

- Serious tropical diseases, such as malaria, could spread to temperate countries such as Ireland.

- There may be a higher risk of skin cancers among pale-skinned people such as the Irish.
- Trends in world tourism could be dramatically altered.
- Mediterranean regions may suffer a decline in tourism, as temperatures may be too high.
- Winter holiday resorts, for example ski resorts like Zermatt in Switzerland, could have much-reduced snowfalls, which would negatively affect their tourist industry.
- If trends continue, predictions indicate that sea levels will rise by 0.2–1.4m.
- Temperatures may rise by as much as 3°C over the next 100 years.
- This means that there would be greater extremes of weather, with freak storms and droughts, causing local starvation and the mass extinction of plants and animals.
- Millions of people would be forced to migrate as their lands become swamped by the rising oceans, e.g. Bangladesh.
- In Europe the polderlands of the Netherlands and much of the Wexford coast may be submerged, unless it is protected by higher dykes.

Desertification in North Africa

The Sahel in Africa has suffered from extreme desertification over past decades

Causes of desertification

- Desertification threatens the lives of hundreds of millions of people in sub-Saharan Africa.
- The Sahel region stretches for almost six thousand kilometres, east to west, across Africa.
- Until recent times, 70 per cent of the Sudan was covered with tropical forest vegetation or savannah woodland. Many of the trees were cut down as the demand for cash crops increased to meet national debts.

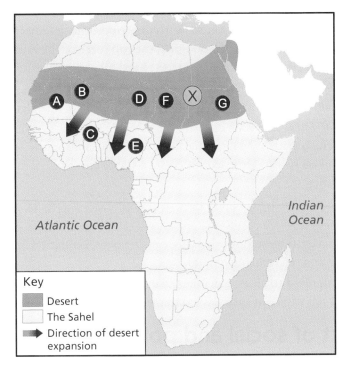

Identify the desert labelled X and each of the countries A–G

- Throughout the 1960s, countries in the Sahel became part of a global economy.
- They began producing goods such as cash crops for a global market.
- Because of this, the area devoted to agricultural crops such as groundnuts increased.
- Farmers became dependent on cash crops for their livelihoods.
- When the rains failed, the soils were left exposed to the winds, which caused erosion of the soil.
- This deforestation, in association with global warming (the greenhouse effect), has led to desertification. Climate change is brought about by the interaction between the forest and the atmosphere.
- As global temperature rises, the ability of the air to hold more moisture increases. Consequently, less rain falls, especially in those regions that have been deforested. This causes deforestation and drought.

Study the effects of people's activities on biomes on pages 287– 290.

Consequences of desertification

- When trees are absent, so are clouds. With no clouds, the land becomes dried up by the equatorial sun. When rain does fall, the full force of the rain reaches the ground, and **sheet erosion** occurs. Nutrients and topsoil are washed into rivers and estuaries, creating problems of silting.
- Crops have failed, farm animals have died and people have been left without adequate means of survival.
- The West African state of Mauritania alone loses 100 million tonnes of wind-eroded topsoil each year. Dust storms create a stable atmosphere that reduces rainfall amounts.
- Many children in the Sahel region have died of diseases associated with malnutrition, such as kwashiorkor.
- Many people have migrated southwards, causing overpopulation and further overcropping and overgrazing of land.
- Many have migrated to cities, e.g. Niamey in Niger. This has increased the demand for wood as fuel, which in turn has led to more deforestation.

The impact of social and political decisions

Rural-to-urban migration in the Third World

- Rural unemployment caused by increased migration has led to urban migration in Third World regions. Small landowners cannot compete with agribusiness companies so they sell their farms.
- More than two-thirds of all the world's city dwellers now live in developing countries. Cities such as Mexico City, São Paulo and Kolkata have all added millions to their populations over the past 30 years.
- Thousands of people in the Sahel region of sub-Saharan Africa have migrated southwards as a consequence of desertification in the area. These people were farmers who tilled the land or grazed cattle in their traditional homelands.
- Rural migrants have poured into cities out of desperation due to civil unrest, poverty and hunger, rather than having been drawn by jobs and opportunities.
- Because these migrations have mostly been composed of teenagers and young adults, an important additional impact has been exceptionally **high rates of natural population increase** (high birth rates with low death rates).

Patterns of migration movement

Rural-to-urban movements

- Most migrants are searching for employment, better education and health services.
- Many are fleeing ecological disasters, such as desertification in the Sahel.
- Millions flee from civil unrest such as civil wars, as in Sudan in 2004–2005.

Between Third World countries

- This accounts for 80 per cent of all international migrations.
- It results from a number of causes, such as employment-seeking, ecological disasters, war and persecution.

From Third World countries to the developed world

- This occurs from Central and South America to the USA.
- There is also migration from Africa, the Middle East and China to the EU and the USA.
- Poverty and lack of employment at home cause these migrations.

From Eastern Europe to Western Europe

Up to 2 million people migrated from Eastern to Western Europe between 2001 and 2006. This was because of:

- the sense of freedom created by the collapse of the communist system in Eastern Europe
- poverty or poor living standards, creating a search for a better standard of living
- the persecution of ethnic or cultural groups such as gypsies.

More recently, this trend has slowed, due to a difficult economic climate in the Western countries, such as Ireland and the United Kingdom.

From peripheral regions to core regions

This is fuelled by:

- the need for a safe place to live and work
- a search for employment and higher living standards
- a search for better social and cultural centres, from education to nightlife.

Migration from the Middle East and Syria to Europe

- The political instability of Iraq and the presence of civil unrest in Syria have led to civil war that has forced people to migrate westwards to Europe. Most Syrians have migrated because they have given up hope for their country, whose war shows little sign of ending.
- Four years of fighting have left the Syrians without homes, education for their children, work and without hope for the future. At this stage, it is almost impossible for Syrians to gain legal entrance to most other Arab countries.
- About 4 million people have already managed to get to Turkey, Lebanon and Jordan, but Europe is an increasingly attractive option for them since they have no secure legal status in the countries where they now live. Getting to Europe has been difficult in the past; one such method involves sailing from North Africa to Italy in dangerous boats and sea conditions.

- Germany offered asylum, sanctuary and work if Syrians arrived within their borders. The non-EU Balkan countries laid on special trains to transport them across their territories. Over 1 million migrants have arrived in Germany. The lack of a cohesive common European Asylum policy has not helped this unprecedented migration.

Migration to Ireland since the 1990s

- Ireland was an area of out-migration, rather than in-migration, since famine times.
- The Celtic Tiger economy in the late 1990s and early 2000s created a need for many workers in all sectors, including:
  - returning Irish emigrants who had worked abroad in the UK, EU or America
  - foreign nationals for work in the service industries
  - refugees, both political and economic, in search of sanctuary and a new life with hope for a better future.
- Emigration since 2007 has left Ireland without many of its young adults.

Prepare two sample answers to explain this statement:

We live in an interdependent global economy. Actions or decisions taken in one area have an impact on other areas.

Discuss this statement with reference to one multinational company that you have studied.

- In the first prepared answer, focus on three issues (a) economic and political refugees, (b) migration patterns and (c) human rights issues.
- In the second prepared answer, focus on the impact of global trade patterns in (a) producer regions and (b) consumer regions.

Questions 14, 2013; 15, 2014; 13, 2015.

28 Linking Economic Growth with Human Development

 aims You need to be able to:
- assess the impact of debt on developing economies
- explain how human development can lead to economic development
- explain how economic development can involve exploitation of people at local and global level
- discuss the role of women in society.

International debt and cycles of poverty

Causes of Third World debt

- The rapid rise of oil prices in 1973 triggered a worldwide recession and caused debt repayments of Third World countries to escalate.
- Profits of oil-producing countries could not be reinvested due to world recession.
- So the banks offered huge loans to Third World countries as development aid.
- Many of these countries were ruled by dictators who invested unwisely in arms or useless development programmes.
- In the 1980s the United States raised their interest rates to attract overseas funds.
- This set in motion a spiral of increased rates throughout the developed world; so debts went out of control and poor countries could not repay even the interest.
- The IMF (International Monetary Fund) was set up by the banks of developed countries to restructure loans so Third World countries could repay their debts by:
  1. increasing cash crops
  2. reducing spending at home on services such as education
  3. stopping subsidising the price of foodstuffs, so essential foods became very expensive
  4. introducing wage control to reduce inflation – but this made living even more difficult

5. devaluing national currencies to make exports cheaper, but that made imports more expensive

6. allowing the repatriation of profits of MNCs.

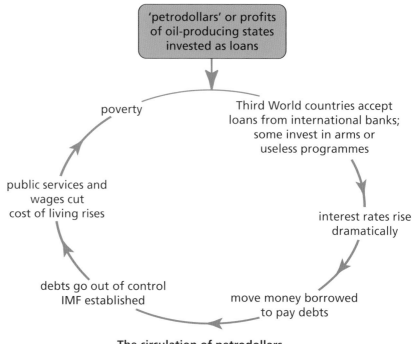

The circulation of petrodollars

Some solutions to international debt

- By 2000 the world's richest countries agreed to cancel about 30 per cent of total Third World debt, and 100 per cent of some individual countries' debt.
- Debt of the poorest African countries was cleared by the G8 countries in 2005.
- A large percentage of profits of multinational corporations in a Third World country should be reinvested in new industries or services in that country.
- Debt repayments should be reduced further to a level that allows these countries to develop their economy.
- Developing countries that have their debts reduced are required to invest existing repayments to promote the development of self-reliance programmes throughout their country.

Types and advantages of aid

Who benefits from aid?

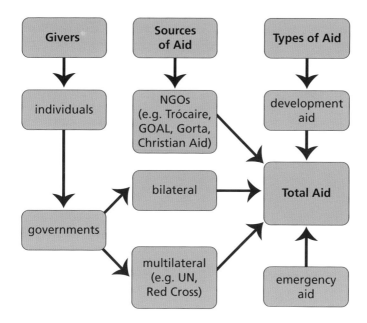

International aid to the South

Aid sources and who benefits

1. **Non-governmental organisations (NGOs)**
   Voluntary organisations such as Trócaire, Concern and Gorta provide both emergency and development aid.
2. **Bilateral**
   This is direct aid from one government to another. Generally this type of aid is used to improve agriculture, education, health services, etc.
3. **Multilateral**
   International institutions such as the Red Cross, the United Nations and the World Bank provide both emergency and development aid.

Emergency aid

Countless lives have been saved from hunger and disease caused by natural disasters such as earthquakes, famines and flooding, by the provision of:

- food, clothing and shelter
- emergency personnel
- medical aid.

Advantages of emergency aid

Emergency aid is essential to save lives in crisis situations

- The supply of food, fresh water, medicines and shelter has saved countless lives.
- Modern transport systems have made the delivery of emergency aid much easier and more effective than in the past.
- Emergency aid does not disadvantage local food producers.

Development aid

Development programmes in the LDCs (least developed countries), such as Zambia, Ethiopia and Lesotho, include projects such as clean water supplies, farm livestock improvement and adult literacy.

Advantages of development aid

- Vital infrastructure such as water supply pipes and wells, sanitation and new roads can give an initial boost to an emerging economy.
- Farm improvement schemes and education programmes help people to cater for their own future long-term needs.
- Health clinics develop skills of local people to cater for their communities' basic needs.
- Development aid is called 'appropriate aid' because it serves the needs of local communities.

Human development

- People who feel the need to help are given the opportunity to act as volunteers.
- APSO (Agency for Personal Service Overseas) recruits people to work on aid programmes.
- Development education provides workshops, seminars and resource packs to inform the Irish people and people from other countries of the dangers of xenophobia.

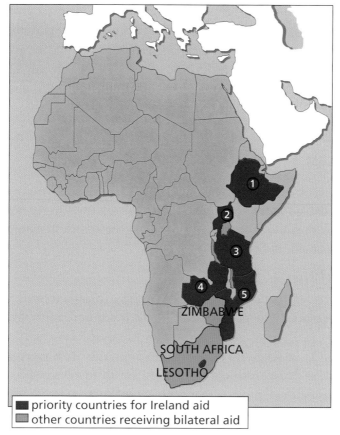

Sub-Saharan African countries that receive Irish and bilateral aid
Activity: Identify the countries 1–5 that receive Irish bilateral aid

Disadvantages of aid

- Tied aid may benefit the donor more than the receiver.
- Aid may cause the receiver to become dependent on the donor country. Military aid could be used by a government against an opponent who may be justified in their opposition to certain government programmes.
- Much tied aid is given to better-off Third World countries that may serve the political or economic needs of donor countries.
- Some powerful countries use aid as a means of political control over weaker countries. For example, the US government requested the use of Turkish airports as bases from which to bomb Iraq. When the Turkish government refused this request, the US immediately withdrew millions of dollars of aid from Turkey.
- Battles were fought in developing countries because governments and opposition groups were supported by US or Russian aid. Their Cold War was fought on others' soil.
- Aid has been used to encourage global free trade, which exposes the markets of poor countries to the products of rich countries.

- Loans may be given in the form of aid. Some of these loans are given on standard commercial terms, and may create crippling debt over long periods.
- The United Nations agreed that developed countries should set aside 0.7 per cent of their GNP as aid. Few countries have achieved this, with only Denmark, Norway, the Netherlands and Sweden having fulfilled the agreement. US aid, for example, is just 0.1 per cent of GNP.

The role of NGOs

What are NGOs?

- NGOs are non-governmental, private agencies that provide aid to developing countries. They include such agencies as Trócaire, Concern, Goal, Afri and Oxfam.
- They provide the following types of aid: emergency relief, development aid, empowerment aid, and education awareness.

Advantages of NGOs

- Their independent status allows agencies such as Trócaire to work independently for justice in places such as South Africa, which was under apartheid policies up to the 1980s.
- Because NGOs are relatively small organisations, they do not get involved in mega-projects such as dam construction. They are mostly involved with community-based 'appropriate aid' projects that get local support.

Disadvantages of NGOs

- Competition between NGOs can lead to the agencies adopting 'starving baby' images that may distort the First World's view of the Third World.
- The scale of funds at the disposal of NGOs is relatively small when compared to national government funding. Nevertheless, the funds of the leading Irish agencies Trócaire and Concern help reduce poverty.
- Some NGOs use 'child sponsorship' schemes where individual children in the Third World are sponsored by individuals in the First World. However, this could make such Third World children feel personally in debt to these sponsors and so may reduce their sense of individuality.

Human exploitation

World trade and global exploitation

- It is believed by some people that Third World poverty has increased as a result of global trading.
- The richest 20 per cent of the world's people control 84 per cent of global trade.
- The poorest 20 per cent control less than 1 per cent of global trade.
- Multinational corporations such as Volkswagen have turnovers of twice the GNP of Bangladesh.

- The turnover of Nestlé Corporation is 20 times greater than the entire GNP of Nicaragua.

Reasons for lack of control of global trading by Third World countries

Reliance on a single commodity or raw material

- Third World countries were colonies that supplied commodities such as coffee, tea and cotton for factories in rich countries.
- Prices for these commodities from developed countries are controlled by powerful multinational corporations, such as Chiquita and Nestlé.
- Some Third World countries are totally reliant on a single commodity for export, so if the price for that commodity falls it is a disaster for that country.

Unfair trading

- The prices of goods from developed countries to Third World countries have risen hugely, but the prices of goods from Third World countries to developed ones have fallen.
- So they have had to sell more and more to buy the same amount of goods.
- In 1972 Uganda sold 6 tonnes of cotton to buy one truck.
- Today it must sell 35 tonnes of cotton to buy a similar truck.

Fluctuating prices

- Because prices of commodities vary greatly from year to year, Third World countries are unable to make long-term plans for development. Sometimes this is due to poor advice from the World Trade Organisation (WTO).
- As more commodities are grown for sale to pay debts, there can be a glut of some commodities in a particular year. This causes a fall in prices.

Fair trade is one way of increasing the earnings of commodity growers

Case study: Coffee

- Coffee is the world's second most important commodity after oil.
- Some countries, such as Burundi and Ethiopia, depend on coffee for most of their income. A bad harvest or a sudden drop in price can bring bankruptcy to such countries. For example, in 1989 the price of coffee fell by one-third in a single week.
- The price of coffee was regulated in the past. But rich, coffee-consuming countries and the World Trade Organisation ended this practice.

Cheap labour

- Many manufactured products, such as clothing and footwear, are now produced in Third World countries. New technology and multinationals (or TNCs – transnational corporations) have been responsible for this trend, creating globalisation.
- New technology has reduced the need for highly paid, skilled labour.
- Multinationals have brought welcome work for Third World countries, but they gain their profits from poorly paid and badly treated workers.
- Most of the profits of TNCs return to where they have their headquarters.
- For example, the legal minimum wage in Indonesia is $1.27 per hour: but 12,000 factories pay less than 40 per cent of the minimum wage.
- Female workers make up 80 per cent of the workforce.
- A normal working week is 50 hours, with no payment for overtime.

Gender roles

- Certain societies, such as Muslim societies, allow daughters to inherit only half as much as sons. Women cannot file for divorce against their husbands.
- The Taliban regime in Afghanistan forces women to cover their entire bodies, even their faces. They cannot attend schools or work outside the home.

> **key point**
>
> Tradition, injustice and poverty are three factors that have seriously affected the role of women in society.

- China's 'one child per family' policy led to the deaths of many infant girls, as there was a preference for sons to carry on the family name. It also led to selective abortion of many unborn baby girls.
- In many poor countries, boys are given preference over girls for facilities such as education.
- Girls can be forced into arranged marriages with distant cousins many times their own age.
- Women must play many roles, as wives, mothers and subsistence farmers, sowing and reaping the crops.
- Women in transnational corporations must work for less pay than men.

Ways of changing gender roles

Self-help

Organised groups of women can challenge their position, assert their social rights and improve their income.

Breaking the cycle of poverty

Education

- Lack of education creates cycles of poverty.
- Improved school facilities can include necessary skills learned in apprentice-type programmes.
- Adult education programmes can help mothers to learn and pass on their new knowledge and desire for learning to their daughters.
- Social education for men may help them to encourage women into education and economic services.

Workplace reform

- Strong trade unions are needed to work for women's rights in places where they are exploited.
- Laws need to be introduced that force equal pay for equal work. In Ireland, the Employment Equality Act was introduced in 1997.
- Additional facilities, such as crèches and maternity leave, encourage mothers to work outside the home.

Aid for women

- Better-designed aid packages would help to facilitate the economic empowerment of women.
- Banking structures should be rethought so that poor women can take out loans to invest in small economic projects. The Grameen Bank in Bangladesh loans money to poor women to buy seeds, cattle, farm machines and even land.

Questions 15, 2013; 15, 2015.

29 Sustainable Development – The Way Forward

aims You need to be able to:
- examine the idea of sustainable development as a model for the future
- discuss the development of fair trade and its impact
- explain how sustainable development involves justice for minorities
- explain how self-help can lead to sustainable development.

The sustainable use of resources

The Kyoto protocol

The Kyoto Conference held in Japan in 1997 set a target of an overall reduction of 5 per cent in the production of greenhouse gases by 2012. This was agreed by all participating countries, including all those of the developed world.

key point

Using resources sustainably means meeting the needs of the present without endangering the requirements of future generations.

However, since then:
- the USA and Japan demanded the right to buy 'pollution quotas'
- in 2001 the USA abandoned its Kyoto commitments.

Ireland agreed to keep its 2012 emissions to 13 per cent above its 1990 levels, but by 2000 Ireland's emissions had exceeded 20 per cent. However, Ireland intends to do the following:
- phase out coal burning at Moneypoint or change it to natural gas supply
- source more energy from wind power
- reduce carbon emissions from vehicles, with higher taxes on fuel to reduce consumption
- introduce energy-efficiency certificates for houses for sale that were built before 1991
- initiate a grant-based tree-planting programme to reduce carbon emissions.

The sustainable use of forests

Sustainable use of forests means:
- conserving some forest regions
- managed use of other forests
- afforestation programmes.

Forestry in Scandinavia
- Over 200,000 hectares of forest are harvested each year.
- Seventy per cent is reforested manually. Natural regeneration occurs in the remaining area.

- Disease in forests is carefully controlled.
- Improved land drainage helps trees grow faster.
- Careful use of fertiliser increases yields.

The sustainable use of fish stocks (See page 186)

Fair trade

The meaning of fair trade

- All producers should be enabled to earn an adequate living by prices for produce, such as coffee, being index-linked to the prices charged by developed countries for manufactured goods such as coffee products.
- Fair wages and safe working environments should be provided for workers.
- Goods sold should be economically and ecologically sustainable.
- Third World countries should gain a reasonable degree of control over their own country's economy.
- Small-scale producers should be able to contribute to a country's exports.

key point

Globalised trade is driven by the aim of achieving constantly greater profits for multinational corporations.

This policy increases inequalities between rich and poor regions.

Globalised trade is not aimed at improving levels of human development.

The unfair existing global trading system

- The prices of Third World commodities fluctuate widely on the world market. This policy is encouraged by wealthy nations to their own benefit.
- The products of most multinationals are made in poor countries by people who work in poor working environments, such as sweat shops, for minimum wage.
- Some products, such as tropical hardwoods, are produced by destroying tropical forests.
- Trade barriers are created against some poor countries for political or other reasons.
- Multinationals (transnational corporations) have increased their control of world trade. Seventy per cent of global trade in wheat is now controlled by six multinationals.
- Changes by the International Monetary Fund (IMF) have reduced the control of governments over the activities of multinational companies.

Fairtrade Mark Ireland

- The Fairtrade Mark Ireland and other Fairtrade labelling organisations have been established to promote fairer trading practices of quality products.
- The Fairtrade Mark is a guarantee to consumers that the producers have been paid a fair price for their produce and that the producers work in safe and decent working conditions.

The Fairtrade system in practice

- The First World importers deal directly with the producers to eliminate middlemen.
- The producers are offered a guaranteed minimum price that is higher than the international market price.
- Some money is paid in advance to the producers and an additional premium is given for some local community projects.
- The producers must guarantee to provide a safe working environment and an eco-friendly production system.
- The Fairtrade Labelling Organisation International (FLO) certifies that the production process of the coffee has met its standards.
- The consumers are willing to pay about two cents extra per cup for this Fairtrade product.

How has Ireland and Europe responded to Fairtrade produce?

- Sales of Fairtrade-certified products in Ireland in 2009 were €33 million. Sales in the UK topped £800 million. Fairtrade products can now be found in over 3,000 independent Fairtrade shops and over 6,700 supermarkets all over Europe.

How has Fairtrade affected some producers?

- In the Volta Rivers Estate in Ghana, workers are now paid twice the national minimum wage and own 25 per cent of the company's shares.
- Toilets and showers are installed on the estate and water is piped to the workers' village.

How does Fairtrade produce affect the consumer?

- Fairtrade systems produce healthier foods.
- A more eco-friendly production system uses fewer chemicals than other growers.
- Banana crops are sprayed only 10 times annually, compared to 40 sprayings on other plantations.
- Chemicals such as paraquat are no longer used on Fairtrade crops. Some 20 per cent of male banana workers in Costa Rica were left sterile in recent years after handling toxic chemicals.

Justice and minority groups

Bonded labour

- Bonded labour is the most common form of slavery in the world today.
- About 20 million people are in bonded labour.
- About 4 million people are in bonded labour in Pakistan.
- Bonded labour exists in several Third World countries.

key point

The level of development of any society can be measured by the degree of justice with which that society treats its weakest members.

- Bonded labour begins when a person borrows money from an unscrupulous moneylender. In return the borrower agrees (bonds) to work for the moneylender until the loan is paid.
- Wages paid by the moneylender are low and insufficient to meet the interest, so the loan continues to increase.
- The bonded labourer/borrower is persuaded/forced to work indefinitely and without wages for the lender.
- Other family members may be forced to work against the loan and this can continue for generations, so that some family members are born into slavery.

In 1991 the Pakistani government banned the practice of bonded labour. But:

- moneylending landlords are people of influence and few are charged with the crime
- the Pakistani government denies that bonded labour is common in Pakistan
- they state that there are only 7,000 people in bonded labour. Human rights groups claim that over 4 million Pakistani people are in bonded labour
- there are no work-related government schemes for people who are freed from bonded labour.

The campaign for an end to bonded labour

- High Court rulings have helped free over 12,000 bonded labourers.
- The Rugmark label is an indication that no illegal child labour was involved in manufacturing.

Self-help development in Third World and peripheral regions

- It is increasingly important that people-centred development is undertaken by self-help development schemes in which responsibility rests with members of each scheme.
- Such groups can link up with and gain financial and other support from larger, well-established development bodies. These include:
  - NGOs such as Trócaire, Oxfam and Christian Aid
  - women's movements that work for basic salaries and the abolition of discrimination against women
  - cultural movements that help strengthen local cultures to counteract influences from westernised globalisation.

Case study: Self-reliance in Kerala, India

Regional government initiatives in Kerala have achieved the following results:

- The people of Kerala in southern India live on average more than 10 years longer than other Indians.
- They enjoy better health, education and transport services.
- There are fewer inequalities between males and females and between castes.

These results have been achieved through land reform and financial security.

- Over one million people were given direct access to land.
- Local co-operative credit was arranged to buy livestock and inexpensive hand tools.
- Community-based schemes provided clean, fresh water and primary healthcare to reduce disease and death rates.
- As people became more financially secure they had fewer children. Local family-planning campaigns helped reduce birth rates.

Case study: Self-help project in eastern Ethiopia: The eastern highlands project

Activities

- *Crop production:* farmers are provided with plentiful supplies of seeds and trained in crop-production techniques.
- *Livestock production:* farmers are assisted in animal breeding, poultry-rearing, bee-keeping and the production of animal feed.
- *Soil and water conservation and afforestation:* seed nurseries are established and trees and grasses planted in gullies to reduce erosion.
- *Education:* primary schools are being established in the area. Adult classes are conducted in environmental awareness, HIV awareness and family planning.
- *Public health:* the project supports the staffing and training of clinical staff, who focus on community vaccination programmes, health education and child nutrition.
- *Women's programme:* helps women to generate an income by learning skills such as needlework, dressmaking and market gardening.
- *Water supply:* wells are bored for small irrigation systems and domestic water supplies.

key point

Aims of project:

- to increase foodstuffs and farm income in a sustainable way
- to improve basic services
- to restore local natural resources.

exam Q

Questions 13, 2013; 14, 2015; 14, 2016.

Option 2: Geoecology

You must write your answer in **paragraphs** or you may lose cohesion marks.

MARKING SCHEME

Choose three or four headings/aspects for your answer. The marking scheme will be as follows:

Number of aspects:

- 3 aspects @ 20 marks each **or** 4 aspects @ 15 marks each
- Identifying heading/aspect — 4 marks
- Discussion — 8 × SRPs or 6 × SRPs
- Overall coherence — 20 marks graded
- Select scheme according to number of headings/aspects discussed
- Allow credit for up to 2 examples from SRPs.
- Allow for 2 labelled illustrations (different illustrations in different aspects).

Note: Some questions have alternative marking schemes, depending on the answers required.

30 The Development of Soils

aims You need to understand that soils develop from the weathering of rocks and from redeposited weathered material.

The scientific study of soils is known as **pedology**. Soil is the surface layer of loose material that covers much of the earth's land surface. It contains both organic and inorganic matter. It is part of the natural environment that links the relationship between bedrock, climate and vegetation.

Soil composition

All soils contain mineral particles, humus, water, air and living organisms such as bacteria.

Mineral matter

- A soil gets its mineral content from its parent material. The parent material can be bedrock that has been broken down by physical and chemical action, glacial deposits, river deposits or wind-blown deposits.
- Mineral content refers to minerals such as calcium, phosphorus, potassium, potash and other compounds.
- These are the foods that plants need in order to grow.
- The parent material determines the soil colour, depth, texture and pH value.

Organic matter

- Organic matter is also referred to as **humus**.
- Humus forms from decayed plants, and to a lesser degree from animal life through the action of bacteria and other micro-organisms.
- Humus also improves the texture of a soil.
- Humus binds soil particles together, which increases the soil's ability to hold moisture.
- Plant roots help to bind soil particles together.

Climate

- The distribution of the various soils coincides with the distribution of the world's climate.
- So climate influences the type of vegetation that grows in a region.
- The greater the amount of vegetation that grows in a region, the greater the humus content of the soil.
- Climate influences the rate at which weathering of the soil and decay of its plant matter occur.

- Heavy rainfall causes **leaching** of the soil's minerals.
- **Weathering** is the first state of soil formation.

Slope and water movement

- Steep slopes encourage the removal of fine particles by rainwater.
- Gentle and flat slopes encourage the accumulation of fine particles.
- When rainfall is greater than evaporation, water moves from the surface layer to lower layers, carrying nutrients down with it. This process is called **leaching**.
- The downward movement of water may create a hard pan that can prevent drainage and lead to waterlogging.

Air

- Air is vital in the soil for **oxidation**, which converts parts of the organic matter into oxygen.
- Air is also vital for the bacteria present in the soil, which require oxygen and are therefore said to be **aerobic**.

Soil characteristics

Texture

- Texture refers to the proportions of sand, silt and clay particles that make up the soil.
- Texture determines the soil's ability to:
  1. retain and transmit moisture
  2. retain nutrients
  3. allow roots to penetrate it.
- **Sandy soils** consist of 70 per cent or more sand particles by weight and have few nutrients. They feel gritty to rub.
- **Clay soils** consist of 50 per cent clay particles by weight. Clay soils are rich in nutrients, but are likely to become waterlogged. They feel sticky or plastic when wet.
- **Silty soils** are intermediate between sandy and clay soils. Silty soils have a smooth, soap-like feel.
- **Loam soils** are ideal for agriculture. They contain a mixture of particles of many different sizes. Loamy soils are well aerated, with some moisture and plant food.

Colour

- Humus-rich soils are dark brown or black in colour.
- Brown soils of temperate forest lands, such as Europe, get their colour from decayed leaves and plant particles.
- Organic matter, such as leaves, in rainforest soils decays rapidly owing to the high humidity of the forest floor.
- Dark soils absorb more sunlight and so are warmer than light-coloured soils.
- Warm soils aid germination of seeds and have a long growing season.

- Soil texture can be determined by examining a soil sample. This can be done by mixing a soil sample with water in a jar.

Soil structure

- Soil structure refers to the shape of the soil grains or particles.
- In undisturbed soils, the clustering of particles forms different shapes known as **peds**.
- The shape and alignment of the peds, together with their size, determine the size and number of pore spaces through which air, water and organisms can pass.
- Soils with a **crumb structure** give the highest agricultural yield because it provides the best balance between air, water and nutrients.

Water content

- Water moves downwards by **percolation** and upwards by **capillary attraction**.
- Water in the soil becomes a weak solution of many mineral compounds.
- The chemical processes that take place in a soil do so mainly in solution.
- Water content varies between soils, from almost nil in arid climates to waterlogging in wet clay soils.
- Constant percolation of water downwards in mid to high latitudes, owing to high rainfall, causes leaching.
- **Leaching** is a process whereby minerals are drawn downwards from the upper horizon at the surface, to lower horizons. Leaching creates **podzol** soils.

Organic content

- Organic matter includes humus, and is formed mostly from decaying plants and animals.
- Humus gives the soil a dark colour.
- The highest amounts of organic matter are found in the **chernozems** or **black earths** of the North American prairies, Russian steppes and Argentinian pampas.
- Fallen leaves and decaying grasses and roots are the main sources of organic matter.
- Soil organisms, such as bacteria and fungi, break down the organic matter.
- Where soil organisms are present and active they will mix the plant litter into the A horizon, where it decomposes into humus.

pH value

- A soil's **pH** measures its acidity or alkalinity.
- A soil with a low pH value is said to be **acidic**. This happens when minerals such as calcium, magnesium and potassium are leached by heavy rain.
- A very low pH, or acid soil, slows down decomposition and may even prevent decay, as in the creation of peat.
- A high pH means an **alkaline** soil. This indicates it has a high calcium (lime), magnesium and potassium content.

Questions 18, 2013; 16, 2014; 16, 2015.

31 Factors that Affect Soil Characteristics

 You need to know:

- the factors that affect soil characteristics
- how people interfere with these processes.

Factors that affect soil formation

Parent material

- If the soil is composed of unconsolidated deposits such as boulder clay, soil formation will occur more rapidly than if it were bedrock.
- Soils inherit their characteristics from parent material.
- Soil from limestone areas will contain calcium and other minerals and will become alkaline.
- Soils from sandstone regions will be free-draining and sandy and will heat up quickly in spring.
- Soils from clay regions will have poor drainage and may become waterlogged.

Climate

Effects of temperature and precipitation include:

- constant heat and moisture encourage constant growth
- soils in hot, wet regions tend to have lots of vegetative cover, such as rainforest or monsoon forest
- decomposition occurs rapidly
- chemical weathering occurs rapidly, creating deep-red soils
- heavy rainfall causes leaching
- long spells of drought, such as may occur in grassland regions, tend to increase the amount of minerals, such as calcium, by evaporation.

Topography

- Deep soils develop on level surfaces.
- Where slopes are steep, thin soils develop, owing to erosion by runoff and gravity.
- Gently sloping ground helps drainage.
- High ground is exposed and is cold.
- Soils on high ground are generally thin, with few minerals.
- South-facing slopes are generally warmer and encourage growth early in the season.

Living organisms

- Plant roots help to bring soil particles together, which is especially important on steep slopes.
- Plant roots absorb moisture and nutrients.
- Worms, beetles and other insects help to aerate the soil.
- Insects, fungi and bacteria break down plant matter.

Time

- Soils develop over long periods, often thousands of years.
- Soils can also be eroded away in short spells, over years or even months. Example: wind erosion in the Dust Bowl of North America.
- Soils may develop quickly or slowly, depending on the parent material.

Water-retention properties

- Water in the soil is essential for plant growth.
- When water is absent plants wither and die unless they are adapted to drought conditions, as desert plants are.
- Water-retention rates are determined by soil structure and texture.
- Clay soils can hold more water than sandy soils.
- Too many clay particles lead to waterlogging.

Processes that influence soil formation

SAMPLE EXAM QUESTION AND ANSWER

Question:

Examine two of the natural processes which influence soil formation.

Answer:

Aspect 1 – Leaching

- Leaching is a process whereby soluble minerals are dissolved by percolating ground water and are washed down to lower horizons in the soil where they are deposited. Leaching is widespread in the wet climate of the West of Ireland and at the Equator in latosol soils.
- Tropical latosols (equatorial soils) are exposed to daily torrential downpours. Iron compounds in the soil are oxidised and turn the soil a red colour. These red soils are called laterites. Laterisation is a form of extreme leaching. The high temperatures of the tropics contribute to leaching/laterisation by speeding up the chemical reactions of water on rocks, such as the oxidation of minerals like iron.
- Latosols are very poor in nutrients due to the leaching process. Nutrients are mainly confined to the surface where there is decomposing leaf litter and dead plant matter.
- The chemical weathering of rainforest soil creates many important mineral deposits through a process called 'secondary enrichment'. This occurs

because chemical weathering and percolating water together concentrate the small amounts of metals that are widely scattered throughout the soils into economically valuable concentrations.

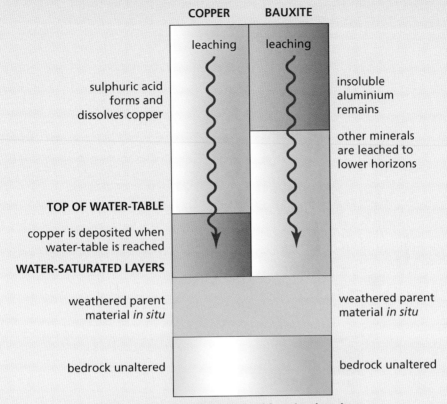

Soil profile of leached mineral-bearing laterite

- For example, **bauxite**, the principal ore from which aluminium is made, is formed due to leaching. When aluminium-rich soils are subjected to the intense and prolonged weathering of the tropics, most of the common elements, including calcium, sodium and silicon, are removed by leaching. Because aluminium is extremely insoluble, it becomes concentrated at the surface as bauxite.
- Secondary enrichment of **iron ore** may also occur when soluble iron compounds are washed down through leaching and deposited in lower horizons to form a concentrate of iron ore, such as magnetite.

Aspect 2 – Podzolisation

- Podzolisation is an extreme form of leaching by acidic ground water. It occurs in cool areas of heavy rainfall such as on many of Ireland's uplands and highlands. It also occurs in Boreal regions of coniferous forest or moorland vegetation. Groundwater is generally acidic but becomes more acidic when it percolates through decayed or dead vegetation. Acid rain also increases podzolisation.
- Podzol soils form under coniferous forests because pine needles are slow to compose and form acid soils. Regions of coniferous forest such as bogs in

the West of Ireland and mountain regions such as the Scandinavian highlands may create acid soils due to the rotting of the granite rocks that form them. The acidic ground water dissolves all soil minerals except silica in the form of quartz. Quartz is a very weather-resistant mineral.

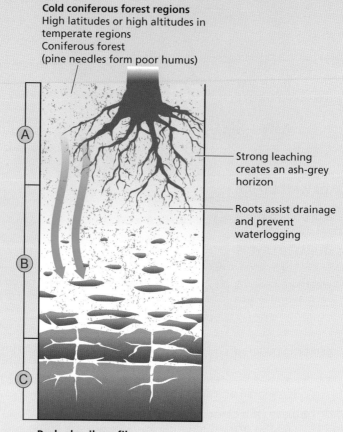

Cold coniferous forest regions
High latitudes or high altitudes in temperate regions
Coniferous forest
(pine needles form poor humus)

Strong leaching creates an ash-grey horizon

Roots assist drainage and prevent waterlogging

Podzol soil profile

- Podzol soils have a very distinctive soil profile. The A horizon has a bleached or very pale colour due to the presence of these quartz crystals and because it has been drained of coloured minerals.
- The B horizon below is enriched with the dissolved minerals and is darker in colour. The B horizon may also contain a layer of reddish iron oxide (rust). This rust acts as a cementing agent and forms an impermeable layer through which percolating ground water cannot pass. This layer is called the hard pan.
- The stony C horizon sits directly on the bedrock.

Aspect 3 – Salinisation

- Hot, dry regions experience the reverse process to leaching. **Evaporation** and **capillary attraction** cause salts in ground water to rise through the soil and build up in the upper layers. Salt is deposited on the surface as a hard white crust. If the salt concentration becomes too high, plants are poisoned and die. The roughing of the surface soil helps reduce the effect of capillary attraction and evaporation.

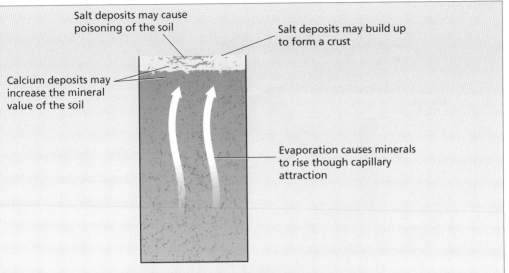

Salt deposits may cause poisoning of the soil

Salt deposits may build up to form a crust

Calcium deposits may increase the mineral value of the soil

Evaporation causes minerals to rise though capillary attraction

Calcification and salinisation

- Salinisation is a problem for farmers who have to wash the salt away or break up the crust before their crops can be sown.
- Irrigation is a process where reservoir or well water is sprayed on surface soil to water plants in dry regions. The evaporation of this water causes a salt deposit to build up over time and may lead to soil poisoning if it is not carefully managed. This effect can be reduced by growing crops that need less water. Irrigation salinisation in Australia is estimated to cost the farming community €307 million each year. Southern California is also a hot, dry region that is intensely irrigated and has salinisation problems.
- **Calcification** results in calcium being built up close to the surface of the soil. This helps make the soil very fertile. Chernozem soils, or 'black earth' soils of the steppes of Russia and the Ukraine are grasslands where calcification occurs naturally. Chernozems are also found in the prairies of North America.

Classification of soils

World soil maps do not always show the soils as they exist in reality; instead they show the zonal soil most likely to occur in a region.

There are three basic soil groups: **zonal**, **intrazonal** and **azonal**.

Zonal soils

Zonal soils are classified according to the climate zone in which they occur. They are mature soils with distinctive profiles and clear horizons. They include the following.

Tundra soils

- These are soils in Arctic regions. *Examples:* northern Canada, Scandinavia, Russia.
- Vegetation consists of lichens, shrubs and mosses.
- They have a shallow, brown to dark-grey A horizon.
- The subsoil is permanently frozen (**permafrost**).

Latosols

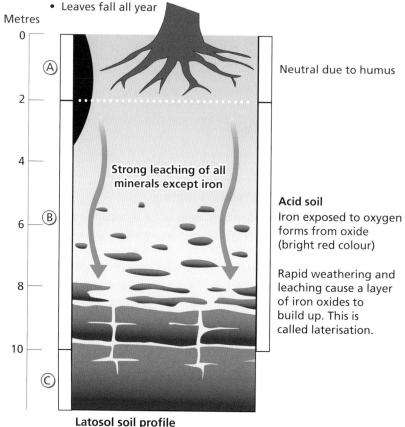

Tropical regions
- High rainfall and temperatures
- Bacteria alive throughout the year
- Roots on surface or close to surface
- Leaves fall all year

Neutral due to humus

Strong leaching of all minerals except iron

Acid soil
Iron exposed to oxygen forms from oxide (bright red colour)

Rapid weathering and leaching cause a layer of iron oxides to build up. This is called laterisation.

Latosol soil profile

- These are soils of hot, humid regions in the tropics. *Examples:* India, Indonesia, Brazil.
- High rainfall has leached out most minerals except for iron and aluminium oxides.
- Iron oxides in the B horizons tint the soil a red colour, forming laterite.
- Chemical weathering is dominant and plant matter is broken down quickly.
- They are generally soils of a tropical region such as rainforest or monsoon forest.

Podzols

- These soils occur in the coniferous forest belt in northern latitudes.
- Pine needles form the ground cover beneath the forest canopy.
- Percolating rainwater leaches out surface minerals that are redeposited to form a hard pan, which creates waterlogging.
- They are acidic and need large amounts of lime and fertiliser to make them fertile.

Chernozems (Black earths)

- These are found in temperate grassland regions. *Examples:* the steppes of Russia and the Ukraine, the pampas of Argentina, the prairies of North America.

- Because rainfall is low, the A horizon is black owing to a high humus content and little leaching.
- Calcium deposits are deposited in the B horizon.
- They are neutral soils with a crumb structure and are very fertile.

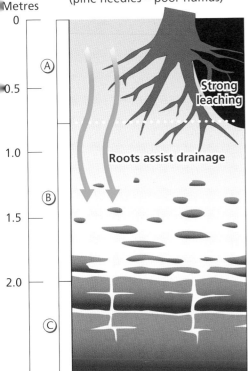

Cold regions

High latitudes or high altitudes in temperate regions
Coniferous forest
(pine needles – poor humus)

Strong leaching

Roots assist drainage

Podzol soil profile

Temperate regions

Grassland

Water washes calcium down (calcification)

Chernozem soil profile

Desert soils

- These occur in hot, dry regions of arid and semi-arid regions in temperate and tropical areas. *Examples:* the Atacama in Peru and Chile, and the Californian and Nevada deserts.
- Humus is limited, owing to the almost complete absence of vegetation.
- Intense sunshine creates salt deposits from evaporation of ground moisture. This process is called **salinisation**.

Identify some plant characteristics in this photograph that help desert plants survive long periods of drought

Intrazonal soils

Intrazonal soils are individual soils that develop within regions of zonal soils where local factors such as parent material or drainage may have a more dominant effect than climate.

Peat soils

- Peat soils are black and the surface material consists of partially decayed vegetation. The remaining soil consists of dead plant matter.
- They form in regions of cold that have persistent rainfall.
- They support only acid-loving plants such as rhododendron and heathers.

There are two types of peat soil in Ireland:

Blanket peat

- Blanket peat covers hill and mountain tops inland and along the counties of the west coast.
- Acid groundwater prevents decay of plant matter.
- It is shallow: only about two metres deep.

Raised peat

- Raised peat developed in shallow lakes.
- These may be 10 metres or more in depth and have been exploited commercially.

Gley soils

- These form in waterlogged regions because of the presence of impermeable soils such as shales or clay.
- They have a blue-grey colour owing to lack of oxygen, and that prevents decay.
- They are found in the Cavan–Dundalk drumlin landscape, in Antrim–Derry coastal regions and in South Clare.

Rendzinas

- These form in limestone and chalk regions, and their surface cover consists of grasses.
- The A horizon is black or dark brown. There is no B horizon.
- The surface soil sits directly on the bedrock.
- This kind of soil is suited to beef cattle rearing, as in the Burren or karst regions.

Terra rossas

- These are mature, limestone-based soils.
- Iron minerals in the soil have been oxidised, creating a red soil.
- Terra rossa soils are found in the Mezzogiorno in southern Italy and in the coffee-growing regions of Brazil.

Azonal soils

- Azonal soils are soils with an immature profile that have not had time to develop fully.
- The parent material may be weathered rock or debris that may have been transported from some other location by ice.
- Their location is not confined to any specific climatic zone.

Lithosols

- These are stony, shallow soils formed from the weathering of the bedrock.
- Erosion and sometimes mass movement may prevent the development of a soil profile.
- They are common on upland slopes.

Regosols

- These are derived from volcanic deposits, sand deposits or alluvial deposits.
- The A horizon is light in colour.
- There is no B horizon.
- The C horizon consists of silt or sand or a mixture of both.
- These soils form alluvial deposits on river floodplains, such as the Tigris–Euphrates rivers in Iraq and the Indus and Ganges flood plains in India and Pakistan.

A sample exam question and answer on brown earth soil can be found on moresuccess.ie.

Human interference with soil characteristics

Overcropping and overgrazing

Irish example: the Burren in Co. Clare (see page 287).

See how people interact with biomes on pages 287–290.

SAMPLE EXAM QUESTION AND ANSWER

Question: Various soil patterns have developed in different regions of the world because of the action of different soil forming processes. Discuss. (2016)

Answer:

Soils contain many minerals that are determined by the parent rocks from which they form. Other factors, such as climate topography and time, interact with these minerals to form various soil profiles.

This answer may be used to answer alternative questions, e.g. soil profiles are the result of the operation of soil-forming processes. Discuss.

Laterisation

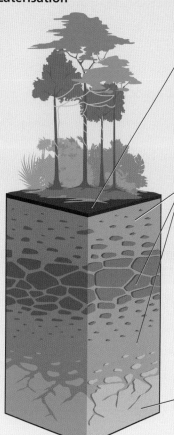

O horizon
There is a thick **litter layer** with a continuous supply of litter from falling leaves and branches

There is a very thin but fertile **humus** layer

Decomposition of organic matter, aided by bacterial activity, is rapid, taking just a few days

A, B and C horizons
Soil horizons are not very distinct due to the continuous abundance of **mixing agents**

There is a great depth of soil as a result of extreme weathering (including laterisation)

The soil has a **red colour** due to the presence of iron oxide (rust), which remains in the soil after other minerals have been removed by leaching

Nutrients rarely reach these lower layers. If they do, they are rapidly leached downwards, leaving the soil infertile

Bedrock
The bedrock is also subject to rapid **chemical weathering**

Profile of a laterite soil

- Laterite soils have developed in **regions of tropical and equatorial climate** where chemical weathering occurs at intense rates. These climates **support rainforest or tropical savannah vegetation**. Tropical forest experiences heavy rainfall, approximately 2,000 mm, and constant high temperatures of 30°C annually. Tropical savannah experiences almost these same conditions for six months of the year.

- World examples include the Savanna grassland in Africa; the Congo Basin in Zaire.

- The drenching rains and high temperatures of these climates promote **extensive soil leaching**, which removes humus and the other soluble minerals. The remaining insoluble minerals undergo intense biological and chemical weathering. The **rapid leaching means that horizons are poorly developed** and the soil does not retain its fertility and so can be infertile, yet they can support a luxuriant forest cover due to the nutrient-rich thin top layer. The nutrient cycle is short. Plants grow rapidly, otherwise they will not get the nutrients before they are leached by high rainfall.

- Some minerals absorb water through **hydration and hydrolysis**. The minerals expand, causing stress within the minerals that break them apart to form soil. The **presence of heat and water oxidise the insoluble minerals such as iron compounds** that remain to give the soil a red or yellow colour. This distinctive soil type is known as latosol. The texture of latosols varies from clay, silt, sand or loam because the parent rock may also vary. Latosols are wet soils once they have a cover of vegetation. If this is removed, they dry up very quickly and can form a hard brick-like crust that is impossible to till.

Humification: Brown earths

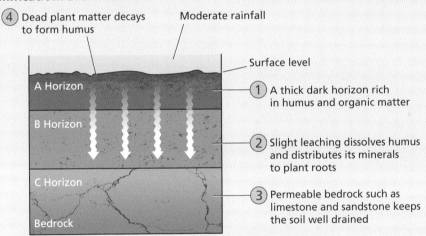

The makeup of brown earth

- Brown earth soils are generally **located between 35° and 55° north of the equator.** This is a region with a humid temperate climate where rainfall totals are approximately 600–1,000 mm per year, and temperatures range between 4°C in winter to 18°C in summer. These temperature and rainfall totals allow them to be well-drained soils with well developed A and B horizons with a pH of between 5 and 7.

- World examples of brown earths are found in the lowlands of **Central Plain of Ireland** and the **lowlands of Western Europe**, such as the **Paris Basin**.

- Brown earths have a high organic content. They were formed in low-lying areas of temperate climate **where deciduous forests grew.** The forests provided an abundance of leaf fall and dead organic matter, such as plant litter from dead oak, beech, chestnut and elm branches, and trunks that decayed and accumulated on the forest floor.

- The organic content develops because of the **process of humification**. Humification is the way dead organic matter is converted into a black gel called humus by the action of fungi and bacteria on dead things. The rain washes the humus into the soil, which raises its fertility. The **humus also helps bind soil particles together** and so it influences the crumb structure of the soil. This structure determines the size and amount of pore spaces between the soil crumbs and the amount of water a soil can hold or release as runoff.

- In these climatic conditions, leaching is the process by which humus and other plant nutrients are washed by rainwater down through the soil. Slight leaching has the beneficial effect of dissolving humus and distributing it to plant roots that absorb soluble minerals. The **pH levels of 5 to 7 favour the growth of most Irish agricultural crops**, including grass and barley.

- Due to the mild climatic conditions, the original deciduous forest cover and brown earths support a wide variety of creatures, such as earthworms, which aerate the soil by creating burrow holes for drainage and aeration. They also carry humus from the A horizon to lower horizons, and carry minerals from lower layers back to the surface, thus enriching and mixing the soil minerals and particles.

Podzolization

- Podzols are most common in mountain areas at high altitudes and in **Boreal regions** of the world **between 50° and 70° north** where coniferous forest, called taiga, grows. The soils of the Boreal Forest are at their most extensive in the northern hemisphere where the landmasses are at their broadest, and they extend right across the North American and Eurasian continents.

- World examples of podzols are found in the **coniferous forests of Scandinavia**, the **coniferous forest regions of Eurasia and North America**.

- The podzols of the Boreal Forest have mostly conifers of spruce, pine, cedar and larch trees, with some shallow-rooted deciduous species, such as birch, aspen and willow. The vegetation must withstand very cold average annual temperatures of –5°C to +5°C. Summers are short, about 1–3 months and always less than 4 months. Winter temperatures may drop as low as –50°C. These cold temperatures throughout the year limit the decay of vegetation. Snow may remain on the ground for as long as nine months in the most northern regions of the forest.

- The evergreen needles create acids, which leach the soil of the limited minerals with the exception of quartz, that form during the year. This leaching creates the typical profile of a podzol with its greyish subsoil colour. Moisture is also limited due to the presence of permanently frozen subsoil, called permafrost. Taiga soils tends to be very acidic, with a pH of 4.5, undeveloped and poor in nutrients. It lacks the deep, organically enriched profile present in temperate deciduous forests. The thinness of the soil is due largely to the cold, which hinders decay.

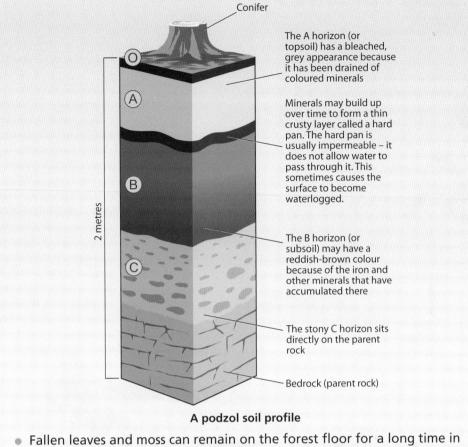

Conifer

The A horizon (or topsoil) has a bleached, grey appearance because it has been drained of coloured minerals

Minerals may build up over time to form a thin crusty layer called a hard pan. The hard pan is usually impermeable – it does not allow water to pass through it. This sometimes causes the surface to become waterlogged.

The B horizon (or subsoil) may have a reddish-brown colour because of the iron and other minerals that have accumulated there

The stony C horizon sits directly on the parent rock

Bedrock (parent rock)

2 metres

A podzol soil profile

- Fallen leaves and moss can remain on the forest floor for a long time in the cool, moist climate, which limits their organic contribution to the soil. The forest floor has only pine needles, lichens and some mosses growing on it. The soil is leached and displays the typical podzol profile with a greyish subsoil profile. In clearings in the forest and in areas with more Boreal deciduous trees, there are more herbs and berries growing. Diversity of soil organisms in the Boreal Forest is high, comparable to the tropical rainforest.

exam Q

Questions 18, 2010; 16, 2012; 17, 2016.

32 Biomes

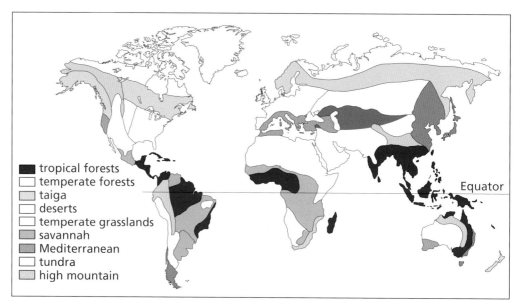

- tropical forests
- temperate forests
- taiga
- deserts
- temperate grasslands
- savannah
- Mediterranean
- tundra
- high mountain

Equator

The nine major biomes of the world

Temperate deciduous biome in Europe

An Irish and European example: Brown earths – An Irish soil profile

- **Brown earths** are found in temperate regions of deciduous forest.
- Because there is little leaching there are no distinct horizons. However, the A horizon is a little darker than others.
- They have a crumb structure and are naturally very fertile.
- Many earthworms and living organisms are found in them.

Location

Found on the western side of continents, between 40° and 60° north and south of the Equator.

Climate – Influencing factors

- Close to mild, moist ocean conditions.
- Affected by warm, moist south-westerly winds.
- Average winter temperatures 4–6°C.
- Average summer temperatures 15–16°C.
- Moisture throughout the year, with a winter maximum of 1,000–1,500 mm.

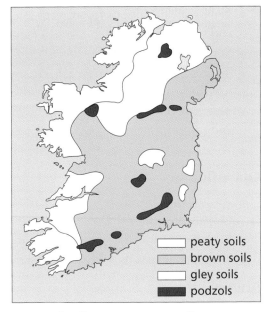

Ireland's most common soil types

peaty soils
brown soils
gley soils
podzols

Natural vegetation

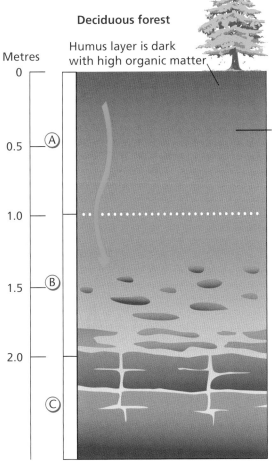

Deciduous forest

Humus layer is dark with high organic matter

Metres

Rich in mineral matter called **topsoil**. Many living organisms

- Soil is brown, well aerated
- Soil originally developed under deciduous forest cover (before agricultural practices) and influenced by **glacial deposits**

Brown earth profile

- Temperate deciduous forest, with ash, oak, elm, beech, chestnut, hazel, hawthorn and sycamore.
- Some layering.
- Tallest: oaks; second layer: ash, chestnut, elm and beech; third layer; hazel and hawthorn.
- Tree type influenced by soil type, as local soils vary depending on slope, bedrock and soil composition.
- Forest floor has many plants, such as ferns, mosses, brambles, orchids.

Soil influence

- Autumn leaf fall allows recycling of nutrients, humus is created by bacteria, and osmosis absorbs nutrients into the trees, creating new leaves.
- Earthworms mix this plant debris throughout the A horizon.
- These are deep soils, with some tree roots reaching and breaking up the bedrock.

Animal life

Grey and red squirrel, badger, fox, rodents, wild boar, wolf, rabbit, hare. Many of these have become extinct in some regions as a result of human interference.

Human interference

- Most woodland has been cut down to make way for agriculture.
- Grazing animals keeps landscape open (without trees).
- Oaks were cut down for large wooden galleons during colonisation.
- Farming has added many nutrients by means of artificial fertilisers.

Case study: The Burren in Co. Clare

- Woodland cover was cut down for farming.
- Soil was tilled by early farmers and exposed to strong westerly winds.
- Soil was eroded, leaving bare, rocky, limestone landscape called karst.

Equatorial Forest biome

SAMPLE EXAM QUESTION AND ANSWER

Question: Describe and explain the main characteristics of one biome that you have studied.   (2013–2016)

Answer:

The Equatorial Forest biome

1. Climate

- This region extends right across the globe between latitudes 5° north and south of the Equator, so it has an equatorial climate. The angle of the noonday sun varies only from 90 degrees, when the sun is directly overhead at the Equator, to 66 degrees, when it is directly over the Tropic of Cancer (on 21 June) or the Tropic of Capricorn (on 22 December). So sunlight hits the earth directly, **not at an angle**. Average temperature each month is about 27°C and the annual range is only 2°C.

- The temperature rarely gets higher than 35°C or drops below 24°C. This is due to consistent cloud cover that blankets the equatorial skies over the forest. In reality, rainforests can feel much hotter than this due to the intense humidity of the region.

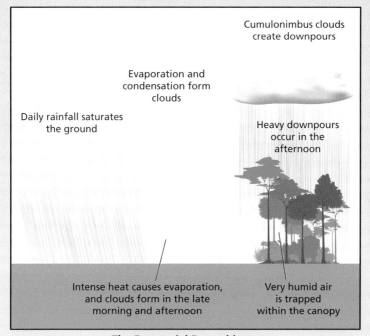

Cumulonimbus clouds
create downpours

Evaporation and
condensation form
clouds

Daily rainfall saturates
the ground

Heavy downpours
occur in the
afternoon

Intense heat causes evaporation,
and clouds form in the late
morning and afternoon

Very humid air
is trapped
within the canopy

The Equatorial Forest biome

- **Relative humidity** at ground level may often reach as much as 88 per cent. Transpiration from the trees generates high levels of water vapour and the high temperatures increase the ability of the air to hold this moisture.
- Rainfall amount varies as the sun travels from the Tropic of Cancer to the Tropic of Capricorn. This gives a slight dry-season effect at the edges of the forest zone. Rainfall totals vary but it is always in excess of 2,500 mm in each of the forest zones across the globe. Parts of Sumatra gets 4,500 mm annually.
- **Rain falls in short, heavy downpours**, with strong winds that often shake the canopy. The forest floor becomes temporarily flooded but quickly filters through the soil cover.
- The largest and most famous rainforest is in the Amazon Basin that includes parts of Ecuador, Venezuela, Peru, Bolivia and Brazil. Other regions include the Congo Basin, Indonesia and northern Australia.

2. Soil

- The latosol is the zonal soil associated with tropical rainforests. Latosols are **poor in nutrients** due to leaching by the heavy rains over thousands of years. The soil has a red colour due the oxidation of iron compounds.
- **The rainforest has a very short nutrient cycle.** Nutrients are mainly found in the living plants and the layers of the decomposing leaf litter on the surface

(the O horizon). The high humidity and the various decomposers such as insects, bacteria and fungi quickly convert this dead plant and animal life into humus. Plant roots absorb these nutrients the moment they are released. Ninety-nine per cent of nutrients are held in the root mats of the forest floor.

- Only 5–8 per cent of sunlight reaches the forest floor, so the soil and undergrowth are deprived of this source of energy.

- The chemical weathering of rainforest soil creates many important mineral deposits through a process called 'secondary enrichment'. This occurs because chemical weathering and percolating water concentrate the small amounts of metals that are widely scattered throughout the soils into economically valuable concentrations.

O horizon
There is a thick **litter layer** with a continuous supply of litter from falling leaves and branches

There is a very thin but fertile **humus** layer

Decomposition of organic matter, aided by bacterial activity, is rapid, taking just a few days

A, B and C horizons
Soil horizons are not very distinct due to the continuous abundance of **mixing agents**

There is a great depth of soil as a result of extreme weathering (including laterisation)

The soil has a **red colour** due to the presence of iron oxide (rust), which remains in the soil after other minerals have been removed by leaching

Nutrients rarely reach these lower layers. If they do, they are rapidly leached downwards, leaving the soil infertile

Bedrock
The bedrock is also subject to rapid **chemical weathering**

Profile of a laterite soil

- For example, Bauxite, the principal ore from which aluminium is made, is formed due to leaching. When aluminium-rich soils are subjected to the intense and prolonged weathering of the tropics, most of the common elements, including calcium, sodium and silicon, are removed by leaching. Because aluminium is extremely insoluble, it becomes concentrated at the surface as bauxite.

- Secondary enrichment of iron ore may also occur when soluble iron compounds are washed down through leaching and deposited in lower horizons to form a concentrate of iron ore, such as haematite.

3. Plant life (flora)

- There are four distinct layers of vegetation in a rainforest: the emergers; the canopy; the understorey; and the forest floor.

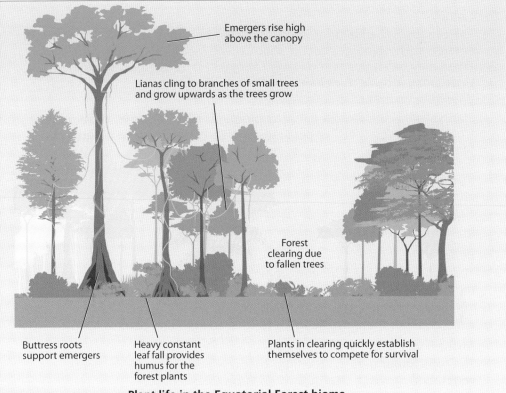

Emergers rise high above the canopy

Lianas cling to branches of small trees and grow upwards as the trees grow

Forest clearing due to fallen trees

Buttress roots support emergers

Heavy constant leaf fall provides humus for the forest plants

Plants in clearing quickly establish themselves to compete for survival

Plant life in the Equatorial Forest biome

Emergers

- The **emergers are the tallest trees** (up to 80 metres high). They are spaced far apart with umbrella-shaped branches that stand well above the canopy. Because these trees are exposed to drying winds, they tend to have small, pointed leaves.

- These giant trees have straight smooth trunks with few branches. Their root system is very shallow but they have large buttress roots that spread out as much as nine metres to support such tall trees in the wet soils. Many of these trees are tropical hardwoods, such as teak.

Identify the buttress roots on these emergers

The canopy
- The canopy is the main forest cover of tree tops that form a layer below the emergers. The canopy is found about 20–40 metres above the ground. There may be an upper and lower canopy in some regions. Some plants of the canopy include thick **lianas** and epiphytes, like mosses, lichens and flowering orchids.
- Plants such as the orchids get their inorganic nutrients from the air and from rainfall and they live perched on branch joints. Unlike plants in the temperate deciduous biome, some of these plants have drip tips to shed water quickly. Some waxy jug-like leaves allow plants to gather as much water as possible during downpours and then discard it before it stagnates and breeds bacteria.
- Some leaves are able to turn with the sun so they always absorb the maximum amount of sunlight.

The understorey
- The understorey is a dark environment that is under the canopy. Most of the understorey of a rainforest has so little light that plant growth is limited.
- There are short, leafy, mostly non-flowering shrubs, small trees, ferns and vines or lianas that have adapted to filtered light and poor soil.

The forest floor
- The forest floor gets so little light that few plants grow here. Dense vegetation grows in clearings when large trees fall.
- Plants such as lianas cling to the tiny branches of young plants. As the trees grow so too do the lianas as they hang from forest branches for support.
- Only the most vigorous plants in the clearings survive to reach the sunlight.

4. Fauna (animal life)
- **Camouflage** is one very effective way in which animals adapt to their environment. One of the most effective ways to adapt and be safe is to look like a leaf. Moths and other insects may look like dead or living leaves and are difficult to see amid the surrounding foliage.
- The rainforest floor is littered with dead leaves: insects are abundant here and may be in danger from predators, so they adapt their camouflage to their surroundings. There are many varieties of stick insect that look like a twig. Tree frogs also use camouflage.
- Animals also use colour to warn predators that they are poisonous. For many this is just a bluff but some, such as the poison arrow frog and some snakes, are poisonous. Bright colours generally indicate danger.

Tree trunk environment
- There are many environments within rainforests and each environment has its own population of insects and animal life. For example, woodpeckers drill holes in dead tree trunks because the wood is soft and easy to penetrate. They use these holes to make their nests. Living trees are also used by some woodpeckers. Tree sap seeps from these tree-wounds and acts as an irritant to snakes that try to seek out the woodpeckers' nests.
- Other animals, such as some monkeys or birds, use these holes once they become unoccupied.

- Some birds feed on insects going up a tree while other birds feed on them as they come down, depending on the location of insects in the bark.

Pollination
- Plants use nectar in their flowers to attract insects to aid pollination. Other plants, such as kapok, have fluffy tops attached to their seeds for dispersal by the wind. Kapok is an emerger so it needs its seeds to be carried far away to ensure its survival.

Desert biome

A desert region is an area characterised by little or no rainfall, where vegetation is sparse or absent.

Small local areas may have lush vegetation if water is available close to the surface. Such areas are called **oases**.

Desert characteristics

- Deserts may be either hot or cold, with less than 250 mm of precipitation annually.
- Desert surfaces are generally boulders, gravels, bare rock or sand.
- All deserts have their own characteristic fauna and flora.
- Desert moisture is unpredictable in distribution and amount.
- Rainfall may occur in sudden downpours in localised areas, creating flash floods.
- Coastal mists may affect coastal deserts where there are cold currents offshore.
- Hot deserts lie between 15° and 30° north and south of the Equator.
- They are affected by the trade winds, which create high-pressure zones.
- Compression of the descending air causes it to heat and retain its moisture.
- Clear blue skies and sunny weather dominate.
- Some hot deserts result from the rain-shadow effect, for example the Atacama and the Kalahari. Here coastal mountains create rain on the windward side, and are sufficiently high so that winds are dry as they descend on the rain-shadow side, creating drought.
- Temperate deserts lie between 30° and 40° north and south of the Equator.
- Some deserts are also affected by rain-shadow and cold ocean currents, for example the Patagonian Desert in Argentina.

Case study: North American deserts

- The North American deserts include four regions: the Chihuahua Desert, the Sonora Desert, the Mojave Desert and the Great Basin.
- They lie between the Rocky Mountains and the Sierra Nevada mountains.
- The Mojave, Sonora and Chihuahua are hot deserts.
- The Great Basin is colder because it is more elevated than the others.

Climatic characteristics

- All suffer extremely long drought periods.
- Localised summer downpours create flash floods.
- Temperature in winter is about 8°C, while summer temperatures average 30°C.
- Diurnal range can be as great as 30°C, owing to lack of cloud cover.

Soils

- Soils are aridsols.
- Soil texture varies from fine sand to gravel and stony.
- Some regions have deep soil deposits from continuous deposition of surface streams.
- Soils are poorly developed, owing to the absence of moisture for break-up of minerals and the lack of plant matter.
- Intense evaporation creates alkaline soils with calcium, sodium and gypsum minerals.
- Calcification is the dominant process.
- Salinisation is also common, creating salt deposits in saltpans.

Vegetation

- Some plants have adapted well to the short downpours. These are **ephemerals** that complete their life cycle in two to three weeks.
- Ephemerals open their seed pods during the downpours as a physical reaction to the water. They sprout quickly, flower, pollinate and die within a short time.
- Some plants, such as the giant saguaro, store water. It has the following characteristics:

  1. needle leaves to break the wind, creating a cooling effect for the plant

  2. vertical grooves to direct water to its base, where its roots absorb it quickly

  3. waxy bark to prevent evaporation.
- Cacti are common in American deserts.

Fauna

- Desert regions have few animals owing to the lack of water supply. Those that do live in these hot, dry regions have adapted to their surroundings.
- Nocturnal or early-morning animals include the rattlesnake and the elf owl.
- The tarantula, the desert tortoise and kangaroo rat burrow into the sand to avoid the hot sunshine.
- Some animals, such as the rabbit, are dormant during the hot summer.
- Reptiles produce uric acid instead of urine, so they waste little water.
- The roadrunner, a desert bird, runs instead of flying to reduce energy loss.

Questions 17, 2013; 18, 2014, 18, 2015; 18, 2016.

33 How People's Activities have Altered Biomes

 aims You need to understand how people's activities have interfered with biomes.

Early settlement and the clearing of forest cover

- Farming, more than any other activity, has led to deforestation on a world scale.
- The knowledge of farming spread from the Middle East to Europe. It was first practised in the Middle East about 10,000 years ago.
- It reached Ireland about 6,000 years ago.
- It led to deforestation on a large scale in some regions, when trees were cut down to create tillage and grow crops.

Deforestation in the Burren, Co. Clare

- The Burren had a gritty soil cover after glacial times about 10,000 years ago.
- Early farmers cut down the trees so they could till the crumbly soil.
- Overexposure to coastal winds and rain led to erosion and loss of soil.
- Today most of the Burren is a barren, rocky landscape.

The felling of tropical forests

- Large regions of tropical forest have been cut down over the past four decades.
- In Brazil this deforestation was carried out for hardwood timber supplies, such as teak and mahogany.
- Large ranches were also created in the cleared forest land to supply fast food chains with meat.
- Soil erosion is common where deforestation has occurred.
- Plantation agriculture and wood demand in India have led to large loss of forest land.
- Native tribes lose their homeland and their way of life as they are forced from their lands.
- Big industrial projects such as hydroelectric dams lead to large-scale deforestation. Valleys are also flooded behind dams. *Example:* the Tucurui project in Brazil.

Intensive agricultural and industrial activities

- Most agricultural lowlands that are intensively farmed were once covered by deciduous woodland.
- Such regions include Western Europe and America. Most American houses are timber-framed. This means that large quantities of wood are needed for construction.
- California's redwoods were cleared by lumber companies and miners.

- Over 500 square kilometres of natural habitat are lost to development in California each year. This includes semi-desert land around Los Angeles.
- Las Vegas has become a large, sprawling, urban region that was built in a desert environment.

SAMPLE EXAM QUESTION AND ANSWER

Question: Biomes are altered by human activity. Discuss. (2015, 2014, 2012)

Answer:
The Sahel is a long, narrow region that runs east-west across the southern edge of the Sahara Desert in North Africa. It is a transition zone between two biomes – a hot desert biome to the north and a tropical grassland biome to the south. It also is a region particularly prone to political conflict and social unrest, which adds to the region's difficulties.

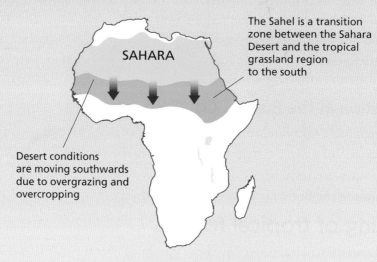

The Sahel is a transition zone between the Sahara Desert and the tropical grassland region to the south

SAHARA

Desert conditions are moving southwards due to overgrazing and overcropping

The location of the Sahel

Deforestation

- **Deforestation** is a serious problem in the Sahel region that has a negative domino effect on the environment locally and regionally. The countries that make up the Sahel region are all part of the Developing World and night-time temperatures can drop by as much as 20°C below daytime temperatures due to the clear night skies. **Firewood** is an important human need in the Sahel because fossil fuels for cooking and for heating are expensive. In Africa, an estimated 90 per cent of the entire continent's population uses firewood or dried dung for cooking, and in sub-Saharan Africa, firewood and brush supply approximately 52 per cent of all energy sources.

- **High population growth** rates of 2.5–4 per cent, which averages 6 children per woman, is a pressing problem, especially as health improvements are decreasing infant death rates without a corresponding lowering of fertility rates. The regions around cities are

exam focus

These headings can be used to explain how human activities can influence soil erosion.

devoid of trees and brush. The rapidly expanding cities of the Sahel, such as Darfur in the Sudan, are consuming almost all of the country's wood supply. Humanitarian and peacekeeping forces are adding to the problems as house rents have increased 4 to 16 times, when compared to 2003 levels in Sudan.

- **Investment in urban property** is now one of the most secure forms of investment/money since political unrest began (pre-conflict, livestock was the preferred form of capital). The demand for housing increases the demand for wood. Previously, trade in timber and wood fuel used to be a central part of the livelihoods of just a few. Now, large numbers of people are dependent on wood supply for most of their incomes. Deforestation removes the presence of tree roots and exposes the soil to erosion by the wind.

Overgrazing

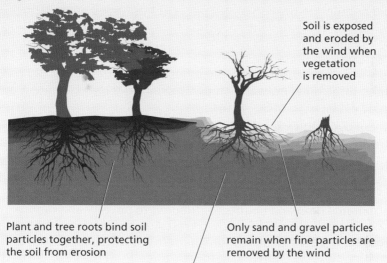

Soil is exposed and eroded by the wind when vegetation is removed

Plant and tree roots bind soil particles together, protecting the soil from erosion

Only sand and gravel particles remain when fine particles are removed by the wind

The soil dries up and becomes barren

The results of overgrazing

- Traditionally, farm **animal ownership** was a measure of wealth and status. As the region's population increased, so did the numbers of cattle and goats. These increased farm animal numbers, which led to overgrazing and a reduction in the cover and quality of vegetation that grew throughout the region. Too many animals beyond its carrying capacity remove the protective grass cover that protects the soil and exposes it to erosion by the wind and rain. Large herds of animals trample on and compact soils with their hooves. This makes the soil less porous by reducing spaces between soil particles and preventing moisture from percolating into the soil. This increases runoff and erosion in times of infrequent but heavy downpours.

- The lack of forest and bush cover, and the additional loss of grass have reduced the effect of **transpiration**, a process whereby moisture is absorbed by plant roots and evaporated through the plants' leaves. Reduced transpiration causes less moisture in the atmosphere, leading to less cloud cover and reduced rainfall.

- Most cattle farmers in the past were **nomadic herders** who moved in search of fresh pastures that had only vague traditional boundaries. This was a sustainable pattern. It allowed soils to renew their fertility by leaving them fallow for long periods of time (in some case for up to 10–20 years). **Increased cattle numbers** have changed this traditional pattern and farmers are forced to keep cattle permanently in fenced-off land. Thousands of wells have been built to cater for the increased cattle numbers, but too many wells in an area lower the water table that has taken centuries to build up; this causes some wells to dry up.
- Overgrazing by sheep has occurred on the natural grasslands of the **Steppes in Mongolia**. Overgrazing has also occurred in **Tibet**, where traditional grazing herds have been increased in recent decades.

Overcropping

- **Rapid population growth** of 2–4 per cent has forced many farmers in the Sahel to overcultivate land to produce sufficient food for themselves and their families. This region no longer gets regular sufficient rainfall totals for agriculture. These farmers did not allow their land to rest and remain fallow in order to restore sufficient nutrients naturally, nor did they fertilise sufficiently between crops. The soil then became barren and its structure started to break down.
- As these overcultivated **areas became less productive**, farmers began to cultivate marginal land towards the north of the Sahel in places such as central Mali and central Sudan. This **marginal land borders the Sahara** region and is close to the desert. It is not fertile enough for sustained agricultural production and it also quickly became barren.
- **International debt and politics** contributed to poverty and famine in this region. The arrival of the French in West Africa in the late 19th century altered the traditional agricultural patterns of the Sahel. French policies that emphasised export crops and east-west trade from the interior to Atlantic port cities led more farmers to abandon the traditional trans-Saharan trade.
- During the 1960s, many countries of the Sahel region received **cheap loans**, which they cannot now pay. They are regarded as highly indebted poor countries. To qualify for debt relief, they must put more of their land under cash crop cultivation, such as ground nuts (peanuts) and cotton for export. The crops are then sold on the world market to pay off these national debts. Cash crops, such as peanuts, that are grown year after year exhaust the soil so much that, following three years of cultivation, the land needs to be fallow for six years.
- This **growth of cash crops** has led to monoculture in the region and the loss of fertility in the soils of the Sahel. This has the domino effect of more farmers cultivating more marginal land to feed their own families. The soils of these marginal lands are not mature or developed, and they lose their nutrients very quickly leading to crop failure, famine and desertification.

Questions 18, 2014; 17, 2015.

Option 3: Culture and Identity

exam focus

You must write your answer in **paragraphs** or you may lose cohesion marks.

MARKING SCHEME

Choose three or four headings/aspects for your answer. The marking scheme will be as follows:

Number of aspects:

- 3 aspects @ 20 marks each **or** 4 aspects @ 15 marks each
- Identifying heading/aspect – 4 marks
- Discussion – 8 × SRPs **or** 6 × SRPs
- Overall coherence – 20 marks graded
- Select scheme according to number of headings/aspects discussed
- Allow credit for up to 3 examples from SRPs
- Allow for 2 labelled illustrations to a max of 2 SRPs (different illustrations in different aspects).

Note: Some questions have alternative marking schemes, depending on the answers required.

34 Populations: Physical and Cultural Factors

Racial groups

- A person's race or racial group cannot be changed.
- Race is a biological inheritance.
- Race refers to physical characteristics such as skin colour, height, hair type, physique and shape of head.
- These characteristics are passed through genes from parents to offspring.

Ethnic groups

- **Ethnic** refers to a minority group with a collective self-identity within a larger host population, such as Italians or Irish in New York, or Chinese in Ireland.
- The Aboriginals of Australia, who were cut off on the once-isolated island continent, are an ethnic group.
- The Kalahari Bush people, who were isolated in the Kalahari semi-desert region of southern Africa, are another such group.

Skin colour and race

- In the past, racial groups were classified by skin colour: white, yellow, red, brown and black.
- Scientists today believe that dark- and light-coloured skins developed because of humans' adaptation to their environments.
- Skin colour is a result of the presence of melanin-producing cells in our bodies.
- We all have the same number of melanin-producing cells.
- In dark-skinned people these cells produce 43 times more melanin per cell than in light-skinned people.
- Melanin is necessary to combat the effects of ultraviolet light by absorbing dangerous rays, and so it protects us against cancer.
- The greater the amount of sunlight, the greater the need for melanin to protect against skin cancer.
- Dark skin was also needed to protect against the effects of strong sunlight on the production of folic acid.

- Groups further away from the Equator needed some ultraviolet light to create vitamin E, so humans developed genes for creating light-coloured skin.
- Therefore, different skin colours developed at different latitudes, so that people could live healthy lives in those places.

Race and genetic make-up

- Any person's race accounts for only 1.5 per cent of his or her genetic make-up.

There are five recognised ethnic or racial groups:

Caucasians

Europeans and people of European ancestry; brown-skinned people, such as Arabs and people of the Indian subcontinent.

Northern, Central and East Asians

Chinese, Inuit, Samis and American Indians (Amerindians).

Africans and black people of African descent (such as African Americans).

Black Australian Aboriginals

The Bush people of the Kalahari

The impact of Europe on world migration and racial patterns

The colonisation of the Americas

exam focus

Revise explorations and colonisation on your Junior Certificate History course.

- Emigration to the Americas was a 'release valve' for many overpopulated European regions.
- The European-settled lands of North America, Australia and New Zealand, parts of South America and South Africa provided:
  1. cheap food supplies for Europe's growing population
  2. raw materials for its industries.
- The effects of European colonisation on the Native American people were catastrophic.
- The native people of what is now the USA declined from 5 million in 1500 to 60,000 in 1800.
- These native people were devastated by epidemics of infectious diseases such as smallpox and measles.
- Over 12 million Africans were transported to the Americas as slaves.

Multiracial societies

Case study 1: France

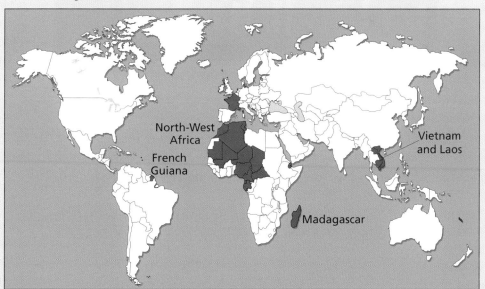

The extent of the former French Empire

- Like Great Britain, France is a former colonial power.
- About 14 million French citizens, nearly one-quarter of the total population, have at least one immigrant parent or grandparent.

- A large share of the post-war immigrants and their offspring come from former French colonies in North Africa, sub-Saharan Africa, and from countries in South-East Asia.
- Immigrants also came from colonies in the Caribbean.
- This population is concentrated in the suburbs and urban centres such as Marseilles and Lyon.
- Most immigrants live in **ghetto-like communities**.
- Large past migrations and high birth rates among immigrants have made Islam the second-largest religion in France.
- Many immigrants, especially those from Algeria and Morocco, came to France as 'guest workers' in the 1960s and 1970s.

Case study 2: Brazil

Brazil's soccer team show evidence of a varied ancestry

- Brazil has a population of 167 million people. About 80 million of them are people of **black African descent**.
- These are **descendants of the slaves** who were brought to Brazil by the Portuguese to work their sugar and cotton plantations along the north-east coast.
- Of the 80 million black people, about 67 million have combined European, African and Amerindian ancestries.
- The remainder, forming 55 per cent of the population, are mainly of European origin, the descendants of immigrants from Portugal, Italy, Germany and Eastern Europe.
- The Japanese population numbers about 1.3 million.
- **Ethnic mixing** is so great that hardly any group is unaffected.
- Only about 275,000 Amerindians survive. In the hunger for land and minerals, many have been forced from their forest homelands.
- Few black people are involved in politics and even fewer have positions of power within government, even though they form almost half of Brazil's population.

Case study 3: The United States of America

- America is a **multiracial society** where racial mixing has been slow to occur.
- The African-American group is the only group to have involuntarily emigrated to the USA.
- Only 44 per cent of black people agree that race relations in the USA will eventually improve.
- **Racial mixing has increased**, especially among the young population. For example, 70 per cent of Italians born after 1970 have mixed ancestry from outside their ethnic group.
- Roughly 99 per cent of African-American women and 97 per cent of African-American men marry within their ethnic group.
- Many black people live in ghetto communities; and ghettos have come to symbolise the place of the poor within cities.
- Some people believe that with no work, no income and no property the only way to achieve a **masculine identity** is through crime and gang membership.

SAMPLE QUESTION AND ANSWER

Question: Discuss the impact of colonisation/migration on ethnic/racial patterns.

Answer:
The African-American cluster in south-eastern USA

Revise explorations and colonisation on your Junior Cert History course.

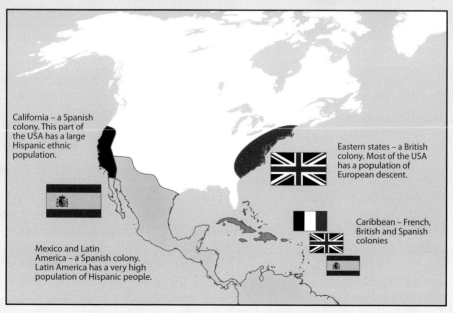

California – a Spanish colony. This part of the USA has a large Hispanic ethnic population.

Eastern states – a British colony. Most of the USA has a population of European descent.

Caribbean – French, British and Spanish colonies

Mexico and Latin America – a Spanish colony. Latin America has a very high population of Hispanic people.

Some colonies that influenced racial distribution in the United States

- The **Portuguese, French, Spanish and British were the main colonists** in the Americas. Black slaves were introduced into Virginia in North America in 1619. They were **needed to work the cotton plantations** of the southern states. The soils of central Alabama and north-east Mississippi were dark and fertile, and the term 'Black Belt' became associated with plantation agriculture based on enslaved black/African-American labour. During the first half of the 19th century, as many as **one million enslaved African Americans were transported** through sales in the domestic slave trade to these south-eastern states in a forced migration to work as labourers for the regions' cotton plantations. After having lived as slaves for several generations in the area, many remained as rural workers, tenant farmers and sharecroppers after the American Civil war and emancipation.

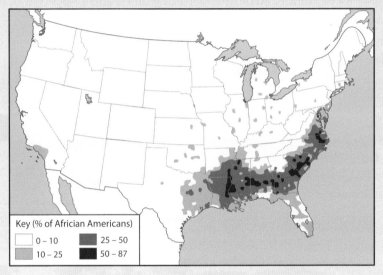

Key (% of African Americans)
- 0 – 10
- 10 – 25
- 25 – 50
- 50 – 87

The distribution of African Americans in the USA

- Beginning in the early 20th century and up to the 1970s, a total of six million black people left the South in the Great Migration to find work in industrial cities, especially in the north, midwest and west coast. They became highly urbanised.

- All African Americans living in the North were free in 1860 and only 6.2 per cent of African Americans living in the South were free, yet there were more free black African Americans still willing to live there. One of the reasons why a large majority of freed African Americans remained living in the South was that among the immigrants arriving were freed slaves fleeing the West Indies during the 1791 slave revolt against the French in Saint-Domingue (now Haiti).

- There was a second surge of free black slaves when Napoleon Bonaparte, exhausted and in need of cash from France's defeat by the slaves, sold his country's vast Louisiana territory to the Americans. There was also an influx of racially mixed people who were the offspring of black slaves and French and Spanish colonists. By 1810 the South had a free black population that was there to stay. Most free black people in the South preferred to live in cities because that is where jobs were available.

Hispanic-Americans in Latin America and North America

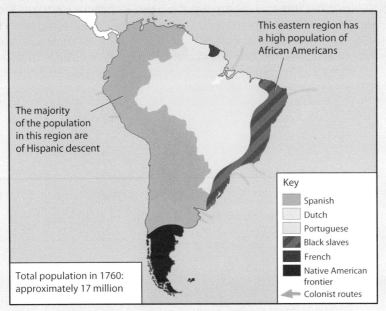

The majority of the population in this region are of Hispanic descent

This eastern region has a high population of African Americans

Key

- Spanish
- Dutch
- Portuguese
- Black slaves
- French
- Native American frontier
- Colonist routes

Total population in 1760: approximately 17 million

The pattern of Hispanic Americans in North and South America

- During the Age of Discovery, the Christian Church invested a major effort to spread Christianity in the Americas by converting Native American peoples, such as the Navajo and Apache. They attempted to pacify and Hispanicise (make Spanish-like) these people. These Catholic missions were established by the Spanish Empire during the 14th to the 19th centuries in an area extending from Mexico and the south-west parts of the USA, southwards as far as Argentina and Chile. The Jesuits and Franciscans were the main missionaries in what are now the western states of the USA, such as California, Arizona, Texas and New Mexico. The missions were a series of religious and military outposts. The **Spanish settlers** who came in search of land and wealth introduced livestock, fruits, vegetables cattle and horses. The **descendents of these Spanish settlers** are now **the dominant ethnic group in the Americas**. Today, these missions are some of the oldest and most visited historic monuments.

- Christopher Columbus, who led four **voyages of discovery for Spain**, colonised the West Indies. Hernán Cortés conquered the Aztec Empire in Mexico and Central American countries. Later, other Spanish conquerors, such as Francisco Pizarro, conquered Peru and eventually Spanish influence spread southwards as far as Argentina and Chile.

- These colonisations introduced the Spanish language, customs and culture throughout Latin America, with the exception of Brazil, which was colonised by the Portuguese. **The Treaty of Tordesillas** divided South America between the Spanish and Portuguese to prevent conflict between these two nations.

- Dutch settlers from the Zealand region colonised Guiana. Sugar, cotton, indigo and coffee were the main exports. Black slaves were also imported to work the plantations here. Neighbouring French Guiana, controlled by the French since 1946, is now part of the EU and its official currency is the Euro. In the past, it began as a plantation development with black slaves transported to work the plantations. **Asians also were attracted to work in the Guianas.** There is a substantial population of Asian people living in Latin America due to historic links with Europeans.

Black African Americans in Latin America

African Americans and Caucasians live in this eastern region

Caucasians and Native Americans live in this region

1.3 million Chinese (Asian) in this region

The pattern of black African Americans in South America

- The Portuguese colonised Brazil and introduced black slaves from Africa **to work on their cotton plantations**, which were mostly located along the east coast. **This is called forced migration.** The black people brought to Brazil were from different ethnic groups and from different African regions: The West African and the Bantu people. **The West African group** were native to Guinea, Ghana and Nigerian regions. Some of these people spoke Arabic and many could read and write in this language. Many of these slaves **were better educated than their European masters** who could not even read or write in Portuguese. These slaves of Arab and Berber influence were largely sent to Bahia. Even today, the typical dress of the women from Bahia has clear **Muslim influences**, such as the use of the Arabic turban on the head.

- Most of the slaves brought to Brazil came from the **Bantu regions of the Atlantic coast** of Africa where today Congo and Angola are located, and also from **Mozambique**. In general, these people lived in tribes. The people from the Congo had developed agriculture, raised livestock, domesticated animals such as goat, chicken, pig and dog, and produced sculptures in wood. Some groups from Angola were nomadic and did not know agriculture.

- The slave trade was a huge business that involved hundreds of ships and thousands of people in Brazil and Africa. There were officers on the coast of

Africa that sold slaves to hundreds of small regional dealers in Brazil. In 1812, half of the thirty richest merchants of Rio de Janeiro were slave traders. Only 45 per cent of the Africans captured in Africa to become slaves survived. It is estimated that as many as **12 million Africans were captured to be brought to Brazil**. Slavery ended in Brazil in May 1888. Today there are **14.5 million people of African descent** living in Brazil, who mostly live near the east coast in both urban and rural regions. Interior Brazil is settled mostly by people of Spanish, European and Native American descent.

Black Africans in France

- There are about **1.6 million black people living in France**, which is equivalent to just under **4 per cent** of the population. It is estimated that 4 out of 5 black people in France are of African immigrant origin, with the minority being of Caribbean ancestry. France was a colonial power and had many colonies in North Africa and in the Caribbean region where these migrants came from in search of better opportunities.

- **Racism is on the rise in France**, with half of the French population admitting that they have a racial prejudice. French researchers have little to back up any racial facts because ethnic statistics are forbidden in France by the constitution; acknowledging differences based on race, religion or sex is discriminatory. Though there is a deeply engrained racist culture, many French people pretend that it does not exist. Many black people in France live in ghetto communities in Paris and Marseilles, and evidence suggests that there is discrimination in employment, education and career opportunities for black French people. **Major riots** have occurred in these ghetto communities in recent decades as a backlash against discrimination in French society.

Racial conflict

Racial conflict in the United States

- The African-American group is the only ethnic group that emigrated to the United States involuntarily.
- Slavery was introduced into the southern states to create cheap labour for cotton and tobacco planters.
- At the end of World War II, Americans showed increasing concern over racial discrimination.
- In the 1950s, the emergence of the Civil Rights Movement resulted in a revival of Ku Klux Klan organisations. The most important of these was the White Knights of the Ku Klux Klan, led by Robert Shelton.
- In the South, especially in the states of Alabama and Mississippi, violence against black people by white people was rarely fully investigated. Lynching was still used as a method of terrorising the local black population.
- In 1987, a civil court action by a mother against the Klan over the lynching of her son was successful. She was awarded $7 million and the Klan had to sell all its assets to pay the fine.

- Most civil rights demonstrations stressed non-violence. But the demonstrations sometimes caused tension that resulted in violence.
- Martin Luther King Jr, the black leader of the Civil Rights Movement, who was a Nobel Peace Prize winner, was assassinated in 1968.

Racial conflict in India

Racial conflict in India may be looked at under two headings:

1. the caste system
2. northern and southern Indians.

The caste system

- The **caste system** usually refers to the groups of society into which the people of India are divided by religious customs.
- In general it means a **hereditary division** of any society into classes on the basis of **occupation, colour, wealth or religion**.
- India has four castes, the highest-ranking group being the **Brahmins**. People who do not belong to any of these four groups become outcasts or **untouchables**.
- With the introduction of British systems to India, the castes became **rigid social divisions**. No one could rise to a higher caste than the one into which they were born.
- India today has become more flexible in the customs of its caste system. Urban people are less strict about the system than rural people.
- In cities, different castes of people intermarry and mingle with each other.
- In rural areas there is still discrimination based on castes and against the untouchables.
- Most of the degrading jobs are still done by the Dalits or untouchables, while the Brahmins remain at the top of the hierarchy: many Brahmins are doctors, engineers and lawyers.

The caste system is a form of racial discrimination

Northern and southern Indians

- The people of India belong to all the major racial groups. However, **Caucasians make up 90 per cent of the population**.
- The British promoted religious, ethnic and cultural divisions among their colonised peoples to keep them under their control.
- The British promoted the idea that India is a land of two races – the lighter-skinned Aryans, in the northern half of the country; and the darker-skinned Dravidians, in the southern half.
- European thinkers of that time believed in a racial theory of mankind that was based on colour alone. They saw themselves as belonging to a superior 'white' or Caucasian race.

Questions 20, 2014; 19, 2015; 20, 2016.

35 # Language and Religion as Cultural Indicators

aims You need to know that language and religion are indicators of ethnic origin.

Language as a cultural indicator

- **Cultural regions** is the general term for areas where some portion of the population shares some degree of cultural identity.
- The culture's language is clearly evident in the place names of such regions, e.g. Gaeltacht.
- The choice of language on signs is another visible symbol of culture in the landscape.

The major language families

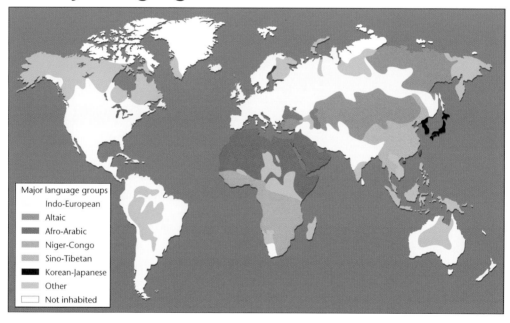

Major language groups
- Indo-European
- Altaic
- Afro-Arabic
- Niger-Congo
- Sino-Tibetan
- Korean-Japanese
- Other
- Not inhabited

The major languages of the world

The Indo–European family

- About half the world's population speaks languages from this family.
- It began in the region now called Turkey; its speakers migrated to various regions and the language changed along the way.

The Sino–Tibetan family

- The second most widely spoken language, with over one billion speakers.
- Includes Chinese, Thai, Burmese and Tibetan.

Arabic–Semitic family

- Includes Arabic and Hebrew.
- Mostly spoken in north and north-east Africa, the Middle East and the Arabian peninsula.
- The spread of the Muslim faith across Africa brought Arabic to this region.

The Ural and Altaic family

Includes Finnish, Hungarian and Turkish, as well as the languages spoken in the Asian part of Russia.

Niger–Congo family

- This language family is also called Bantu.
- The region where these languages are spoken stretches from the Sudan in the north to South Africa in the south.
- It includes Swahili, which developed as a pidgin language from contact with Arabic traders along the east African coastline.

Japanese and Korean family

Limited to Japan, North Korea and South Korea.

Dravidian family

Spoken in southern India and Sri Lanka. Includes Tamil.

Gaeltacht regions

In 1925 Gaeltacht regions in Ireland were divided into two categories:
- **Fíor Gaeltacht** regions, where 80 per cent or more of the population spoke Irish
- **Breac Gaeltacht** regions, where 25–79 per cent of the population spoke Irish.

At this time Gaeltacht regions covered substantial areas of the West of Ireland. Today, however, Gaeltacht regions have reduced in size and number and are confined to scattered regions along the west and south coasts. They have a total population of about 86,000 people.

Initiatives for the survival of the Irish language

- Festivals that promote the language through art exhibitions and music.
- An audio-visual industry that promotes Irish culture within the Gaeltacht and throughout Ireland. These influences include:
  - Raidió na Gaeltachta
  - the TV station TG4
  - local radio stations
  - Irish-language schools (na Gaelscoileanna)
  - summer colleges in the Gaeltacht areas.

Supports for minority languages

- Article 22 of the European Charter of Fundamental Rights states that the EU respects cultural, religious and linguistic diversity.
- The **European Bureau of Lesser-used Languages** (**EBLUL**) works on behalf of those in the EU who speak minority languages. It creates and supports policies that support these languages.
- The EU gives financial aid to EBLUL.
- International conferences are held to identify ways to improve the situations of these minority languages. These are organised by the **Foundation for Endangered Languages** (**FEL**).

Religion as a cultural indicator

Religion creates landscapes by the construction of religious buildings: there are churches in Christian regions, and mosques with their minaret towers are found in Muslim areas. There are no bars in Muslim areas.

Personal indicators:

- Sikh men wear turbans and have long beards
- Muslim women wear chadors
- there are differing attitudes, for example towards women, to birth control, to materialism.

The world's major religions

Judaism

- There are only about 16.5 million Jewish people in the world.
- The religion's origins are traced back to Abraham, who migrated from Mesopotamia, now called Iraq, to Palestine with his followers.
- Isaac, who was Abraham's true heir, became the ancestor of the Israelite people.

Christianity

- Christianity is the largest religious group: over 33 per cent of the world's population are Christians.
- Christianity has its origins in Judaism.
- Christians believe that Jesus Christ was the messiah prophesied in the Old Testament.
- Christianity spread rapidly through the work of St Paul and other missionaries.
- The Romans persecuted the Christians for many years until the Emperor Constantine granted them freedom of religion.
- The Edict of Milan in AD 313 granted religious freedom to Christians in the Roman Empire.
- The rulers of Spain and Portugal were Christian and they helped spread the Christian faith to Latin America.
- The British and French, also colonial powers, spread Christianity to the USA, Canada and Australia.

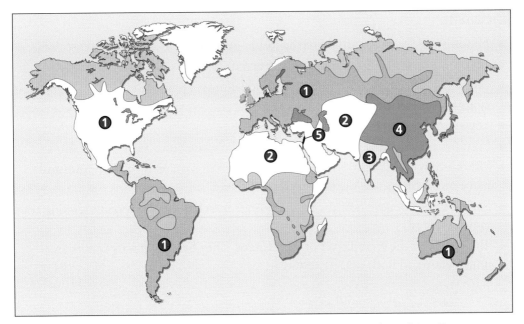

Identify the main religions in each of the regions numbered 1 to 5

- The Jesuits carried Christianity to China.
- Christianity had spread throughout Russia before the Russian Revolution.

Islam

Muslims always face Mecca during prayer

- Islam is the name given to the religion preached by the Prophet Mohammed in the 7th century.
- Mohammed was an Arab who was born in Mecca in about AD 570.
- He preached that there was only one god, Allah.
- Those who believe in Islam are called Muslims.
- Islam has its origins in Judaism and Christianity.
- Mohammed believed that Christ was a prophet of Islam.

Hinduism

- Hinduism is mostly confined to the Indian subcontinent and South-East Asia.
- It is not promoted through missionary activities.
- Hinduism traces its origin to tribes of Indo-European migrants who brought their language, Indo-European, with them.
- The sacred texts of Hinduism are the Vedas.
- Hindus are monotheists, which means they believe in one high god, Brahman.
- Hinduism is divided into three sects, each with its own view of the nature and name of the high god: Vishnu, Shiva or Shakti.
- Some Hindus believe that the three gods are merely different ways of looking at the same high god.
- The Ganges is the sacred river of the Hindus. They believe that its waters are immaculate and nothing can pollute it.

SAMPLE QUESTION AND ANSWER

Question: **Examine the importance of religion as an indicator of culture**

Sikhs and their identity

- The Sikhs are a minority cultural group in India who belong to a religion that was founded by Guru Nanak about 500 years ago to unite Muslims and Hindus of all castes into a single faith. This faith gained millions of followers in the Punjab region.

Turbans are worn by Sikh men

Strong beards are a symbol of the Sikh appearance

A Sikh man

- As members of the same cultural group, all Sikhs resemble each other by wearing five symbols, called 'K' symbols. They are 'Kesh' (uncut hair), 'Kanga' (wooden comb), 'Karra' (steel bracelet), 'Kachha' (short breeches) and 'Kirpaan' (blade 6" to 9") to symbolise self-respect.

- Sikh men wear a dastar, or turban, to show their commitment to Sikhism. Turbans are made from a strip of material, 5 metres × 1 metre, that is turned clockwise around the head.

- Women are required to cover their heads, usually with a long scarf, called a chunni. Sikhs who follow all of these traditions are called **Khalsa**. People who follow only some of these conditions are called **Sahajdharis**. Sikhs are clearly different from other Indian people in their appearance and dress code. This symbol of identity is called bana.

- Many Sikhs seek political independence from India. In order to satisfy this demand, the Indian government made Punjab a separate Punjabi-speaking state where the Sikhs are the majority rulers. However, some Sikhs want full independence in a newly renamed state they call **Khalistan**.

- The holiest shrine of the Sikhs is the **Golden Temple in Amritsar**. During British colonial rule, many Sikhs won the respect and trust of the British and many thousands were employed as policemen and soldiers. As a result, a large Sikh middle class developed in the rich agricultural region called the Punjab.

- The culture of the Sikhs is largely affected by their religious beliefs and every important Sikh ceremony is performed in the presence of the **Holy Granth** (Sikh Bible). In order to unite Hindus and Muslims, the Sikh faith asked its followers to throw off all divisions of caste, colour and race.

Jews and their identity

Clothing

- Clothing has long played a significant role in Judaism, reflecting religious identification, social status, emotional state and even the Jews' relation with the outside world. The ancient rabbis taught that maintaining their distinctive dress in Egypt was one of the reasons the Jews were worthy of being rescued from slavery.

The kippah, or skull cap, is worn by Jewish men as a sign of reverence and respect.

A tallit katan is a white undergarment worn by Jewish men. It has fringes or tassels dangling from the waist.

A Jewish man

- Most Jews dress similarly to non-Jews when outside synagogue. Orthodox Jews are often recognisable by their distinctive garments worn for reasons of ritual, tradition or modesty. In particular, Orthodox (and some non-Orthodox) men cover their heads with a **kippah** (skull cap), and some cover these with **black hats** or a **shtreimel**, a type of fur hat.

- More traditional Orthodox men often wear black suits. Many Orthodox men also wear a tallit katan or a **tzitzit**, a four-pointed garment with fringes on the corners, underneath their shirt.

- **Many Orthodox women shun pants** and instead stick to **dresses and skirts**. Also, Orthodox women generally wear modest clothes that cover much of their bodies, although the amount that is covered varies from community to community. In some ultra-Orthodox communities, women are discouraged from wearing bright, attention-grabbing colours. Once married, most Orthodox women cover their hair with a hat, wig or scarf.

- In some cases, over time the Jews adopted **distinctive dress voluntarily**, to separate themselves from the prevailing culture, e.g. **covering the head** with a hat or **kippah** as a sign of submission to differentiate themselves from Christians, for whom the removal of the hat was a sign of respect. In others, they were required by law to dress in a particular way, e.g. in Medieval Spain, Jews had to wear special hats and badges.

Food/cuisine

- Jewish cuisine is a diverse collection of cooking traditions of the Jewish people worldwide. It has evolved over many centuries, shaped by dietary laws, Jewish festival and tradition. It is referred to as **kosher**. The laws of keeping kosher have influenced Jewish cooking by prescribing what foods are permitted and how food must be prepared. Kosher is usually translated as 'proper'.

- Certain foods, notably **pork and shellfish, are forbidden**; meat and dairy may not be combined, and **meat must be ritually slaughtered** (by a ritual slaughterer, called a shochet) and salted to remove all traces of blood. Observant Jews will only eat meat and poultry that is certified kosher. Before it is cooked, it is soaked in water for half an hour.

Muslims and their identity

Clothing

- Islamic dress in Europe, especially the variety of headdresses worn by Muslim women, has become a prominent symbol of the presence of Islam in Western Europe. In several countries, the adherence to 'hijab', an Arabic noun meaning 'to cover' has led to political controversies and proposals for a legal ban. The Arabic word hijab literally translates into English as 'veil'. Followers of Islam believe that it was originally implemented by God in order to secure Muhammad's privacy and create a distinction between public and private lives from outsiders and to protect one's honour. The veil re-emerged as a topic of conversation in the 1990s when there was concern regarding potential western influences of Muslim practises in Islamic countries. The veil had a new purpose of shielding Muslim women from western influence. Some religious leaders reinforced that an additional purpose of the hijab was to protect the Islamic people and customs.

A burqa is a covering for the face and body worn by some Muslim women. It has an opening for the eyes only.

A niqab is a veil for the face with the eyes and upper part of the face exposed. It is worn by some Muslim women.

A Muslim woman

- There are lots of different kinds of coverings worn by Muslim women all over the world. The most controversial are the niqab which is a veil for the face that leaves the area around the eyes only clear. The niqab is worn by an accompanying headscarf and the burka that covers the face and body, often leaving only a mesh screen to see through.

Muslim landscapes
- Mosques with their minarets or towers are visibly different from churches and contribute to the differences in Muslim and Christian landscapes. A minaret is a distinctive architectural structure found adjacent to mosques. It is generally a tall spire with a conical or onion-shaped crown that provides a visual focal point that is traditionally used for the Muslim call to prayer.
- The absence of some building types, such as bars and pig farms from Muslim communities, occurs because alcohol and pork are taboo in Islam.

Religious practises
Certain sacred practises and rituals are very important to Muslims, such as the **Kibla**, which is the direction that should be faced when a Muslim prays. It is fixed as **the direction of the Kaaba in Mecca**, Islam's holiest shrine. Muslims all praying towards the same point is traditionally considered to symbolise the unity of Muslims worldwide. Daily prayers for Muslims are an obvious act and may be practised at work, at home or on the street.

The relationship between Church and State

The Irish Constitution

The Irish Constitution was introduced in 1937. It:
- recognised the special position of the Catholic Church in Ireland
- guaranteed freedom of conscience and the free profession and practice of all religions.

The power of the Catholic Church was used to influence government decisions such as the withdrawal of the 'Mother and Child' scheme.

Case study: Northern Ireland
- Sixty-two per cent of Church of Ireland members and almost all Presbyterians lived in the same nine Ulster counties.
- Political control was predominantly in the hands of Protestants.
- The Plantation of Ulster gave rise to the large Presbyterian population and the spread of Calvinism.
- The Orange Order represented the wealthy landowners, industrialists and the Presbyterian community.
- Social segregation of Catholic communities from Protestant communities led to ghettos in city regions.
- **Gerrymandering** was common. This was the arrangement of voting so that only those who held property were entitled to vote for local councils, and those who had many properties had many votes.

- There was widespread corruption and discrimination against Catholics.
- Civil rights marches were organised by the Catholic communities to demand equal treatment with Protestants.

Religious conflict

Case study: Religious conflict in Northern Ireland

Discrimination in Northern Ireland caused conflict between Catholics and Protestants during the Troubles

- Between 1966 and 2000, over 3,600 people were killed and 36,000 wounded as the conflict spread into mainland Britain and the Republic of Ireland.
- This period is known as 'The Troubles'.
- Since 1997, a ceasefire has held among the main paramilitary groups, such as the IRA, the UDA and the UFF.
- The **Good Friday Agreement** was signed on 10 April 1998.
- The Former US Senator, George Mitchell, was chairman of the all-party talks that led to the agreement.
- Tension has existed between the two faiths since the reign of **King James I** in 1609, when the Protestant faith was introduced to Northern Ireland.
- The **Treaty of 1921** recognised this religious division by dividing the country into the predominantly Protestant Northern Ireland and the predominantly Catholic Republic of Ireland.
- The Good Friday Agreement created a 108-member assembly and a 14-member executive body in which both Catholic and Protestant members sit together in government.

exam Q

Questions 19, 2014; 20, 2015; 19, 2016.

36 Nationality and Nation States

aims You need to know about the complex issues that can be created by national boundaries, including the conflict that can arise between ethnic and cultural groups as a result of the concept of nationality.

key point

NATIONALITY

Nation state refers to a country that occupies a specific area of land, and this area is occupied by a national group who share a common culture.

The concept of nation state combines three elements:

- **nation** (or ethnicity)
- **state**: the type of government or regime in power
- **territory**: the area defined on the ground that is controlled by the state.

Nations

- A nation is a group of people who feel bound together through personal ties and who possess a unity and solidarity that has grown by:
  - following a common way of life
  - sharing common experiences
  - possessing common cultural traits
  - inheriting a common tradition.
- **Nationalism** is the cause through which such groups claim their right to be a sovereign power within a particular area of land.
- Nations rarely consist of just one ethnic group.
- The factors that create and maintain national feeling include:
  - ethnic group or race
  - language
  - religion
  - a common enemy.
- A state boundary sometimes coincides with a physical natural barrier, such as a mountain range (e.g. the Pyrenees) or a river (e.g. the Rhine between France and Germany).
- A **frontier** is a zone or area which separates one ethnic group or nation from another, for example the border between Northern Ireland and the Irish Republic.

Everyday expressions of Irish culture and identity

Drama

There are many plays based on Irish culture and folklore.
The Playboy of the Western World and *The Field* are just two of many such Irish dramas that have been performed in the Abbey Theatre in Dublin and at other venues throughout the country.

Sport

- The Gaelic Athletic Association has promoted Gaelic games and has the biggest membership of all sports organisations in Ireland.
- Every parish has its own GAA club.
- Its most important events are the two All-Ireland Finals that are held in September each year.

Music and dance

- Traditional Irish music and dance are popular expressions of Irish culture.
- Feis Ceoil competitions are held regularly.
- The designs on female costumes for Irish dancing are based on Celtic patterns.

Festivals

- St Patrick's Day parades are held on 17 March every year in all our major towns. The largest parade is held in New York, where a large population of Irish people and people of Irish descent live.
- The Twelfth of July festival celebrates the identity of the unionist community in Northern Ireland.
- Many small towns have special events that celebrate other interests of Irish people, such as the Wexford Opera and Arts Festival.

Summer schools

Summer schools promote learning and interaction among students, poets, writers, politicians and university lecturers in an informal setting.

Festivals and sports in Europe

- The 'Running of the Bulls' is an annual event in Pamplona, in the Basque region of Spain.
- The Munich Beer and Music festival is the largest festival in the world – over 6 million visitors visit each year.
- Ice-skating and skiing are popular sports in snow-covered upland regions such as the French, Austrian and Swiss Alps, and include cross-country skiing, especially in Scandinavia.
- The Tour de France is the most famous of all French sporting events.

Nationality and nation states: Issues relating to physical and political boundaries

Water supplies

- The probability of conflicts over water supplies is great, especially in times of water shortages.
- The rivers that flow through some nations do not rise in those nations. For example, the River Indus in Pakistan rises in India. India takes some water from the river before it flows into Pakistan. If too much is taken, less flows through Pakistan, much of which is desert and relies heavily on this source for its water supply.

Offshore boundaries

- The water, the seabed and their resources – such as oil and gas – within **200 nautical miles** of a country's seashore belong to that country.
- This area is called the country's **Exclusive Economic Zone**.
- Territorial seas extend up to **12 nautical miles** offshore. States must allow the innocent passage of foreign ships through these waters.
- Where states adjoin each other, lines halfway between the nearest shorelines of each state must be decided.

Political boundaries

The political boundaries of a state define its ability to enforce its laws.

Political boundaries and ethnic divisions

Political boundaries often divide an individual ethnic group into two or more divisions.

- The **Basque region** is divided into two parts. The larger part is in Spain; the smaller part lies in France. They are separated by the Pyrenees mountain range that forms the boundary between France and Spain.
- The border area separates the nationalist people in Northern Ireland from their southern cultural neighbours in the Republic of Ireland.

Cultural groups within nation states

Basques in France and Spain, see pages 142–145.

Nationalists in Northern Ireland

- People who live in Northern Ireland and wish to be part of a united Ireland are called nationalists.
- Since partition in 1921, nationalists have lived under British rule and have suffered discrimination.
- Nationalists are Irish in their traditions and customs and most are Catholic.

- Nationalist feelings developed as a consequence of the British occupation of the island of Ireland and the oppressive treatment of the Catholic minority for over 70 years.
- The separation by fear of Protestant and Catholic communities has led to the development of ghettos in Derry and Belfast.
- Demands for civil rights and equal treatment with Protestant citizens led to civil rights marches in the 1960s and 1970s. Thirteen civilians were shot dead by the British forces during a civil rights march on 'Bloody Sunday' in January 1972.
- A minority of extreme nationalists support the IRA, an illegal paramilitary organisation.

The IRA and the British Government

- As a consequence of Bloody Sunday, the IRA intensified its campaign of violence in British cities and army barracks.
- Internment without trial of IRA sympathisers intensified the campaign further.
- Ten IRA prisoners died in prison to highlight their claim for political rather than criminal status.
- Efforts by SDLP leader John Hume and Sinn Féin leader Gerry Adams led to a ceasefire that continues to this day.

A sample question and answer on nationality as a part of identity can be found on moresuccess.ie.

Cultural groups without nationality

Basques in France and Spain

See pages 142–145.

OR

Sikhs in India

- The Sikhs form a cultural group that belongs to a religion founded by **Guru Nanak** about 500 years ago.
- Guru Nanak tried to unite Muslims and Hindus of all castes into a single faith.
- Most people in the Punjab region are Sikhs and followers of Guru Nanak.
- Their holiest shrine is the **Golden Temple in Amritsar**.
- Many Sikhs earned positions of trust in the defence forces during British colonial rule. This gave them a sense of middle-class status when independence came in 1947.
- All Sikhs wear five symbols, called the K symbols: Kesh, Kangha, Karra, Kachha, Kirpaan.
- Sikh male adults wear a dastar, or turban, and have long beards. Sikh women cover their heads with a long scarf, called a chunni.
- Sikhs who follow all these traditions are called Khalsa. People who follow only some of these are called Sahajdharis.

- This symbol of distinct identity, defined by dress code, is called bana.
- Many Sikhs seek full independence from India.
- To satisfy some of their demands, the Indian government made the Punjab a separate, Panjabi-speaking state where the Sikhs are the majority rulers.
- Many Sikhs want full independence, in a state they would call Khalistan.

SAMPLE EXAM QUESTION AND ANSWER

Question:

Many states have different cultural groups within their borders. Discuss. (2016)

or

Examine the effects of political and/or physical boundaries on cultural groups. Discuss. (2015)

or

The existence of different cultural groups within state borders can lead to conflict. Discuss. (2014)

Notes:

- Focus of question is different cultural groups existing within states (2016)
- Focus of question is on impact of boundaries on cultural groups (2015)
- Focus of question is on how conflict can occur when there are different cultural groups within state borders (2014)
- Allow for up to 3 examples to a max of 3 × SRPs (different examples and in different aspects)
- Allow for up to 2 labelled illustrations to a max of 2 × SRPs (different illustrations and in different aspects).

If you use three headings you must give eight SRPs.

If you use four headings you need to give six SRPs.

ALWAYS use three or four headings.

For example, you could write about: the political–religious divide in India (see pages 155–156); nationalists in Northern Ireland (see pages 315–316); and the Basque conflict with the Spanish government (see pages 144–145).

Answer: Political boundaries often divide an individual ethnic or cultural group into two or more divisions. This situation may lead to conflict in some cases.

Nationalists in Northern Ireland

- People who live in Northern Ireland and wish to be part of a united Ireland are called **nationalists**. Since partition in 1922, nationalists have **lived under British rule** and, until recent times, have **suffered discrimination** on many fronts. They are Irish in their traditions and customs and feel a strong sense of being Irish, rather than being British as unionists do. Most nationalists are Catholic and are represented by political organisations such as Sinn Féin or the SDLP.
- The nationalist population developed their sense of **Irishness**, just as the majority of people of the Irish Republic did, as a consequence of the

British occupation of the island of Ireland and the treatment at the hands of the British Forces and Royal Ulster Constabulary (Northern Ireland's police force). The events of 1916–21 and the oppressive treatment of the Catholic minority for over 70 years have cemented nationalist feelings that created an Irish identity.

Derry City is called Londonderry by Ulster unionists

Belfast city has many ghetto communities

Northern Ireland is part of the United Kingdom

- The demand for civil rights and equal treatment with Protestant citizens led to **civil rights marches in the 1960s and 1970s**. These marches led to clashes between police and marchers that reached a peak in the shooting dead of 13 unarmed civilians by the British forces on what is now called **'Bloody Sunday' in the city of Derry**. Over 20,000 people gathered in Derry in 2002 to mark the 30th anniversary of this atrocity.

- A minority of extreme nationalists support the IRA, an illegal armed organisation. At present, a cessation of military activities is part of the peace process that continues to dominate Northern Ireland politics today.

- The distribution patterns of the urban population of Catholic and Protestants has **led to 'ghettos'** in cities such as Derry and Belfast. Ethnic clashes between Catholic and Protestant ghetto communities still occur occasionally.

Palestinians

- At the beginning of the 20th century there were just 44 nation states. The remainder of the world was divided into Empires such as the British Empire, the French Empire and the Ottoman Empire. Nation states are therefore more or less a 20th-century phenomenon.

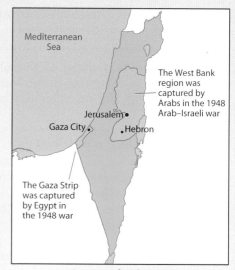

Mediterranean Sea

The West Bank region was captured by Arabs in the 1948 Arab–Israeli war

Jerusalem

Gaza City

Hebron

The Gaza Strip was captured by Egypt in the 1948 war

A map of Palestine

- The **Palestinians are an Arab people** who lived in south-west Asia for thousands of years. Their religion, customs and traditions are different from those of the Israeli people. Palestinians speak and write Arabic. The Jews speak and write Hebrew.

- Palestine has remained in Muslim hands almost continuously since the 16th century. Due to persecution in

Europe before **World War II and the Holocaust**, Jewish immigrants had been returning in large numbers to their original homeland, which they had been driven out of by the Romans. This created increasing tensions between Jews and Arabs. Promises were made during World War II by Britain and the Allied powers, both to Arabs and the Jews, that their ethnic groups would be given a homeland

- The Arabs were given some lands in various separated units in 1947, when the territories of the **Ottoman Empire** were divided after World War II. This division led to the creation of two states in Palestine: (a) a new Palestine State and (b) Israel. Then Palestine lost its national territory, because it and the neighbouring Arab **states did not recognise Israel's right to exist.** They attacked the new state of Israel in 1948 but they lost. Subsequent events have left them without any independent state of their own. Since then, Arabs who had called Palestine their homeland for centuries **have lived as refugees in neighbouring countries.** Israel is now 60 years old and most Palestinians were born after the partition of Palestine in 1948.

- **The Palestinians call themselves a nation without a state** (much as the Jews did before Israel was founded), although they and their descendants make up the majority of Jordan's population today. They demand that their grievances be heard and that a Palestinian state be created. The first steps towards such a state have been taken as part of the Arab–Israeli peace process, and these negotiations continue. Current estimates of Palestinians in the Arab world total about 8.5 million people.

- Palestine is also known as the 'Holy Land', and is **held sacred by Christians, Jews and Muslims,** because some of the most important events in each religion took place here, especially in Jerusalem. Because of its location at the crossroads of Africa, Asia, and Europe, Palestine has been the battleground of the great powers in the region throughout history. In recent decades, the discovery of vast oil reserves has interested the superpowers of the USA and Russia, and they have become implicated in supporting differing political solutions for the region.

Sikhs

- The Sikhs are a minority cultural group in India who belong to a religion that was founded by Guru Nanak about 500 years ago to unite Muslims and Hindus of all castes into a single faith. This faith gained millions of followers in the Punjab region.

- As members of the same cultural group, all Sikhs resemble each other by wearing five symbols, called 'K' symbols. They are 'Kesh' (uncut hair), 'Kanga' (wooden comb), 'Karra' (steel bracelet), 'Kachha' (short breeches) and 'Kirpaan' (blade 6" to 9") to symbolise self-respect.

- Sikh men wear a dastar, or turban, to show their commitment to Sikhism. Turbans are made from a strip of material, 5 metres × 1 metre that is turned clockwise around the head.

- Women are required to cover their heads, usually with a long scarf, called a chunni. Sikhs who follow all of these traditions are called **Khalsa**.

People who follow only some of these are called **Sahajdharis.** Sikhs are clearly different from other Indian people in their appearance and dress code. This symbol of identity is called bana.

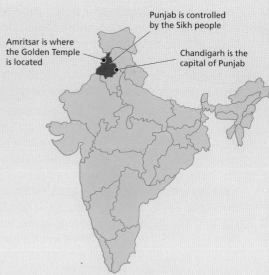

Punjab is controlled by the Sikh people

Amritsar is where the Golden Temple is located

Chandigarh is the capital of Punjab

A map of Punjab

- Many **Sikhs seek political independence from India.** In order to satisfy this demand, the Indian government made Punjab a separate Punjabi-speaking state where the Sikhs are the majority rulers.

- The culture of the Sikhs is largely affected by their religious beliefs, and every important Sikh ceremony is performed in the presence of the **Holy Granth** (Sikh Bible). In order to unite Hindus and Muslims, the Sikh faith asked its followers to throw off all divisions of caste, colour and race. The holiest shrine of the Sikhs is the **Golden Temple in Amritsar.** During British colonial rule, many Sikhs won the respect and trust of the British and many thousands were employed as policemen and soldiers. As a result, a large Sikh middle class developed in the rich agricultural region called the Punjab.

- However, some **Sikhs want full independence** in a newly renamed state they call **Khalistan.** In 1984, an armed uprising by some Sikhs seeking independence from India caused the Indian prime minister, Indira Gandhi, to order the Indian Army to attack the Golden Temple and eliminate any insurgents, called **Operation Blue Star**, as it had been occupied by Sikh separatists who were allegedly stockpiling weapons. Consequently, Indira Gandhi was assassinated by two of her Sikh bodyguards. This caused further bloodshed when a **huge mob**, assured of police non-interference, descended on various localities where mainly Sikhs were concentrated.

- Armed with iron rods, knives and clubs, the mobsters brutally killed people from the Sikh community and torched their houses after putting kerosene on them. Even women and children were not spared from the horror.

- Sonia Ghandi, the President of the Indian National Congress Party and the widow of Indira Gandhi's son, Rajiv, officially apologised in 1998 for the events of November 1984.

exam Q

Questions 19, 21, 2013; 20, 2014; 21, 2015; 20, 2016.